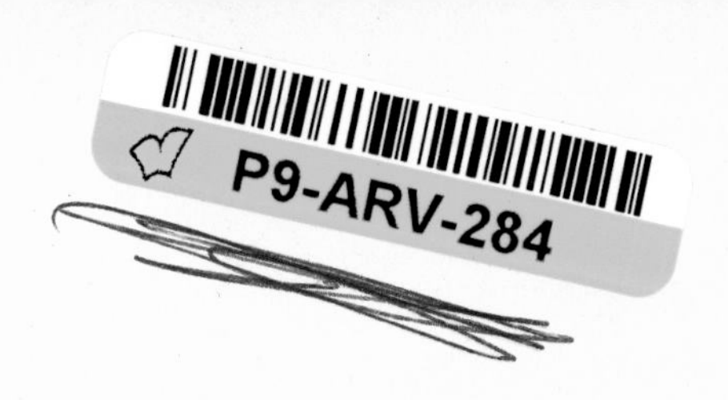
P9-ARV-284

Developmental Management

General Editor: Ronnie Lessem

Spiral Dynamics
Don Beck and Chris Cowan

Managing Organizations that Learn
Steven Cavaleri and David Fearon

Greening Business
John Davis

Ford on Management
*Henry Ford**

Integrative Management
Pauline Graham

Charting the Corporate Mind
*Charles Hampden-Turner**

Executive Leadership
Elliott Jaques and Stephen D. Clement

The Rise of NEC
Koji Kobayashi

Transcultural Management
Albert Koopman

Total Quality Learning
Ronnie Lessem

The Great European Illusion
Alain Minc

Managing Your Self
Jagdish Parikh

Intuition
Jagdish Parikh, Fred Neubauer and Alden G. Lank

Conceptual Toolmaking
Jerry Rhodes

The Future of Management
Robert Salmon

Organizing Genius
Paul Thorne

European Strategic Alliances
Sabine Urban and Serge Vendemini

*For copyright reasons this edition is not available in the USA

The Future of Management

All Roads Lead to Man

ROBERT SALMON

Translated by Larry Cohen

First published as *Tous Les Chemins Mènent À L'Homme* ©
1994, InterÉditions, Paris.

This edition published 1996 by

Blackwell Publishers Ltd
108 Cowley Road
Oxford OX4 1JF
UK

Blackwell Publishers Inc.
238 Main Street
Cambridge, Massachusetts 02142,
USA

British Library Cataloguing in Publication Data

A CIP catalogue record for this book is available from the
British Library.

Library of Congress Cataloging-in-Publication Data

Salmon, Robert, 1930–
[Tous les chemins mènent à l'homme. English]
The future of management : all roads lead to man / Robert Salmon.
p. cm. — (Developmental management)
Includes index.
ISBN 0-631-20307-9
1. Forecasting. 2. Management. I. Title. II. Series.
HD30.27.S2213 1996
658—dc20 96-9235
CIP

Typeset in 11 on 13 pt Ehrhardt
by Graphicraft Typesetters Ltd, Hong Kong
Printed and bound in Great Britain by
Hartnolls Limited, Bodmin, Cornwall
This book is printed on acid-free paper

To the company presidents who have guided my working life,
Mr François Dalle and Mr Lindsay Owen-Jones

Contents

Foreword by Lindsay Owen-Jones

Willingness to look squarely at the future is not a common attitude nowadays. Public opinion would rather turn its eyes away from the storm clouds gathering on the horizon. The world has become too uncertain, too complex. The collapse of traditional ideologies has made visionaries suspect. Terrified by mounting risk, voters seek comfort in conservatism, in clinging to old ways. As for politicians, they tailor their programs to this resistance to change. Even if they are aware of how dangerous it is simply to maintain the social and economic status quo, they dare not swim against the current. The unavoidably cautious policies that result from this situation reveal little or no real ability to anticipate events; for the most part, our political leaders are just handling things one day at a time.

Yet this general syndrome of resistance to vision must stop at the gates of the modern company. For us industrialists, doing nothing cannot be an option. Those who rest on past achievement without looking forward are rapidly penalized. Cautiously following the beaten path that led to success just a short time ago is the surest way of failing. Future success cannot be achieved with tried and tested recipes. As Gaston Berger, the founder of futurology, put it, "Tomorrow will not be like yesterday; it will be new and it will depend on what we do. It is less something to be discovered than something to be invented."

It is thus in the vital interest of today's companies to welcome visionaries, however disturbing they may be, and to listen to them with curiosity and indulgence. "How difficult it is to make predictions, especially regarding the future!" warned Alphonse Allais. When change of every kind accelerates, it is a serious mistake to confine ourselves to solving the most urgent problems. Short-term preoccupations prevent us from perceiving decisive transformations. Paradoxically, we are confronted with a lack of visionaries at a time when the future seems increasingly opaque.

I have known the author of this book for many years. His activities in international trade and his great curiosity led him, long ago, to travel extensively. He has taken advantage of this opportunity to consult the most innovative politicians, sociologists, scientists, and economists for hints as to what the future might bring. I can attest to his keen desire to discover what people of different races, languages, and cultures, living in countries at diverse stages of development, do to take charge of their own fate.

A number of years ago, I gave Robert Salmon the opportunity to turn his sensitivity and experience into a genuine occupation: that of prospecting for the future. It can therefore be said that I bear a certain objective responsibility for the writing of this book. I am in no way surprised that the author has given central importance to human factors. He thus reveals concerns that are totally in keeping with the traditions of L'Oréal and the thinking of Eugène Schueller and François Dalle. This emphasis on the full, unhampered development of all human potential could well take us beyond the mere solving of current economic problems.

It is my hope that this book will arouse more than just interest in its readers, for it calls upon each and every one of us to become aware of his or her own co-responsibility. It might even inspire emulators, some of whom thus finding a new vocation. The author would certainly be delighted; in any case, it is my fondest wish for him.

Lindsay Owen-Jones
Chief Executive Officer of L'Oréal

Foreword by Peter Schwartz

At the dawn of a new millennium powerful winds of change are transforming our world in unimaginable ways. We are nearly desperate for helpful maps and guides to a landscape shaped by rapidly shifting features and profound uncertainties. This book in your hands is exactly that: an insightful diagnosis of where we are, where we are headed, and most of all, what we ought to do.

The powerful forces for change interact on several levels and in complex ways, creating major discontinuities and turbulence. The end of the Cold War has unleashed a new and varied array of interests which shape geopolitical relations and events. The dramatic rise of Asia, economically and politically, heralds the end of 500 years of world rule by European civilization. The growing availability of nearly 800 million new highly skilled workers in Asia, at a fraction of the cost of European and American workers, is transforming production and employment. The sheer impact of nearly 2 billion teenagers is difficult for an older generation to foresee. But it is clear that the widening gap between the older and far richer 300 million and their far more numerous, younger, poorer neighbors will reshape politics and economics. Underpinning all of these changes are radical developments in technology: from the broad and deep impacts of today's information technology to the emerging prospects of biotechnology and nanotechnology. Yet the enormous economic success of the past century has also led to new problems which threaten continued economic success in the century ahead. Many of these are environmental impacts with a global reach such as climatic instability, ozone holes and soil, fisheries, and water depletion.

Not only is the world changing, but how we think about the world is changing as well. The sciences are in part being transformed by supercomputers and the Internet. In nearly every discipline, the rate of change is accelerating as more and more researchers employ ever more powerful tools and are more tightly interconnected. Among the most significant new frontiers is complexity. We are developing powerful new paradigms to understand how complex systems like ecosystems, the climate, or financial markets go through dramatic and sudden change.

At the same time what we believe about the world is also changing. With the death of Communism, old ideological struggles have faded only to be replaced by new ones. Ethnic identity and spiritual aspirations are increasingly organizing the new boundaries of the human condition. The worlds of Christianity, Islam, and Confucianism/Buddhism may be the new organizing dimensions of international relations. Ethnic identity may become the basis for nationalism; human values the emerging core of the new global politics.

Understanding the interaction of all of these forces, events, models, and values requires a similarly complex set of sensibilities. There are at least three ways people relate to the world around them. Some people want to change the world. These are the doers and are often found in business. The explorers want to know everything. They are ruthlessly curious and very rare. And, finally, there are true intellectuals who want to observe, reflect, and think about the world, and often from their ivory tower in the university. Robert Salmon is exceptionally well balanced along all three dimensions. Robert has been a successful businessman, helping to build one of the world's great companies, L'Oréal. He is an insatiable explorer, roaming the most interesting and unusual corners of the earth. And finally he is a serious thinker. This book is the fruit of all these aspects of Robert Salmon. It moves fluidly among the various levels of change and modes of understanding. Ultimately, it is a valuable guide for individuals, business, and other organizations seeking to navigate the dimensions of global change.

Peter Schwartz
Chairman, Global Business Network

Preface

This book aims to present a synthesis of our economic, social, and moral evolution, based on the views of renowned specialists, and then to draw a number of lessons for business management in the broadest sense of the term. And yet I hardly have the typical profile of a brilliant student or writer of dissertations. In a family of career officers, graduates of the École Polytechnique, and top-ranking civil servants, I was actually considered something of a failure, above all since I chose a business career – in the field of perfume and cosmetics to boot.

When I was a boy, I found school much less exciting than reading adventure stories. I envied all those heroes who set out to discover new worlds and whose courage was rewarded with the opportunity they had to encounter still-intact, authentic civilizations. I dreamt of leading that kind of life.

Most of these adventure novels were written in the nineteenth century. They described a world of strong, clearly defined cultures that were soon to disappear. Over the past hundred years, humanity's technical ability to solve the various problems of existence has greatly increased, but to widely differing degrees. It could be said, for example, that, whereas our contemporaries are fed and housed twice as well as in the nineteenth century, they possess ten times as many clothes, their opportunities for movement are a thousand times greater, and their capacity to communicate has been augmented a million fold. Geographical limits have also been swept aside, although our mental limits have yet to be broken down.

Be that as it may, the fact remains that, unlike the explorers of yesteryear, I have never had to contend with the obstacles to free movement or the indigent means of communication that helped to keep traditional societies intact. Today, air travel makes it possible to go several times a year to the four corners of the earth. For three decades now, I have been covering some 200,000 miles a year on business trips. I have had the privilege of visiting virtually every region of the world, of working in most existing countries. I will undoubtedly never be able to express the full measure of my gratitude toward the successive presidents of our company, who gave me this unique opportunity to carry on the life of a modern adventurer.

To be sure, once-forbidden cities have now been opened up to tourists, and the ambushes that await us along the highway are of a different nature. The world is steadily shrinking, and its already blurred borders are fast disappearing. All international airports look alike. Yet encountering other cultures remains an adventure, one that requires attentiveness and openmindedness. Making all due allowances, I can claim to have shared with yesterday's explorers, whom I idealized in my youth, a thirst for distant expeditions that has formed the guiding thread of my existence since the very start of my career. It still does.

Since I was fascinated by things foreign, I set out for the Far East as soon as I had finished my studies, on a sort of initiatory quest. After several journeys, I felt more mature, better equipped to begin my working life. Thus, when I got a job as a salesman upon my return home, I quite naturally gravitated toward overseas operations. I just felt too hemmed in in France, a country whose Cartesian rationalism often fails to recognize the value of intuition. Adventure livened up my life, giving me the impression that I was breaking new ground on markets on the other side of the globe, that I was forging into uncharted territories, where I encountered different cultures the way you discover a new fragrance.

Through regular world travel, I feel I have developed the ability to grasp intuitively why people in a given country, who are the products of their civilization, think, dream, eat, and dress the way they do. At the same time, however, I may have become somewhat atypical, since I tend to look at French society in rather the way an outsider would.

France seems to me to be dangerously out of step with our epoch. Ours is the arrogance of people who used to be something special. Others are charitable enough to view us first and foremost as the land of human rights, while we ourselves are more likely to dream of the faded glory of the Napoleonic era. We forget that French power in Europe is dead and buried. Considering what our country has become, our vision is too grandiose, to such an extent that it impairs our credibility on the world scene.

None the less, France unquestionably remains a symbol of good taste, of the *art de vivre*, of the things that make life worth living. In that area, we have unchallenged leadership. For example, the Colbert Committee, in keeping with the values of traditional craftsmanship, strives to maintain the highest possible standards of workmanship in those crafts that have made France the envy of the world. But instead of taking pride in this reputation, we Frenchmen have developed a fully fledged complex about it, and yearn to gain recognition for our technical accomplishments (the high-speed train, the Concorde, or our nuclear-power plants) which, however undisputable they may be, have no lack of competitors.

L'Oréal has become a world leader not only as a result of its own technological and creative strengths, but also because of the intrinsic competitive advantage that the French enjoy in this particular line of business. Not long ago, our company president still had to take a back seat in employers' organizations, for the steelmakers and directors of the rising electronics industry found it hard to take our branch seriously. Times have changed, of course, but even today, when a foreign decision-maker sings the praises of French champagne, fashion, or cosmetics at a reception in a French embassy, you still may hear one of our attachés declare with obvious injured pride: "True, but I would also like to stress that we are a major high-tech nation as well."

One of the incontrovertible assets of our culture lies in our ability to see things in universal terms, but it would not hurt us to get rid of some of our dogmatism, to acquire some flexibility and modesty. We measure universality exclusively by our own yardstick, while closing our eyes to the fragmentary, contrasting realities that make up a world in which nothing stands still.

My new position in our company has led me to fight for a different approach, one based on a willingness to open our windows wide onto the outside world. I feel greatly encouraged by the attitude of young people in France, who differ considerably from their elders. While concerned over their inadequate preparation for the international context, they state loudly and clearly that everything that comes from other countries is relevant to them and deserves ample examination. Whenever I talk to them about exports or world geopolitics, my viewpoint is enthusiastically received.

Three years ago, after 27 years as operational director, I was asked to set up and to run a company-wide "social research unit" whose task it is to monitor not only technological and business developments, but also societal, legislative, geographical, and even geopolitical trends. Needless to say, this also means taking an interest in managerial, scientific, and philosophical questions, an endeavor that has led me to travel increasingly around the world in search of both technological and marketing innovations as well as new ways of thinking.

Although I feel confident that I have taken into account a large number of extremely suggestive observations from the brilliant personalities I have encountered, I don't claim to have made an exhaustive, impartial assessment of the views expressed, even those coming from the most respected intellectual figures. I was certainly bound to work toward a synthesis of the contacts my colleagues and I have established over time. Yet I was also motivated by the desire to take a stand, to stress that both the *raison d'être* and the very survival of our economic and social organizations are inseparable from the unhampered development of human beings.

At present, there is a growing awareness of this basic truth, in response to an increasingly felt lack of meaning, a spiritual deficit that is slowly undermining Western society. In practice, however, our organizations continue to use people instead of being useful to them. Experience has taught me, on the contrary, that ultimately, it always pays to take disinterested action aimed at letting individuals develop freely, and that companies that place special emphasis on human potential, an essential building block of our social edifice, invariably achieve greater balance as a result.

An economic order based on human dynamics is more likely to enjoy lasting good health than one that is hooked on short-term results. It is obviously possible to hold up impressive quarterly statements that were achieved at the expense of employees' aspirations, distributors' loyalty, customer satisfaction, research quality, team creativity, and environmental protection. But with that kind of success, companies are digging their own graves.

It seems clear today that continuing to apply the formulas of the past will only lead to failure. This book strives quite simply to persuade each and every manager that devoting him or herself to human potential is the best way to be consistent, authentic, efficient, and to become more than a mere manager – to become a real leader.

Acknowledgments

I would like to stress how indebted I am to the various personalities that it has been my privilege and my pleasure to meet. Their anticipatory thinking has left a profound impression on me, and this book would undoubtedly never have been written without the extremely fertile discussions they were kind enough to have with me. They include the following.

- Nobel prize-winning professor Ilya Prigogine

In the United States:

- Stanford professors Jerry Porras, William Pasmore, and Robert Burgelman
- Itchiaque Rasool, of NASA
- Harlan Cleveland, professor at WFS
- Harvard professors Abraham Zaleznik and Chris Argyris
- MIT professors Peter Senge and Nicholas Negroponte
- The remarkable organizers of the Global Business Network (GBN), Peter Schwartz and Napier Collyns
- Michael Doyle
- The president of the Noetic Institute, Willis Harmann
- Berkeley professor Fritjof Capra

In Japan:

- Professor Shosaburo Kimura (Todai)
- Kuniyasu Sakai

- Masao Yukawa
- Dr Kawamoto (TRC, Tsukuba)

In Europe:

- Jacques Lesourne
- Dr Jean-Marie Pelt
- André Comte-Sponville, professor at the University of Paris-I
- Thierry Gaudin
- Jean Staune
- Dr Giuseppe de Rita (Rome)
- Michel Godet
- André-Yves Portnoff
- And my friend, Dr Serge Airaudi (CRC)

In expressing my gratitude, I would particularly like to single out Pierre Wack, in France, and Dr Jagdish Parikh, in India, who is well aware how fond I am of him. My warmest thanks to all of them for having opened up new horizons for us.

Last of all, I wish to express my deepest appreciation to my lifelong friend, professor Antoine Faivre, to the book's illustrator, Denis Meillassoux, and to the members of my team, Yolaine de Linares, Gérard Delaplace, Pierre Petrus, and Patrice Kobis, who all contributed to enriching this work, especially with their documentary research and their judicious observations.

Introduction

In the 1960s, work and technical progress seemed to bring us closer each day to a future far brighter than the present. Remember the predictions made at the time about the closing years of the twentieth century? Futurologists painted an idyllic portrait of the world of the 1990s. A society centered on leisure time, with colonies in outer space, was supposed to have done away with poverty and unemployment, held major epidemics in check, stabilized birth rates, built new cities free from overcrowding and coexisting harmoniously with the surrounding countryside, and, of course, wiped out malnutrition and illiteracy in the Third World.

Today, however, at a time when the gap between rich and poor has doubled and the boundary between affluence and destitution runs right through the middle of most of our towns, there no longer exists any Third World, a combat area of competition between two systems, since that *annus mirabilis* which put an end to the Communist bloc and thereby to an entire historical era. What is left is a complex, polymorphous, chaotic world in which everyone appears to be completely at sea. The threat of global nuclear war seems to be fading away (although this is largely an illusion, given the likely proliferation of atomic weapons) and, with it, the sense of obligatory alliance, leaving in its wake a more diffuse kind of risk.

The same generation that saw a man walk on the moon has also seen millions of others walking toward shantytowns and refugee camps. It won sexual freedom, but also encountered AIDS. It found a symbol of individual freedom in the automobile, yet it also discovered the joys of traffic jams under clouds of carbon monoxide. The euphoria of economic expansion for some and the perspective of social change for others have since been overshadowed by a deep, underlying anxiety.

Whereas 1989 gave rise to hopes for a new departure, the years that followed have been marked by a terrifying tendency toward disintegration. Even in families untouched by unemployment, which have maintained, or even increased, their purchasing power, parents now fear for the future of their children, for whom they increase their savings (as well as for themselves, in order to have some insurance against the risk of declining retirement payments). Reflexes of unrestrained consumption, which developed in countries obsessed with the privations experienced during World War II, have now been replaced by extreme financial caution in the face of an uncertain future.

Uncertainty is indeed the key word in the era that has just begun. What we don't know seems everywhere to outweigh what we do. A period full of upheaval, the second half of the twentieth century is characterized in particular by the discovery of black holes and antimatter. It might well be argued that just such an uncontrollable void now constitutes the dominant metaphor of the universe and of our existence, although we have always attempted to see it as a continual, logical chain offering certainty and security.

While technical, social, psychological, and political change is accelerating, no one seems to know where we are going any more. In the midst of "the lonely crowd," everyone is trying to rebuild a world view on the basis of, or perhaps in spite of, the avalanche of images and information which forms a sort of uninterrupted noise from the whole world. For the unifying effect that the omnipresent mass media have on beliefs and values that evolved through centuries of cultural differentiation remains more superficial than real, and generates more confusion than clarity. Our planet has been united in the immediacy of communications, but at the cost of mental cohesion.

This situation not only throws off balance individuals who feel lost since previous social and ideological frames of reference have fallen apart; it also affects the way in which our political and economic institutions operate. Indeed, any decision in which the future of the community is at stake requires collective motivation, or at least a shared vision of goals. The fact is, however, that for the first time in history, our world no longer recognizes any standards that could adequately structure consciousness and society, with the possible exception of human rights and democracy, whose chief virtue seems to be that it gives everyone the right to adopt whatever standards they find most convenient.

However, once we acknowledge change and uncertainty as the dominant, inevitable features of life, rigid, ossified institutions are no longer appropriate. The challenge is not merely to modernize and adapt them, but to reconsider the purpose and the means of all their basic structures, in a continual process of questioning. From now on, every organizational form (political, social, or economic) will have to be conceived of as a work in progress. We need to invent new strategies based on the idea that mobility is here to stay, both inside the company and in the overall economy.

Technological success is necessarily fleeting, and all organizations are doomed to entropy. They must constantly be regenerated. The only competitive advantage that makes that possible, and that thereby appears to have lasting value, is the quality of the people involved. Developing human potential is a long-term investment, one that bears witness to the company's faith in its own future.

Recent upheavals have underscored the inanity of both planning and extrapolating in the face of changes driven by increasingly fragmentary, random, and elusive forces. Even the most reliable of statistics have ceased to reassure today's technocrats, who find it highly disturbing that reality is beyond their control. Tomorrow's world will belong to explorers eager for creation and adventure, who "put their money" on the idea of unlimited possibilities, and who would rather experience change, anticipate it, and participate in it than be passively subjected to it.

Pessimistic observers claim that humanity is blindly heading for a disastrous future over which it has no influence. This gloomy, anguished vision leads them to advocate a fatalistic brand of *laissez-faire.* I see things quite differently. My aim is to adopt the attitude of an explorer, who lucidly scrutinizes reality with the sole intention of developing his ability to deal with it, to be ready for battle when the time comes. Only by deciding to look risks squarely and positively in the face can we properly harness our creative resources and adjust to the twists and turns that real life takes. We must learn to consider the "voids" that characterize a situation (the indeterminate, the unpredictable, the unquantifiable) as a potential for renewal. Paradoxically enough, it is by "going with the flow" that we will be able to reach a new kind of inner balance, or even control over events.

Our warehouse of conventional responses is empty. We will only find new ones to the extent that we give up the narrow economic and financial frame of reference that has concealed until now phenomena that are more intangible, but also more essential. The current phase of economic stagnation is nothing but a ripple on the ocean's surface. At a much deeper level, what is at stake is the part that people and their free development should play in our society. The risk of ecological catastrophe, of social disintegration, and of lost cultural identity may well turn out to be much more threatening in the long run than economic failure. We can no longer treat the economy as something separate from other aspects of human development. The word "economy" itself originally meant "household management" in Greek. It should be stressed, however, that there will be little left to manage in a house built on land that has subsided.

Potential for economic development is conditioned by efforts to preserve the equilibrium of the planet. In this regard, mobilizing human energy depends, as it did in the past, or even more so, on the authenticity of the answers we give to major questions of existence such as "Why work? What are we living for?" Companies that help people to work out satisfying answers to these questions will be building up a decisive competitive advantage over those who don't or can't.

PART I

Of Beaten Paths and Dead-ends

1

The Ubiquitous World TV Screen: a Source of Confusion and Cultural Resistance

If an abstract equality triumphs, the century of individualism may well take place without any real individuals. Through a continual process of levelling and division of labor, society is becoming everything and man nothing.

Henri-Frédéric Amiel, *Fragments d'un journal intime*, 1851

The power of information technology and the mass media is erasing all borders.

A ubiquitous world screen alleviates individual loneliness and serves to generate a collective memory.

Although the world screen is ostensibly neutral, it often turns out to convey elaborately constructed messages.

Facts as such have lost all significance; the only thing that matters now is the way they are presented.

Various cultures are resisting media levelling and seeking refuge in an extreme cult of local identity.

The national framework has lost its relevance, whereas the citizen of the world has yet to be born.

We must resolve the contradiction between thinking globally and acting locally.

Telephones, fax machines, the packet switching network, optic fibers, and satellites could not care less about mountains, oceans, and distances. From North to South and from East to West, the world is interconnected.

Just as time periods are being reduced, approaching the zero point, spatial distances are rapidly disappearing too. In this context, it is worth recalling the story of Dr Armand-Delille. Obsessed by the rabbits that were devastating his crops, he decided to innoculate those on his land with myxomatosis, convinced that the fence surrounding his property would prevent massive contamination. Myxomatosis thus spread throughout the entire world.

THE GLOBAL VILLAGE IGNORES ALL BOUNDARIES

In this new situation, territorial principles no longer carry much weight. Both labor and capital are increasingly international. For example, the official French telephone directory is partly produced on the other side of the planet, with keyboard work being done by operators in the Philippines. Nearly every country in the world is currently the scene of vast migrations of foreign workers, whether seasonal or not, who flee disadvantaged areas in the hope of finding zones of prosperity and employment.

We can no longer reason in terms of nations and protectionism. Today's companies are not only multinational, but also transnational, and they even tend to be "multidomestic." Decision-making centers are becoming mobile, as political and economic leaders cover hundreds of thousands of miles each year, crisscrossing the entire planet. They discover that nothing looks more like an international airport than another international airport. The articles in the showcases are roughly the same. As for new technology, it is also exported to every corner of the world as fast as planes and satellites can carry it.

NO AUTHORITY HAS ANYTHING TO GAIN FROM RETAINING INFORMATION

Communications travel practically at the speed of light, and are decentralized to such an extent that the power advantages they once brought no longer exist. Cabinet members often get wind of events by watching television – at the same time as their aides do.

It used to be that tom-tom signals could determine the survival of a tribe, or that, by using carrier pigeons, someone like Rothschild could make a fortune as the first to announce the outcome of the Battle of Waterloo. Those times are far behind us now. Today, what happens on one money market is instantaneously communicated to all the others, and the slightest change in exchange rates sends out immediate ripple effects.

Similarly, all the TV channels in the world are interconnected, which means that at any given time, identical news scenes reach homes throughout the world. Little by little, the way in which individuals and entire peoples view the world depends on a huge network of shared thoughts, signs, and images. The very words we use to describe the media (channels, cables) bring to mind the meshes of a mental network that interpenetrates all existing cultures and languages.

WORLD MEDIA ARE GENERATING A STEREOTYPED WORLD PSYCHOLOGY

It would be simplistic to imagine that information is a matter of collecting data on our environment, the way an observer might look at and describe scenery from his window, without the act itself modifying our manner of being or acting. We are watching a "non-stop show" that not only offers us occasional entertainment, or items of curiosity or discovery, or even a few rare courses for expanding our knowledge and awareness of our environment. Simultaneously present everywhere under different guises (TV, radio, newspapers, computers, telecommunications), the global screen of the mass media constantly provides a way of constructing (and of reconstructing) our vision of the world.

This flood of images obviously and inevitably results in the spreading of stereotypes. With aggressive modernity, it crushes any cultures and traditions it encounters and promotes a standardized mental landscape along with life-styles that often have no relation to local realities. Thus, younger generations that have lived since their childhood in the media galaxy are naturally much more receptive to international subjects than their parents were, and they sometimes feel stifled in the traditional, narrow national framework, which they perceive as outmoded and ill-adapted to contemporary life.

As far back as 30 years ago, during the Algerian War, it was the young draftees' transistors that prevented the generals in mutiny from asserting their control over the French troops. In 1989, the existence of video films and radio broadcasts undoubtedly contributed in a similar fashion to the collapse of the Communist world. The global screen can send out cultural shock waves that enable young people to defy hallowed social conventions such as arranged marriages among the Chinese, the confining of Muslim women, and mutilation in Africa. The sight of a cormorant drenched in petroleum on a beach polluted by an oil slick does more to further the cause of ecology than any debate conducted by experts.

THE GLOBAL SCREEN BRINGS "THE LONELY CROWD" TOGETHER

Modern society is characterized by the steady erosion of any sense of belonging. Rootlessness, social and occupational mobility, the loosening of social strictures, individualism, declining moral and religious values, and widespread disregard for established political and social institutions are the hallmarks of the world inhabited by "the lonely crowd" once described by David Reisman.[1]

Such an atomization of social life reinforces the influence of the media. Television and audio seem to be the sole remaining arena in which people can communicate and interact universally. Only the media can reach everyone in his or her private sphere and connect him or her to the rest of the world; they have replaced the *forum* and the *agora* of antiquity as well as the village square. At present, nothing important escapes the control of TV (and, to a lesser extent, radio), from news reports to the choice of political leaders. Audiovisual information not only mediates all essential collective events, but also acts as an arbiter in social life.

POWERFUL IMAGES ARE CREATING A WORLDWIDE COLLECTIVE MEMORY

Through live reporting, viewers have the feeling that they are participating in events occurring thousands of miles away. Journalists give priority to sensational scenes guaranteed to elicit powerful emotions and thus to capture the audience's attention. This leads to the emergence of a kind of worldwide collective memory, constantly fueled by ubiquitous messages, immediate, simultaneous broadcasting, and the uniformity of the scenes selected. Some powerful images have had considerable impact on public opinion: everyone remembers the inhabitants of Berlin tearing the Wall down with their bare hands, Chinese students blocking a tank on Tienanmen Square, or Boris Yeltsin haranguing Soviet soldiers. These are images that in a sense created events or hastened the advent of decisive changes, both in people's minds and in basic power relations.

News on a massive scale makes it possible to denounce corruption, imprisonment, and dictatorship, although this might be more comforting to know if we could be sure that those manipulating the media were sincere advocates of democracy rather than demagogues. After all, they have control of formidable instruments of propaganda, or even the means to go to war, as Saddam Hussein clearly understood when he displayed his Western hostages to the whole world.

Certain forms of disinformation have just as strong an effect as true information. The staging of the "revolution" in Romania and the doctored news coverage of the Gulf War underscored the need for reliable information – on news reporting and those running the media. Yet however wary people may be becoming, critics never go so far as to call into question the media as such, for they have become part and parcel of daily life itself.

Although a TV viewer may be able at any time to zap from channel to channel, he or she can hardly escape the influence of the screen. Facts or news only become trustworthy and acceptable to the extent that they appear on television. The worldwide audiovisual system serves as the ultimate reference, the village drum. However aware we may be that what we are shown has been consciously faked or manipulated for reasons of propaganda, distorted news always seems preferable to no news at all. If it hasn't been broadcast, it doesn't exist.

Anything or anyone lacking the appropriate "media profile" is therefore eliminated from the public scene and kept out of power. Under the *Ancien Régime* in France, the dauphin did not become king until he had been anointed by the Archbishop of Reims. Nowadays, a presidential candidate cannot hope to gain credibility until he or she appears on one of the leading talk shows. There is clear evidence that some TV debates have decisively tipped the electoral scales, simply because, at the crucial time, one of the candidates was not to be seen in the TV studios. The converse holds true of photogenic, or rather telegenic, politicians and actors (like Ronald Reagan). "The society of the spectacle" seems to like tinsel better than serious-mindedness, and sometimes has trouble distinguishing between commercials and political debate.

REALITY IS MASKED BY THE WAY IT IS REPRESENTED

In a chapter with the suggestive title "From Written Government to Screen Government," Régis Debray points out that "the state emblem began as a symbol, then became an icon, and ultimately a sign, that is, first the coat of arms, then the King's portrait, then the President's photo."[2]

Debray goes on to explain that the French state arose from a symbol, "when the *fleur-de-lis* ceased to represent a reigning family and came to stand for France." Some authors trace the state's birth back to 1545, when the Edict of Montil-lès-Tours made it mandatory to draw up customary law in writing. In any case, universal values became widespread with the development of printing and gave form to a new humanity, "reasonable and critical," instead of a society governed by oral tradition, "unanimous but errant," as Condorcet put it.

Language makes use of symbolic abstraction (the word "sheep" has no wooly hairs), unlike icons (such as traffic signs indicating that animal flocks might cross the road), which employ pictographs but whose sole purpose is, for example, to warn motorists. The photograph of a sheep, however, is a mere result of the effect of light on a photosensitive surface, a "sign" in and of itself without meaning. Presented with one and the same photo, two people holding diametrically opposed political viewpoints will both contend that the picture confirms their ideas.

Present-day culture no longer emphasizes language, which has become the privilege of the learned, while increasingly abandoning icons, which, to be comprehended, require faith or a particular context (e.g. the American flag), and appear to be rather the hallmark of overtly totalitarian societies (witness the vast proletarian iconography in Communist countries).

Our "videosphere," which observes everything through a camera lens, has apparently relinquished any claim to make sense out of experience. Education, a normative term, has thus given way to culture, a purely descriptive notion. Foreign policy, which calls for geopolitical vision, has taken a back seat to humanitarian intervention (i.e. all those who suffer have an equal right to aid). "Visual Esperanto has unified and smoothed out the Babel of different languages, stages of development, and social structures. A new form of cosmopolitanism has emerged, but it is more superficial than real. For misfortune presented in two dimensions loses its third dimension, that of historical depth," writes Debray. "Images of a famine in Somalia, of a massacre in Bosnia, of an earthquake in Armenia do not strike us as uniquely Somalian, Bosnian, or Armenian. The visual sphere speaks all languages because it speaks none of them . . . Television tends to strip these tragedies of their meaning by abolishing the profound differences between them."

Members of the French revolutionary army gave their lives for freedom (an abstract symbol); Iranian children, faced with Iraqi machine guns, did so in order to go to Allah's heaven (a stock image created specially for them by the mullahs); today, right under our eyes, Somalians and Bosnians seem to be dying for nothing. "From afar, all the wounded look alike, as do all wars; there are only bodies, no human beings any more who could convey a particular set of values."

We have indeed traveled a long way from the theatrical catharsis of violence, which has functioned since antiquity with the aid of artistic symbols, to the countless gallons of hemoglobin required to produce a TV series based on horrors depicted with growing casualness. The purpose of catharsis becomes irrelevant compared with the near-biological details of a gored body, a sight by now so trivial that, every now and then, it encourages some morbid creature to reproduce it in real life so as to "do what they do on TV." The loss of meaning could hardly be greater.

PACKAGING THE IMAGE TAKES PRECEDENCE OVER THE EVENT ITSELF

Long ago, in his book *Mythologies*, Roland Barthes noted an "important historical paradox: the more technology develops the spread of information (in particular, images), the more it provides a means to mask the meaning constructed behind the appearance of the meaning offered." Wrought with the same care as medieval illuminations were, some images are authentic icons, concealed by the ostensible spontaneity of live broadcasting.

Edgard Roskis[3] raised questions as to the staging of the "historic" handshake of September 13, 1993 between Rabin and Arafat, for he felt he could detect an "image within the image: the figure of Christ personified by Bill Clinton, with his arms stretched out to each side, uniting a Jew and an Arab in the communion of forgiveness and hope." For the cameramen who were massively invited to this programmed celebration, the fact that the only visual angle they had was frontal "compelled them to center their shots on Clinton, with his arms in the position he had chosen." It is highly unlikely that this was a matter of sheer chance; such an interpretation would, in Roskis's opinion, boil down to:

> underestimating the most recent developments in American tradition, which has always "thought image" first and foremost. On this score, the video replay leaves little room for doubt. The President initially seems to spread his arms *naturally*, just so he can bring the two protagonists together; then, forgetting himself for a moment, he drops them at his sides; recalling at the last minute the vital importance of this gesture, he returns to his former pose in time for the handshake.

The moral of the story is provided by philosopher, architect, and town planner Virilio, interviewed in late October by the magazine *Globe hebdo*: "It's communication that matters, not events. Events are dominated by the way they are presented and staged." According to Virilio, wars were won in the early years of the twentieth century by arms, in the middle of it by science, and today by information "processing." The Gulf War demonstrated that the military could use the media as effectively against Saddam Hussein as their Cold War predecessors had enlisted scientists to counter Stalin. He concludes in the following terms:

"The negative side of over-information is confusion, by which we drown in facts, in which facts are themselves defeated. Our world no longer has any reference points. Over-information is creating a new Tower of Babel."

MEDIA STANDARDIZATION IS STIMULATING DEMANDS FOR THE RIGHT TO BE DIFFERENT

Bereft of any deeper significance, such media shock waves entail the spread of stereotyped patterns throughout the world. However, as Coca-Cola and American TV series invade even the most remote desert regions, people also begin to proclaim their ethnic identity loud and clear, to rediscover long-forgotten cultural roots.

In the face of this destructuring invasion, many feel the need to emphasize what is specific about them. Cultural assertion is taking the place of ideological demands. In international relations, fewer than 200 sovereign states have official status, but it would be more sensible to see the world as a patchwork composed of over 10,000 ethnic communities, most of which exist as minorities that feel no allegiance to the states in which they live. They are "transnations," delimited less by any tangible political borders than by cultural barriers.

The recent demand, formulated by the United States in the context of GATT negotiations, that American products be allowed to exceed their current 58 percent share of the French audiovisual market (European Union members uphold a 40 percent quota for European audiovisual works) unleashed a general outcry in French cultural circles. Régis Debray, himself a proponent of "cutural exception," issued a warning to all those who claim that there is no alternative other than the choice "between local ayatollahs and Coca-Cola . . . If the soul of cultural minorities no longer finds any way of expressing itself, since it has been transformed into an alien in its own country, it may just seek an outlet in the worst forms of fundamentalist regression. For this is exactly the future that the tidal wave of standardized image and sound has in store for us: a world of xenophobic backlash and regression."

At present, minority cultures thus exhibit the greatest need for identity and historical rootedness. Language, religion, even ethnic origins, are the components of a search for new focus. From practical forms of mutual aid to nationalist, autonomist, or fundamentalist movements, there are countless ways to "get back to your roots."

Table 1.1 Ethnic evolution of the US population (in %)

	1981–91	*2030*
White	+6	+25
Hispanic	+53	+187
Asian	+108	+79
African	+13	+68

CULTURES ARE BECOMING GLOBAL AND DIFFERENTIATED AT THE SAME TIME

Even the United States, held up for so long as the prime example of a socially cohesive melting pot, is currently the scene of movements that call into question the country's very historical basis. The existence of increasingly vocal black, Hispanic, and Native American groups clearly points to a re-dealing of the cards.

On the Berkeley campus, for example, the level of cultural diversity is indeed striking. Discussions there now revolve around ethnic background, whereas 20 years ago, the idea was to build a new America for all.

When you look at the ethnic evolution of the American population, you cannot help wondering whether the concept of the melting pot still applies (table 1.1). The massive influx of Latin Americans and the rapid growth of the Latino communities have the effect of "importing" Hispanic culture and promoting the use of Spanish in the country. In such a context, we can hardly assume that the various ethnic groups will blend together everywhere with the same results.

National or ethnic claims come to life to the extent that states no longer have the moral authority (i.e. the legitimacy) or the legal and administrative power to assert themselves as the regulators of society. In any case, they are virtually unable to assert anything, since statesmen are concerned above all with their own short-term popularity, even if that means jeopardizing both the future and their country's financial resources. Apparently, political failure is never due to anything nowadays other than "communication problems," a convenient alibi for u-turns in policy (as the hasty withdrawal of a much-needed reorganization plan for Air France in October 1993 illustrated so well).

At a time when the interplay of established social forces (e.g. trade unions and employers' federations) modeled events, reaching a compromise was relatively easy. Now, however, everything has become much more fluid, public opinion is the ultimate judge, and the increasingly complex art of government looks more and more like political guesswork.

THE THREAT OF A NEW INTERNATIONAL INSTABILITY

In the international arena, when the Communist bloc fell apart, marking the end of a long-standing bipolar balance between the superpowers, nationalist sentiment and regional conflicts received a new impetus. The various national structures consolidated at the end of World War II and subsequently in the period of decolonization have increasingly come under fire, whether internally, by ethnic minorities, or by transnational religious or cultural identity movements like Islamic fundamentalism.

The leading powers of yesterday must now face up to the stagnation of their economies. It appears to be more than mere coincidence that the United States and Russia, which both spent enormous sums on the military in the hope that it would bring them world domination, have experienced economic decline in relation to Japan and Germany, who lost the war and whose defense budgets remained extremely low. Contrary to what is generally assumed, and regularly claimed by the various military–industrial lobbies, the economic "spin-off" of defense research seems to have been modest.

In the vast majority of countries, the dominant mood in public opinion is one of anxiety. To be sure, the risk of global nuclear war appears less ominous since the leading powers have initiated disarmament. Yet the risk has in fact become more diffuse, through a process of fragmentation. With the proliferation of nuclear weapons, sometimes in the hands of unpredictable, uncontrollable dictators, and the real possibility of chemical warfare, terrorism, and regional nuclear blackmail, there are legitimate grounds for anxiety. In this context, it is difficult not to wonder what a Yugoslavian-style conflict would look like if it were to take place between former member states of the Soviet Union, given their impressive nuclear arsenals.

What is needed is an international regulator, able to impose a lasting peace or at least to limit the scope of those conflits that do arise. As for "The New World Order" advocated by former US President George

Bush, it too clearly reflects the power aims of the United States to be acceptable to anyone other than the closest American allies.

As an institution, the UN remains too weak and lacking in autonomy. It has, of course, begun playing an increasingly important role, but without acquiring more stable and efficient means of prevention and dissuasion, which would reduce its dependence on its main financial backers at each conflict, it will never gain the credibility it needs. That the UN observers who went to Iraq following the Gulf War submitted their report to the United States instead of to the UN General Secretary gives some indication of how far we still have to go. More recently, the Somalian fiasco and UN powerlessness in Bosnia have amply demonstrated how futile it is to attempt to replace international political vision with humanitarian interference.

THE NATIONAL FRAMEWORK IS COMING APART AT THE SEAMS

In earlier epochs, when people moved about within the limited radius of clearly defined areas, states differed markedly, and each one dealt with problems in its own fashion.

Today, however, a large number of issues can only be settled on a global basis. The management of energy resources, air space and the seas, telecommunications, environmental protection, the struggle against epidemics, and even the fight against organized crime or terrorism all require a resolutely international approach.

Who, we might ask, is planning to take responsibility for the ozone layer or Antarctica? Given the current set-up, a problem as basic as raw material prices is insoluble. Their constant decline over the past several years maintains entire regions of the world in an unacceptable state of poverty.

Although national governments are in no position to handle them, no one quite knows in what forum such issues should now be discussed, much less what institutions should have the right to make the appropriate decisions.

In light of these crucial questions, which involve the very future of the world, there is something alarming about the way in which short-term, local electoral considerations dominate political life. This discrepancy obviously has an effect on the confidence people have in politicians.

It seems long ago indeed that an authentic statesman said he had "a vision for France." But it is far from clear that the day will come when some true citizen of the world will similarly proclaim that he or she is motivated by "a vision for the Earth," one that can reconcile and mobilize people around the globe.

HUMANKIND HAS LOST ITS BEARINGS

With the disappearance of Communist regimes, history has ceased to be a bipolar, simplistic confrontation between capitalism and socialism, between East and West. It has become an open, multipolar game, unstable and complex, in which attempts at dogmatic conditioning cancel each other out in the long run. The certainties of yesterday, which seem so ludicrous today, have none the less paved the way for the emergence of a new kind of critical outlook.

To the extent that it has increased the number of parameters involved, the shift from a bipolar to a multipolar system has led to a growing awareness of the complexity of the world, a notion which we must now integrate into all our thinking. In the future, political structures will no longer be judged by their ability to defend a given territory, but by their ability to manage such complexity.

What is urgently called for is a more harmonious global functioning that can put an end to all the existing barriers, whether national, social, or even between businesses, and thereby make it possible to respond to new challenges that are beyond the limited grasp of institutions and individuals as we know them. Yet such a requirement is clearly at odds with the perpetual need of human beings to "stake out their territory," to get a sense of who and where they are.

We all grew up with the concept of geographical limits, of borders traced on maps that define a country's contours. Our strategies are still based on similar notions of boundaries and territory, which reflect the deep-seated need of people to feel that they "belong" somewhere. All too often, we consider the space we occupy as a closed, almost self-sufficient entity. At present, however, this "Maginot line syndrome" proves to be increasingly out of phase with a world in which networks and connections are rapidly short-circuiting all imaginable established barriers. For nations, the days of "splendid isolation" are over, as are the days of captive markets.

BARRIERS BETWEEN BUSINESSES ARE ALSO BECOMING BLURRED

While in the political sphere, nation-states are losing more and more of their decision-making power to other, so-called regional or world organizations, a similar phenomenon can be observed in relations between businesses.

It can be said that a world community of technology, finance, and economy already exists *de facto*. Useable information must be derived from the mass of data with which we are constantly swamped, from the faint signals that come from everywhere in the world, sometimes simultaneously. It is essential for organizations to be receptive to such information, and therefore to construct open networks whose main purpose is to gather international data as a prerequisite to intelligent decision-making.

Through these networks, large corporations will be increasingly interconnected in complex groupings. The flow of information, research, trade, and investment will occur through constantly evolving forms of international association, so much so that figuring out just what belongs to a particular company will sometimes be difficult.

Firms will no longer be evaluated as they are today. Traders and investors may even have trouble discerning the boundaries between industrial conglomerates.[4] As a result, our perception of such multinational groupings will probably undergo considerable change.

THINKING GLOBALLY, ACTING LOCALLY

Our society is becoming both nomadic and sedentary. On the one hand, modern transportation, communication, and all possible forms of exchange link us to the rest of the planet, and, on the other hand, our actual emotional ties are still a far cry from world citizenship, for they remain rooted in locally defined groups. Most aspects of daily existence are of a disparate nature (food is local, whereas faxes are global) and bring differing registers of perception, comprehension, and reaction into play.

The disorienting, dizzying effect of the emerging global society is compensated for by a retreat into reassuring, familiar subgroups that help people to recover a sense of reality and that have taken on unusual importance since the waning of traditional village communities. Present-day individuals yearn for contact, neighborly relations, and solidarity based on the activities in which they are interested. Nearly anything can bring them together: sports, clubs, charity work, teenage gangs, or religious sects. What matters is to be part of a social network, however fuzzy its contours may be, that offers some kind of collective frame of reference.

The existence of multiple, overlapping levels of solidarity and social cohesion compels us both to think globally when confronted with vital world issues, and to act locally within structures that promote practical integration, that make daily life liveable.

Paradoxically, we find ourselves on two different planes that are sometimes hard to reconcile: day-to-day reality, with its down-to-earth problems that must be solved within the framework of local ties, and the world "psycho-sphere," to which we are connected through television, and in some cases our computers. In order to go beyond this dichotomy, we need to develop a holistic outlook that enables us to grasp simultaneously the unity and diversity of the new society currently taking shape.

This conception could lead to the emergence of a new kind of regulation, based on forms of cooperation that transcend all borders. The current upsurge in regional or local feeling admittedly stands in the way of this development, but it should be stressed that all such attempts at asserting a cultural identity draw their strength precisely from the present confusion as to goals and direction. In this respect, they serve to reveal a deep-seated need for meaning, a meaning that standardized images cannot embody and that discredited conventional doctrines can no longer provide.

Notes

1 David Reisman, *The Lonely Crowd: a Study of the Changing American Character* (New Haven: Yale University Press, 1960).
2 Régis Debray, *L'Etat séducteur* (Paris: Gallimard, 1993).
3 Roskis, a lecturer in the Information–Communication Department at the University of Paris-X, wrote an article entitled "La poignée de main ou l'actualité programmée" printed in the October 29, 1993 issue of *Libération*.
4 In the majority of Western countries, the usual practice is to consolidate company accounts, a complex procedure that makes for rigid structures, whereas in Japan, it is not. New opportunities should be created that enable firms to establish more flexible links to each other.

2

The Twilight of Dogma and the Unchallenged Supremacy of Economic Relations

Doctrines have become unbelievable.

Michel de Certeau

Today's society is not structured by religion, nor by visions of progress, nor by scientistic dogmas.

Society is also turning away from extreme forms of political centralization and materialistic ideology.

Cooperation between people as well as regional alliances are based solely on economic considerations.

The doctrine of free enterprise is not equal to the task of achieving a harmonious integration of the world.

The free market is not immune to dogmatic distortions.

As the present millennium draws to a close, no one quite knows where the vast upheaval of values currently underway is leading us. If, however, we take a longer, historical view of the situation, we can perceive that over the past 30 years, the Western world has experienced the successive collapse of all the frames of reference that structured its world view since the nineteenth century.

RELIGION HAS BECOME A PRIVATE MATTER

In the late 1960s, a first shock wave was produced by the rapid acceleration of the trend toward dechristianization which had begun in the previous century. By now, people have massively abandoned regular religious practice. Society seems to have lost its sacred framework. What religious practice does subsist only involves social minorities and often develops beyond the pale of established Christian models (the rise of Islam, of Eastern religions, or even of sects).

In any event, the new, decisive phenomenon in the present period that needs to be stressed is that religious beliefs no longer structure social life as a whole, but have become a matter of mere individual, private choice. Everyone now accepts the principle that we are all free to adopt those beliefs we consider most suitable. As a result, any form of religious or moral dogmatism meets with massive disapproval, even if the morality is perfectly secular.

Nowadays, it is for the individual, and no longer for the family or social environment, to define the array of beliefs that satisfy his or her conscience and personal views.

TECHNICAL PROGRESS CANNOT ALWAYS BE EQUATED WITH THE PROGRESS OF CIVILIZATION

A second shock wave has been sent out by the erosion of the classical vision of "progress." Not long ago, it was widely held that the development of science and technology would naturally and automatically lead to general progress for humanity and civilization in all areas of life. What we observe, however, is that impressive advances in the field of scientific discovery and practical invention, while an unquestionable source of improvement, do not inevitably promote the cause of universal progress. As recent developments suggest, such advances are only one of its preconditions.

Toward the end of the 1970s, the awareness that an energy crisis (the oil crisis) could undermine economic expansion shook our society's faith in progress. Having assumed for so long that there were no limits to growth, we finally had to address the painful question of the relative scarcity of the earth's resources. Subsequently, it became clear that great industrial and technological accomplishments could also do tremendous damage, creating forms of pollution that endanger the balance of nature as well as the health of humanity. The Chernobyl disaster was the most dramatic sign of this development.

Lastly, recent high-level discoveries have shown that scientific endeavor leads to increasingly broad areas of uncertainty; modern experiments (particularly in physics) have destroyed the mechanistic, positivistic postulates of the nineteenth century. Furthermore, new ethical problems have arisen in the world of biology that would have appeared inconceivable in times past, when scientists were purported to be able to demonstrate anything and to respond to all questions. The past few decades have essentially taught us that life's dynamics are far more complex than we had imagined.

THE END OF COMMUNIST IDEOLOGY

A third shock wave closed the 1980s: the collapse of the Communist empire. The destruction of the Berlin Wall not only marked the disappearance of an oppressive system once considered unshakeable, but also delivered a mortal blow to Messianic Marxism, one of this century's leading ideologies (even a sort of pseudo-religion) and, in so doing, to any claim to force humanity's destiny to correspond to a single, unified end.

"Communism," as Alain Minc has pointed out, "brought to a fever pitch the following simple idea: reason should govern the world."[1] Here was a socialism that saw itself as scientific, not utopian. Yet several phenomena contributed to its sudden loss of credit. What occurred was not so much a rejection of Communist ideology as the demand for freedom of opinion, national autonomy, and free activity, but above all, a radical change in values and world views among the younger generations.

Our epoch has little affection for top-heavy, unwieldy, rigid constructions, whether they are ideologies, bureaucracies, or overgrown production machines. We have entered the soft era, in which "gray matter," information, and creativity occupy center stage, and which is light-years away from the reign of "soviets and electricity."

The powerful Soviet state fell to pieces, and a similar fate awaits any number of centralized power structures – if they haven't already suffered it. The huge industrial complexes served, in a sense, to illustrate the absurdity of a civilization based on deterministic, mechanistic postulates. Stalinism was the consummate political expression of this civilization, as well as its swan song. We are thus witnessing the end of the race for "bigness," for material power, that contributed toward obscuring the traditional divisions in society. Although the race was above all characteristic of the middle of the twentieth century, its origins actually lie much further in the past, in the Enlightenment.

THE BANKRUPTCY OF REDUCTIONISM AND THE QUEST FOR PURPOSE

The notion that an understanding of the whole requires analysis of each of its parts goes back to Descartes. While perceiving the world horizontally, such a conception ignores its vertical nature. This kind of reductionism, combined with determinism (man can fully comprehend the universe in which he lives, this comprehension constituting in fact the ultimate purpose of his earthly existence), gave birth to modern science, which in turn made possible the prodigious economic and social expansion of our civilization.

This ideological postulate was essential to the development of experimental science. Without it, it would have made little sense to attempt to uncover the workings of a world that some philosophies (such as Taoism) consider by definition fundamentally unintelligible. This doctrine was also applied, quite inevitably, to man himself, also reduced to a set of organs and molecules. It thereby eliminated the coherence that a certain spiritual vision previously gave to man's sojourn in this world, without, however, there emerging any new sense of purpose. The postulates of science were no more neutral than the technologies that were born of them. They destroyed the old social order.

Traditional cosmogony grounded society in an immutable order. The king was central to society, just as the Earth was to the world. Under the

Ancien Régime, society was divided into three estates: the priests were invested with spiritual, religious, and intellectual authority; the nobles exercised temporal, i.e. political, administrative, and military power; and the bourgeoisie held sway over the realm of finance, trade, and production. Such a division is still to be found in many traditional societies, which often even maintain cast distinctions. Although the value system upon which they rest and which their members accept is contrary to democracy, it at least has the advantage of giving clarity and structure to social life.

It took several centuries for technical development to bring about the decline of these societies. Yet already in late eighteenth-century France, the Encyclopedists positively worshiped instrumental reason as Descartes had defined it. The prestige attached to experimental science and the astounding achievements of technology managed little by little to overshadow the traditional criteria used to judge the world and to undermine religious and political authority. Economic progress had become the measure of all things.

The past few decades, however, have witnessed growing disillusionment on this score. Our society has begun to realize that a life based entirely on the accumulation of ever-changing material goods is one of utter absurdity.

Of course, the practical results of experimental science (automobiles, airplanes, telecommunications) have brought considerable benefits to humanity. Yet the feeling of power that they afford have also led us to neglect other values and have discredited the collective standards that once held society together.

THE ECONOMY IS THE ONLY LINK LEFT

Once spiritual, religious authority (or its secular counterpart) and the political power of the state have lost their prestige and are no longer in a position to impose their norms on the community, the economy becomes the only general federative principle left in society. In the absence of ideological empires or official religions, sheer pragmatism encourages the establishment of regional alliances in which trade is paramount.

These alliances, of which the European Community provides a clear-cut example, are in fact continental in scope (figure 2.1). They are set

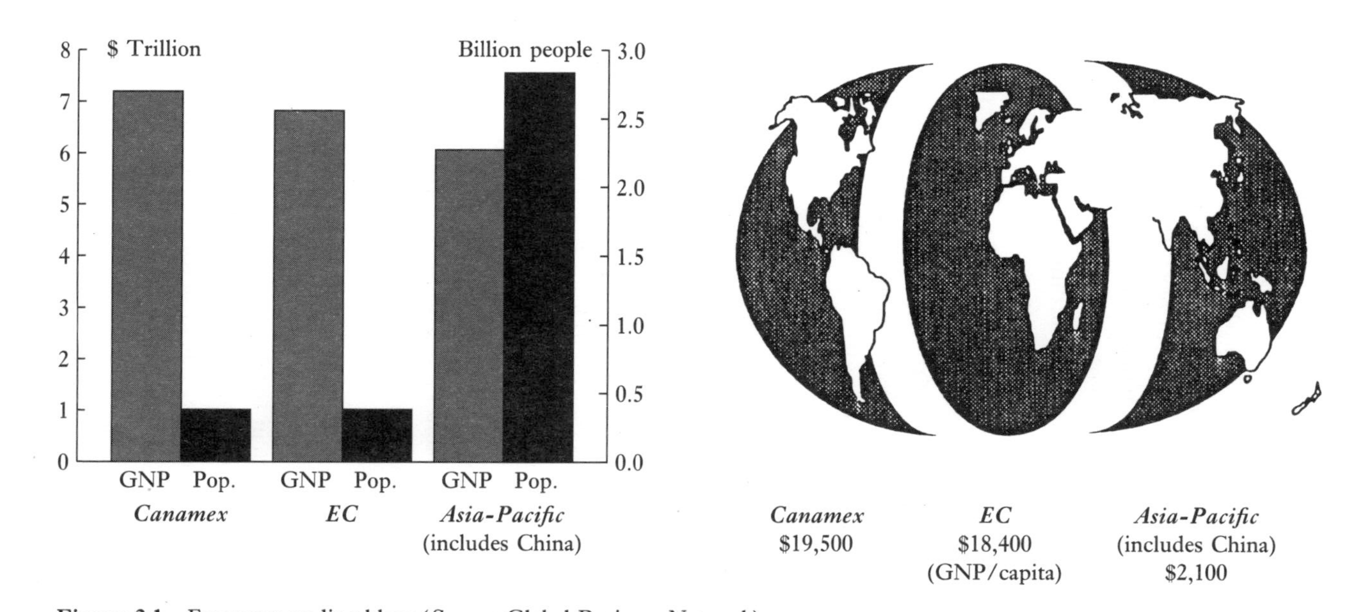

Figure 2.1 Emergent trading blocs (*Source*: Global Business Network)

up to further their members' common interests, which are essentially economic. Although in the case of Europe, there exists a broader social, cultural, and political agenda, its concrete application is slow in coming.

Canada, the United States, and Mexico (Canamex) are also attempting to organize their own common market. Uniting 370 million inhabitants, or slightly more than the former 12 countries of the European Community, this North American community encompasses a newly industrializing country, Mexico, in which wages, social security, and environmental protection are at an incomparably lower level than in the two other member countries. Its proponents see in it the means both to stem the tide of migration from Mexico to the United States and to delocalize labor-intensive industrial activities to the other side of the border. Its detractors claim that it will increase American unemployment. President Clinton succeeded none the less in getting Congress to ratify the agreement on November 17, 1993, while a large number of congressional Democrats (not to mention trade unionists and ecologists) openly expressed their concern over the economic, social, and environmental consequences of this "marriage" and waged a fierce battle against the gradual (15-year) unification process provided for by the treaty.

In the long run, Japan and the ASEAN countries can be expected to follow a similar course in Asia. In spite of all the unpleasant memories of World War II, when confronted with blocs as powerful as North America or Western Europe, the Pacific region may well form an increasingly integrated market centered on Japan and the booming "dragons." Although East Asia is undergoing a primarily pragmatic sort of economic integration, in which market mechanisms play the leading role, the process may take on a new character as the inhabitants of the region become aware of the advantages that such multilateral interdependency offers. The CEAP (the organization overseeing economic cooperation in the Asia-Pacific area) has, for the time being, an exclusively consultative function, but there is every reason to believe that it will have more than that in the future.

Throughout the world, superimposed layers of political decision-making are becoming the rule. For instance, where exactly is Catalonia's future decided? In Barcelona, Madrid, Brussels, or at the UN in New York? The answer is that the region's fate depends at present on the interaction of the four authorities mentioned, and thus on a complex sort of meshwork dominated by economic considerations.

BUT ECONOMIC INTEGRATION ALONE CANNOT UNIFY EUROPE

The European Economic Community, which for 30 years set an example of transnational federation, has been having a hard time pursuing the process of integration since German reunification took place and its member currencies have been fluctuating to a disturbing degree. It is no longer clear whether it is worth continuing in the same direction. Indeed, some observers have begun to question whether a more flexible form of horizontal coordination might not be preferable to the existing arrangement, one able to include the nations of Eastern Europe as well. According to this line of reasoning, it is urgent to forestall the resurgence of traditional demons in the East. Geopolitics, it would seem, require that we focus our efforts chiefly on the economic integration of Eastern Europe and the Mediterranean basin, instead of uniformly distributing them around the world.

However, the economico-financial biases underlying the work of the Brussels officials do not appear particularly adequate to the task of solving the deep crisis in which Europe is bogged down. The successive visions that have accompanied the project of European unity prove to be in contradiction, not only with each other (we have gone from "a Europe of nations" to "the European Union"), but also with the Commission's current practices. It is extremely difficult to discern even a modicum of consistency between the constant hymns in praise of the free market and the countless directives that regulate the totality of production standards down to the most minute details. The result seems to be a kind of downward levelling of the different national legal frameworks. Too bad for the consumer eager for authentic products, who may soon be offered chocolate without cocoa in it, all in the name of free trade, of course.

The main weakness of the European Community lies in its monolithic free-trade vision, which has achieved the status of dogma, to such an extent that it is inscribed in the founding texts of the Community.[2] In addition, this doctrine is meant to apply not only between member nations, which is perfectly appropriate, but even in dealing with other countries. Of the three major economically developed zones today, Europe is the only one that considers moderate protection of its home market a near-diabolical act of regression, rather than simply a possible option that would in no way prevent its 345 million consumers from reaping the benefits of the free market. In the United States, the Buy American Act allows the authorities to suspend imports of certain commodities if they feel that the interests of national producers are in jeopardy.[3] In Japan, both cultural barriers and the country's distribution system ensure that imports never exceed a modest level. In Europe, however, a commissioner who succeeds in reducing the tariffs applied by the EC to non-member countries, which already happen to be among the lowest in the world, sees himself as nothing less than a heroic champion of consumer rights. Partly as a result of such views, the share of the EC member countries in world industrial production is currently declining from 25 percent in 1973 to something like 20 percent in the year 2000.[4] According to Maurice Allais, a Nobel prize-winner in economics, "we are only now discovering the actual scope of the damage done by dogmatic, anarchic, reckless measures aimed at easing international trade restrictions." Over the past 15 years, the OECD countries have lost between 10 and 20 million jobs.

IN SEARCH OF THE ELUSIVE "PURITY" OF THE MARKET

The free market has just knocked out all its opponents. From the underdeveloped countries in the South to the ex-Communist countries and China (which still maintains its socialist label for the sake of appearances), everyone sings its praises, stresses its requirements, and expects that obedience to its commandments will usher in an era of freedom and democracy. Pragmatic and realistic, this new ideal would seem to offer the advantage of not being an ideology. Yet, however unquestionable may be the virtues of the market, this last idea should be taken with a pinch of salt.

Liberal economic views appeared rather recently in world history. As Karl Polanyi[5] demonstrated, in earlier periods (in antiquity, for example) and in other regions (in Mesopotamia, or in the former empire of Dahomey), there existed a flourishing trade that had nothing to do with market laws. Adam Smith was the first to claim that "the invisible hand," i.e. the law of supply and demand, optimally regulates production and distribution. In his view, free trade spontaneously gives rise to wealth and solidarity through the operation of simple mechanisms, and not for moral reasons. According to the father of free enterprise, it is not the kindness of the butcher, the baker, or the beer seller, but the care they take in pursuing their interests that makes it possible for us to have dinner.[6] Specialization enables everyone to function more efficiently. The baker has an interest in producing good bread and selling large quantities of it, so that he can buy shoes from the shoemaker, who, in turn, will not concern himself with baking activites, but rather will buy his bread from the baker. All that is required for the economy to reach optimum levels is *laissez-faire*.

Here was a fully fledged philosophy, which Léon Walras translated into a "pure, perfect" model. If, he argued, the demand for a product exceeds its supply, prices rise, thereby encouraging production; if it is lower, they go down, thus regulating the market by wiping out the least efficient producers.[7] In the meantime, David Ricardo extended these notions to international trade. According to him, nations have just as much reason to specialize as bakers and shoemakers do, with each one enjoying a comparative advantage in a particular branch of production.[8]

All these theories, while highly attractive, not to mention their practical efficiency, none the less have a single flaw: they assume so-called "ideal" conditions that only represent 5 percent of actual transactions at the utmost (a generous estimate, in fact). To take one example, it has recently been observed that production is regulated much more by quantity than by price. Thus, in early 1994, with demand for automobiles stagnant and Volkswagen employees working a mere 29 hours a week, prices for the Golf did not go down in the slightest. In order to operate, the Walrasian model requires the existence of an auctioneer or broker, which is obviously a rare phenomenon in commercial transactions, except on commodity markets. This example also underscores an important point, namely that the market economy is not synonymous with capitalism, contrary to what the Eastern European countries were rather quick to believe. Although the accumulation of capital as a result of profits is necessary to the development of free-enterprise capitalism, it is not in and of itself sufficient. If profits are not reinvested in production, economic activity will remain primarily speculative. In the West, the effects of institutional regulation have not been entirely perverse, or in any case, not nearly to the extent that British and American free-enterprise advocates claim. Capitalism in the Rhineland, which considers itself responsible for social harmony and strives to uphold rules other than purely commerical ones, does not, however, seem to have suffered any notable drop in efficiency.

But, above all, these theories have a great deal of trouble in accounting for the complexity of reality. They have nothing to say about the influence of trust or of ethics. For instance, they are incapable of explaining a phenomenon like blood donation, for they posit the idea that an economic agent always seeks, through his action, to maximize his own benefits. These theories are inherently unrealistic, since they require an unlikely optimization of certain variables (the rationality of the contracting parties, the quantity of information they have at their disposal, etc.), while assuming that others, such as the value of currencies, remain constant. In fact, however, since the international monetary system based on the automatic convertibility of the dollar into gold came to an end, currencies have undergone highly speculative fluctuations unrelated to what they are supposed to be measuring: the productive wealth of the community in which they serve as a reference. There is therefore no standard that could enable us to assess, with reasonable objectivity, "the competitive advantage of nations."

Of course, when it proves to be impossible to reduce the real world to a given theoretical model, one can always try to change the real world so that it fulfills the "utopian" conditions the theory calls for. Current efforts aimed at deregulation, the breaking up of monopolies, and stimulation of international trade can thus be viewed as an attempt to construct a utopian economic model enabling theory to apply at long last to a stubbornly refractory reality.[9] A recent OECD study offers a good illustration of this tendency.[10] It estimates that the world would lose exactly $213 billion in wealth if no agreement were reached at the end of the Uruguay Round of GATT negotiations, and would gain $450 billion if international trade were to be entirely freed of all restrictions. As ostensible proof of their serious-mindedness, the authors worked through 77,000 equations in order to reach these figures. Yet it must be pointed out to the reader inclined to take these equations for an adequate description of actual observed phenomena, that the authors do little more than advance figures for the savings that, according to economic theory, should be possible under the given hypothetical circumstances. "These conclusions," we read, "reflect the hypotheses and choices made by the model's authors." The theory employed thus provides its own justification, with reality serving as a mere source for ballpark figures.

If the goal is to construct models, any number of other ones are possible that have no more scientific value than the one just mentioned,[11] but that lead to diametrically opposed conclusions and that at least offer the advantage of being verified by current trends. Why not start from the assumption of perfect free trade, and then compare the respective competitive advantages of a developed country with a strong currency and of a poor country whose currency has suffered serious depreciation? The former will certainly avail itself of the opportunity to buy goods dirt-cheap in which labor costs are negligible; in doing so, however, it will bankrupt its own domestic producers, unless, of course, they shift their production to low-wage countries. High unemployment thus becomes inevitable in so-called "archaic" industries. On the other hand, this developed nation will attempt to specialize in "nobler" lines of business whose key components are intelligence and high technology, both of which are made possible by the country's excellent educational system and information networks. It will focus all its efforts on these industries, and will manage to maintain a favorable trade balance in value terms. Yet because these new capital-intensive, high-intelligence sectors necessarily create few jobs, the population of this wealthy country is henceforth exposed to chronic unemployment, and a dual society begins to take form. In run-down neighborhoods inhabited by unskilled jobless workers who can't keep pace with social and cultural change, poverty and crime become rampant. As for the poorer of the two countries, the outlook is clearly no brighter. Cities become overcrowded, the farm population leaves the countryside as a result of both the rising demand for unskilled labor and the advent of single-crop industrialized farming using the full range of intensive chemical, pharmaceutical, and biotechnical agricultural methods with which they cannot hope to compete, even assuming a favorable exchange-rate differential. Specializing in low-priced goods, the poorer country lacks the means to create an appropriate social environment for the transformations it is experiencing. Teeming slums and shantytowns are dominated by abject poverty and crime. Another World Bank report concludes that an international trade system devoid of regulation would lead to the "inexorable downward levelling of wages . . . Workers in the North would be impoverished, while those in the South would have roughly the same standard of living as before."[12]

In the current situation, Ricardo's theory cannot be applied to the whole world. A line of reasoning that blithely skips over several magnitudes is bound for trouble. In national terms, it makes little sense to equate France with a baker and Germany with a shoemaker; and even if we were to do so, the European Community would then constitute their village community, rather than a world market in which such enormous differences in social conditions obtain that meaningful comparison becomes impossible, for want of any common standards of measurement. In a continent like Europe, it seems obvious to everyone – especially to the governments involved – that all existing branches of activity, whether industry, agriculture, or services, should be maintained. It would indeed be difficult to imagine a Europe without computer manufacturers, airlines, steel mills, or farms. Under Stalin, the Soviet Union did embark upon a deliberate policy of specialization for the non-Russian republics, but the real goal was not to improve economic efficiency, but to establish as firmly as possible the authority of the country's "center" over the outlying regions. Even today, this policy continues to have profound effects, preventing the Muslim republics from achieving true independence and allowing Boris Yeltsin gradually to reassert traditional Russian influence over the entire former Soviet Union.

In light of the tremendous contrasts between the various versions of the future that the free-trade scenario has to offer, and considering that Anglo-Saxon *laissez-faire* economics has no parallel either in earlier periods of history or in other civilizations, there is legitimate cause for concern regarding its claim to be able to replace defunct ideologies in governing the universe. The following declaration made by US GATT negotiator Carla Hills speaks volumes on the subject: "We want to prohibit nations from imposing health and safety standards that are stricter than the minimum uniform international standards." Needless to say, in such a vision, the trend toward economic globalization leaves little room for ecology and health. We are thus dealing with a new kind of dogmatism that is just as dangerous as its predecessors in so far as it aims to submit social balance and human life to its own expansion requirements.

FREE ENTERPRISE IS NOT IMMUNE TO DOGMATIC DISTORTION

Free enterprise is certainly of mutual benefit to countries that have reached a comparable stage of development, provided that exchange rates remain stable, or at least that their fluctuations do not lead to large trade deficits on either side. At present, however, the system of floating exchange rates, which result almost exclusively from speculative activity, generates chronic economic instability, while keeping these rates far from their equilibrium value, which would accurately reflect economic reality. The interplay of trade relations no longer determines the value of currencies. Every day, the Bank for International Settlements handles an average of $1,100 billion in financial flows, i.e. about 40 times the level of international trade transactions.

Maurice Allais has emphasized an obvious point, namely that trade and exchange rates are indissociable.[13] Attempts at imposing internationally valid trade rules, while allowing the law of the jungle to hold sway in monetary matters, can only be explained either by dogmatic blindness or by the existence of policies designed to protect the interests of the economically dominant nations. This Nobel prize-winner in economics cogently demonstrates that "GATT negotiations on reducing customs tariffs by a couple of points are entirely futile as long as the exchange rates of certain currencies, in particular, the dollar, experience wide, sudden swings."[14]

In these conditions of "unbridled speculation, permitted and stimulated by the monetary and financial system," the resulting exchange rate fluctuations have a "disastrous impact on all countries involved." Such an ill-considered, anarchic easing of restrictions in both capital flows and trade, which places countries of differing weights and with widely dissimilar conditions in the same arena, represents in fact a dogmatic distortion of a free-trade economy that has, until now, made possible considerable prosperity. Maurice Allais concludes one of his articles with the following warning: "The distortions of socialism brought about the downfall of the societies in Eastern Europe. We must by all means avoid letting the distortions of free enterprise lead to the downfall of Western societies as well."[15]

Notes

1 In an interview on RTL, November 20, 1993.
2 In particular, Articles 3A, 102A, 105, and Article 2 of the monetary protocol of the Treaty of Maastricht.
3 The US has at its disposal a veritable arsenal of measures for exerting economic pressure which Europe entirely lacks. Section 301 of the 1974 Trade Act empowers the American administration to decide unilaterally on economic sanctions in the event of disagreement with a trade partner, and the "super-301" even makes the procedure automatic.
4 Gérard Lafay and Deniz Unal-Kesenci, *Repenser l'Europe* (Paris: Economica, 1993).
5 Karl Polanyi, *Les systèmes économiques dans l'histoire et dans la théorié* (Paris: Larousse, 1974).
6 Adam Smith, *On the Wealth of Nations* (Harmondsworth: Penguin, 1970).
7 Léon Walras, *Elements of Pure Economics* (Kelley, 1954).
8 David Ricardo, *On the Principles of Political Economy and Taxation* (London: J. M. Dent).
9 In an article entitled "Le marché fictif et l'économie réelle" ("The fictitious market and the real economy"), which appeared in the November 1993 special issue of the journal *Sciences humaines*, Jean-François Dortier concludes as follows: "The *pure* market would therefore seem to be a mere mirage, a fiction, an economist's dream, at least according to Karl Polanyi's provocative thesis. The author of *The Great Transformation* maintained that the history of capitalism could be analyzed as an attempt to impose a model created out of whole cloth by free-enterprise economists on the real world. The GATT's recent history fairly well corroborates this analysis, for it involves the gradual, yet systematic loosening of restrictions in world commerce in order to realize the ideal of totally free trade . . . The whole history of capitalism boils down to a dual process: on the one hand, constantly renewed attempts at imposing a *utopian* model on reality, and on the other hand, the setting up of institutions meant to control it, to regulate it, and to correct its perverse effects. In the foreground, we have the market; backstage, we find the institutions required for society to function properly."
10 Ian Goldin, Odin Knudsen, and Dominique van der Mesbruggh, *Libéralisation des échanges: conséquences pour l'économie mondiale*, published jointly by the OECD and the World Bank, 1993.
11 See especially Jimmy Goldsmith, *Le Piège* (Paris: Fixot, 1993).
12 Herman Daly and Robert Goodland, in a text published by the Environment Department of the World Bank, September 1992.

13 See his remarkable series of articles published by *Le Figaro*, particularly "Libre-échangisme mondial: les perversions monétaires," June 23, 1993.
14 The main objective of the Uruguay Round was to bring customs duties from 4.7 down to 3 percent on the average.
15 "Un libre-échangisme suicidaire," *Le Figaro*, July 5, 1993.

3

Government: Archaic Practices and Lack of Vision

Official society, with its organizations and institutions, evolves much more slowly than spontaneous society . . . What is on the decline is not citizenship, but traditional mass systems of representation and delegation. The new forms of citizenship are like new forms of vitality. We don't notice them because we don't know how to use them.

Gérard Demuth, President of COFREMCA, *Le Monde*
January 7, 1992

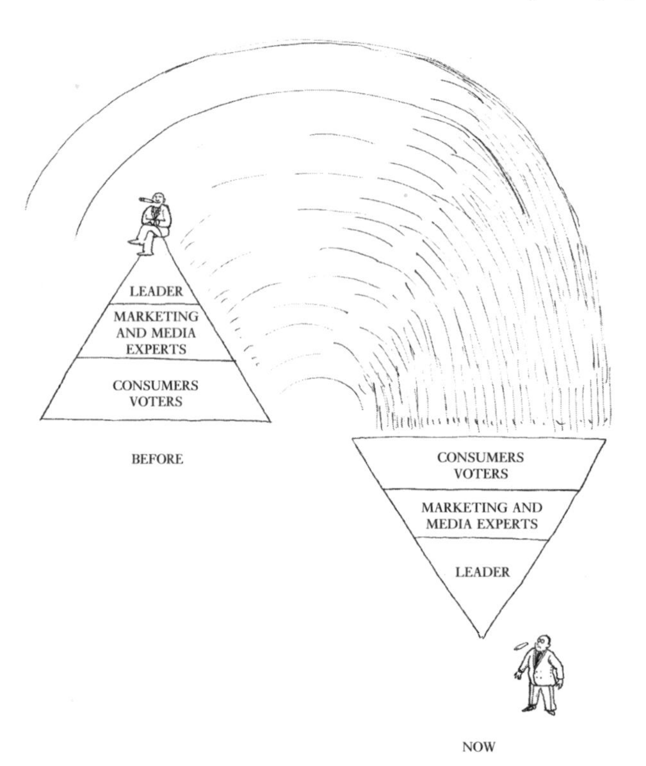

A government that has lost its sacred character no longer controls social evolution.

Traditional power structures have proved to be incapable of anticipation.

Individual choice now dominates the social pyramid.

Constantly on the look-out for fluctuations in public opinion, political leaders are utterly lacking in vision.

The requirements of the race for progress created a school system with a quantitative orientation.

Schools have not gone far enough in the direction of qualitative values, and continue to reproduce a cast system based on exclusion.

Companies could help government in putting a stop to mass passivity and loss of responsibility.

Up until recently, Western society was based on authority, discipline, and secrecy. Under the *Ancien Régime*, the king ruled by divine right; office-holding, fortune, and titles of nobility all depended on the king alone, and in the countryside, even the tax collector, acting on the king's behalf, could wield arbitrary power with impunity. The people were condemned to remain silent, and even if they sometimes had the chance to present their grievances, they were compelled to submit without protest once arbitration was complete. The Catholic Church was organized along the same lines. The Jesuits were committed, according to their motto, to obeying "like a corpse." Society entrusted the Church with the education of a few children of noble birth or from wealthy families, who were intended to reproduce the same complementarity between command and obedience, as God himself had ordained it.

The republican form of government that replaced royal power in France did not derive its legitimacy from God, but from the "cult of Reason." Public education was to be its sacred mission and the school teacher its most faithful missionary, bringing "learning" into the most remote rural areas in order to counteract the previously unchallenged intellectual authority of the clergy. Montesquieu accurately predicted this change. "It is in republican government," he wrote, "that the full power of education is needed." The nineteenth century fulfilled the ambition of giving the masses access to modern scientific reason. This educational effort, which was probably unique in history, has brought considerable benefits. As a result, however, established authority has been called fundamentally into question.

THE POWER PYRAMID HAS BEEN INVERTED

The traditional model of power is currently in a state of crisis. As education, information, and responsibility spread through the population, it becomes increasingly difficult to justify the notion of authoritarian constraint exercised by one individual over another. Whether in the business world or in government, it is no longer possible to maintain the idea of a hierarchical pyramid with the decision-makers at the summit, economics or communications experts in the middle, and ordinary people at the bottom, whether consumers or voters. Nowadays, it is public opinion that conditions national politics, just as consumer choice and demand orient the marketing and production decisions made by company directors.

Millions of individuals, particularly younger ones who are highly educated, consider themselves able to think for themselves. A good many principles have thus been challenged. For example, assertions that were quite common a short time ago such as "Nuclear testing serves an important military purpose," or "The Cold War is here to stay," or "Government has the right to keep some things secret," would today be rejected outright by public opinion. Everything appears to be subject to discussion.

No contemporary state can claim to embody any sacred principle or higher rationality. In practice, actually, governments are now involved much more in a kind of contractual management of changing, and sometimes conflicting, interests. Government may still have sufficient authority to command a certain amount of respect, but it seems doubtful whether it still possesses the institutional means to determine and control social evolution.

OPTIONS ARE NO LONGER IMPOSED FROM THE TOP DOWN

Information has given people the right to choose. This right, which has already led to profound upheavals in society, will remain a driving force of change in the years to come.

The Communist leaders in Eastern Europe were overthrown because of the example set by Western European democracies. When the impatient masses in the East began to travel, they were not motivated by remote, utopian visions, but by information on living standards in neighboring countries. For the inhabitants of Western Europe obviously possessed more goods than East bloc leaders, employers, and planners were able to provide. The Chinese regime was also caught off guard, having failed to take timely action to control the flow of information received by students, who were struck by the affluence they saw in Japan, South Korea, Taiwan, Hong Kong, and Singapore.

For 50 years, social change has been prompted by individual choice, as evinced by growing environmental awareness, the evolving status of women, and the recognition of consumers' and small investors' rights. Leaders or influential figures in politics, business, and religion have had almost no part in all these changes, which were carried out by ordinary individuals themselves. Subsequently, experts, public opinion spokesmen, and businessmen simply fell into step. Last of all, politicians jumped on the bandwagon.

PEOPLE IN POWER IN THE PAST OFTEN PROVED INCAPABLE OF ANTICIPATING CHANGE

Large numbers of Americans opted for compact cars before Detroit factories began producing them. Masses of women stopped having children before churches, schools, and official family planning programs realized what was happening.

Leaders have failed to foresee any number of events, although the signs were already there to see. Development of the nuclear power industry was restrained by a mass movement that considered the experts insufficiently concerned about the population's safety and the handling of radioactive waste. In fact, people were already interested in energy conservation and the use of solar energy, some of them even addressing the issue of global warming, while the world's governments continued to increase our dependence on the oil-producing nations. We now know just where such an attitude has led us.[1]

TODAY, POLITICIANS ARE STILL LACKING IN VISION

Present-day political leaders are concerned above all with conforming to the population's aspirations. Every day, in the highest spheres of government, no decisions are made before the latest opinion polls have been analyzed.

We are living in a society that might be termed a "nobody-in-charge society." Experts and opinion-makers still occupy a central position, but in a pluralistic democracy, no one person can truly control the workings of government. As a consequence, however, nobody holds real responsibility any more. However heartening the extension of democracy may be, we must also take its harmful side-effects into account. Anyone who is unable to put across a vision powerful enough to stir people to action and who merely follows the ups and downs of public opinion hardly deserves to be called a leader.

Governing in the glare of TV spotlights and under the tyranny of opinion polls usually means being more reactive than proactive, giving more weight to the short term than to the long term (especially around election time), and preferring sensational declarations to the accomplishment of real reforms. The main thing is to get the media to talk about you. Yet politicians discredit themselves through their lack of vision. Their rhetoric is both tired and tiresome; it comes across as hollow and devoid of fresh ideas. The Cold War more or less managed to mask this vacuousness by providing politicians with an illusory backbone, but now, with the disappearance of Communism, it has become clear that the emperor has no clothes. The only system left is capitalism, with its multiple scourges of pollution, poverty, and unemployment. As for the remedies suggested, they seem to be inspired by quackery rather than by medical science.

Although politicians of yesteryear attempted to stay "far from the madding crowd," they could not prevent men and women of every race or background from assembling in the parks, right under the windows of official buildings, to make their demands known. At present, political or business leaders are no longer the purveyors of ideology or the guarantors of unfailing certainties. Such a role now falls to those who can make serious proposals that reflect the aspirations of individuals, and who have the leadership qualities required to make them understand and to galvanize the energy of others.

In the absence of social and political projects capable of bringing disparate forces together, the main source of hope seems to be human values and creative talent, most of which emerge from "civil society." Those who seek power and prestige too openly are now viewed with great suspicion. "The major heroes of the modern world," writes Michel Serres, "are those who gave up everything they had in order to live with the most destitute members of our society." Charismatic figures with a vision for the future now best embody society's diffuse aspirations. Collective mobilization can no longer be stimulated from above, but issues forth from the rank and file, through the population's demands.

It is thus appropriate to envision today's actual power structure as an inverted pyramid.[2] The new definition of a leader is in fact close to the one provided by Voltaire: "I am a leader, and therefore follow others." The leader is the representative of a vast movement, with leadership being exercised on the basis of consensus, both in politics and in business.

IF WE DON'T "INVERT THE PYRAMID" WE WILL MEET THE SAME FATE AS THE DINOSAURS!

In his book *Invert the Pyramid*, Jan Carlzon makes a distinction between the boss, who has hands-on power and needs the means to take initiatives, and the leader, "who formulates hypotheses and creates the conditions that make such initiatives possible . . . the contemporary leader delegates responsibility and his autonomy as a traditional boss to those who are in constant contact with the realities of fieldwork. The leader's action requires information. Informing others means making opportunities known, i.e. adopting the opposite approach to someone who merely gives instructions. The leader must be a visionary, a strategist, an informer, a teacher, or in other words, his organization's inspirer."[3]

Carlzon, who brilliantly turned around the Swedish domestic airlines Linjeflyg, illustrates the idea of the inverted pyramid, described in his book, through his own behavior. One day, when he was scheduled to fly on one of his own company's planes, he was informed that it was time for him to board. "Oh really?" he exclaimed in astonishment. "Is everything all set? I didn't hear any announcement."

"No," he was told in reply, "we're letting you board first so that you can choose the seat you want. Then we'll let the other passengers board." Carlzon rejected this "classical way of granting hierarchical privileges. I waited instead for everyone to board, and then I took the last remaining seat. To me, taking precedence over the customer was entirely out of the question."

Innovation invariably involves an element of risk, whether in business or in any other area. Yet refusing to take risks can be fatal.

As Kazuma Tateisi, President of the Omron corporation, so well described, all major organizations or institutions are prone to internal entropy and threatened by the "dinosaur syndrome," which has the following characteristics.[4]

- a highly centralized, swollen bureaucracy
- a proliferation of special forms and permits to handle routine decisions
- increasing numbers of meetings to reach decisions
- the shunting of problems from department to department
- an increasingly laborious process for making definitive decisions, with people in charge less and less willing to take even the slightest risk

The inevitable results are obvious, in the form of poor internal communications, constantly extended time periods for decision-making, and a waning ability to react quickly to events. The sense of efficiency that may have existed when the organization was more flexible is correspondingly weakened.

Official society continues to encourage modes of behavior that are increasingly out of phase with a changing reality, for nothing evolves as slowly as institutional structures. Rooted in nineteenth-century values, our educational system perpetuates long-since outdated beliefs.

IN THE GOOD OLD DAYS, SCHOOLS WERE EXCLUSIVELY CONCERNED WITH THE QUANTITATIVE

At the time of the industrial revolution, developing public, universal education was a means for each country to get ahead in the race to progress. Furthermore, such progress was effective to the extent that society was able to obtain the highest possible quantitative "output," both in production and in education. The goal was to accumulate potential skills and knowledge and to familiarize people with a rational division of labor based on the mechanistic notion of clockwork. Each person was to function as a cog in a vast machine.

This vertical, hierarchical system took root even more inevitably in the modern company, in which the director was at the same time the owner. Everything was decided from the top down. Organized in semi-military fashion, lower-level managers were expected to apply explicit directives, with no questions asked.

Thus, schools were to prepare individuals for their future social rank, according to their qualifications, acquired once and for all. At a time of little social, geographical, and occupational mobility, people set their sights on relatively fixed positions within one of the three major realms that provided that framework for industrial society: production, commerce, or administration and finance.

NOWADAYS, SCHOOLS REMAIN IGNORANT OF QUALITATIVE PERFORMANCE

In the intervening years, however, the world has become less compartmentalized. The development of various means of rapid transportation have made possible a much greater geographical mobility than before, opening up a vast array of new employment opportunities. Owing to the information revolution and mass communication, knowledge once reserved for an elite has become accessible on a mass scale, and previously separated social groups have intermixed. Television made its appearance in millions of households during a period of economic boom, rapid urbanization, and mass consumption. In recent years, written language has given way to audiovisual language.

Yet in spite of all these sweeping changes, school curricula have remained relatively static. Educational principles and methods have barely been modified since the late nineteenth century. Values such as authority and discipline still take precedence over the necessarily interactive character of all learning. Even physical education is still seen in terms of athletic competition and gymnastics (appropriate training for soldiers), whereas there is virtually no concern for the harmony of mind and body (which aikido as well as other martial arts have to offer).

At a time when scientific discovery and technological innovation proceeded at a pace never before witnessed, new functions began to appear in the corporate world. Research and development was added; marketing, the sophisticated art of selling, supplanted traditional sales techniques; and, more recently, human resource departments have begun supplementing the work accomplished by personnel management.

Yet all the while, institutes and universities have stubbornly maintained age-old departmental distinctions; the engineering school has no relation to administration or sales programs. None of these institutions of learning can respond to the demands of the jobs with the greatest impact today. Their graduates are ill-equipped to handle the tasks that companies set for them in the increasingly vital areas of research and development, marketing, and human resources and relations.

To be sure, traditional roles in production and management have not disappeared, but they are no longer decisive for economic competition. Making a real difference now requires other qualites such as the ability to organize the acquisition and operation of new skills.

SOCIETY IS IN GREATER NEED OF DEVELOPED MINDS THAN OF OVERFLOWING ONES

In the heyday of Taylorism, the most important thing was to accumulate as much theoretical knowledge as possible in order to make rational use of the skills thus learned in a highly specialized, predetermined occupation. At present, however, electronic storage possibilities have rendered obsolete a selective system based primarily on human memory. What counts today is not so much the skills you have learned as your *ability* to learn them; in particular, your aptitude for processing and utilizing new, diverse information, which provides the foundation for most contemporary jobs, while constantly giving them new life. Contrary to the logic of Taylorism, which was to separate areas of activity and break work down into distinct, minute tasks, present-day society calls for an ability to establish relations between information from around the world, to blend different scientific disciplines together, and to think in terms of teamwork and networking.

Schools continue to stress the importance of rational qualities (hence the role of math as a means of selection), at the expense of creativity, which plays an increasing part in a society based on innovation. Similarly, universities tend to operate in a vacuum, dispensing theoretical knowledge that is largely irrelevant to the current social context and the actual requirements of the labor market. In reality, we are training growing numbers of future jobless white-collar workers, who will be especially bitter once they discover that the supposedly solid education they got wasn't worth a dime.

"DIPLOMANIA" MAINTAINS A CAST SYSTEM WHILE PRODUCING OUTCASTS

The squandering of educational resources is clearly reflected in the steadily worsening job situation. In France, between 1975 and 1990, the gross domestic product went up 40 percent, while unemployment figures doubled. Among the various possible factors involved, there is the growing separation between the curricula of lower and higher educational institutions and the actual needs of the economy. Thus, some university programs, especially in the social sciences, "churn out" at least a thousand graduates per year in fields with at best about 15 jobs to offer, whether newly created ones or the result of turnover. Conversely, hundreds of highly technical positions remain vacant for want of adequately trained applicants. The academic system then goes on to intensify competition among students in order to make up for the lack of relevance of its programs.

The "paper chase" serves to perpetuate a cast system that is not only ossified, but also absurd and disastrous. Your entire career depends on the degree that you obtain in your early twenties, which, it is hoped, will carry the greatest possible prestige. Both the academic establishment and the influence of the ruling classes contribute to the self-reproduction of an elite modeled on that of the previous century. In France, in fact, as Pierre Bourdieu has demonstrated, this elite can be likened to an authentic "state nobility" that has jealously concentrated knowledge and power in its hands and that lives increasingly cut off from reality.

While swelling the ranks of the over-educated (i.e. both too educated *and* poorly educated), current policies also condemn the majority of the population either to mediocrity or to unemployment. Such social exclusion then has cumulative effects, since the educational system's "losers" quickly get economically left out, often permanently.

Over the past few years, an aggravating circumstance has become apparent. Although the rise in school attendance has practically wiped out total illiteracy in the underprivileged layers of society, the proportion of the population lacking basic reading skills (or able to read only with great difficulty) has increased to alarming levels. According to a recent OECD report, France has eight million functional illiterates. This can be in part explained by the influence of audiovisual media, the use of which takes up time that might otherwise be devoted to reading. In the United States, it is estimated that by the turn of the century, 90 million adults will be incapable of reading a newspaper or magazine.

Yet whatever the explanation, it seems clear that much of this failure can be attributed to the educational system and, more generally, to our antiquated institutional structures, which no longer enable young people to find their place in social and economic life – except those who start out with cultural advantages that make them highly adaptable. One and the same system thus produces both an accumulation of ignorance and over-education; their combined effect is in great danger of breaking society in two.

In this dual society, the losers are rapidly excluded from modern life. They may then be tempted either by crime and drugs, which flourish among the unemployed youth of poor neighborhoods, or by fanatical opposition to a world that apparently has no room for them, as the rise of fundamentalist, extremist currents and of religious sects shows.

PUTTING A STOP TO MASS PASSIVITY AND LOSS OF RESPONSIBILITY

Overcoming the sharp division between citizens (or "subjects") and their government and countering the authoritarian, hierarchical character of traditional state institutions, which are increasingly at odds with present-day values, requires greater participation by ordinary people in the working out of major goals in the common interest. This opens up a new, essential arena for companies, which could step into the gap left by government institutions unable to provide the community with the basic, quality services it needs. This shared responsibility is particularly necessary in the field of training and education. No government in the world has the means to shoulder the burden of updating knowledge and curricula. Joint funding on the part of both industry and different levels of government is thus required if we wish to further the harmonious development of economic and social life.

Notes

1 Harlan Cleveland, in a talk given in Minneapolis in August 1991.
2 Ibid.
3 Jan Carlzon, *Invert the Pyramid* (Stockholm: Albin Bonniers, Förlag AB).
4 Kazuma Tateisi, *The Eternal Venture Spirit* (Cambridge, Mass.: Productivity Press, 1989).

4

Selfishness and the Survival of our Planet

Serious problems such as pollution, the growing gap between North and South, the decay of our cities cannot be resolved without a radical change in ideas and attitudes throughout the world. Scientific and technical experts may find the appropriate means for dealing with them, but in the absence of such a change in values, to which intellectuals must contribute, the future of the world is indeed bleak.

Professor Shuishi Kato, *Leonardo*, 1992[1]

In the face of an ominous future, individualism is on the rise.

Less and less concerned with the fate of his fellow man, the individual wants others to be concerned with his.

It is now the rich who are promoting separatism.

The bipolarization of the world also divides each developed country in two.

The gap between rich and poor has doubled.

Mass migration bears witness to this growing inequality.

Since there is but one ecosystem governing our planet, only worldwide solidarity can save it.

There is widespread acceptance nowadays of the idea that every individual must define her own universe. Her opinions, sensations, and emotions have become the sole criteria for measuring her value system, her life-style, and possibly her allegiances. As a consequence of this emphasis on freedom of choice, on "every man for himself," people now tend to confine themselves to the narrow sphere of their own territory. It takes little time for the micro-sphere of the individual to turn into a cocoon, a refuge for those fleeing the discomfort of social life.

The accentuation of this trend has spawned an impressive array of floating networks that are both contractual and ephemeral. People get together to satisfy short-term needs or the dictates of fashion, joining a sports club, then perhaps a cultural association, participating later in a religious gathering, occasionally defending the interests of their occcupational group. Everyone thus accumulates a large number of fragmentary forms of involvement and loyalty, zapping from one to the next according to what he or she is feeling at any given moment.

ABSOLUTE INDIVIDUALISM LEADS DOWN A BLIND ALLEY

Formed on the basis of shared interests, such groups provide an irreplaceable means of social interaction, while making possible a combination of freedom, i.e. multiple allegiances granted to each participant, and a sort of small-scale tribal structure based on consensus. So far, however, these attempts at enlarging one's protective cocoon have not led to other, less private forms of involvement.

Any "cocooning" (or even "burrowing") strategy reflects both isolation and a need for protection. On the one hand, the individual has particularly good reason to seek new means of communicating with others, of getting in touch with the outside world, since the very fabric of society is increasingly coming apart and generating thousands of individual "republics" that are perfectly foreign to each other. On the other hand, he wants security. Only new bonds of solidarity can overcome the vague feeling of anxiety that accompanies such behavior.

DREADED UNEMPLOYMENT

The future seems threatening indeed. Because of accelerating technological change, trades and occupations are in permanent flux. Many people constantly face the risk that the conditions they had to fulfill in order to get or to keep a job may not be the same tomorrow. As a result, they wonder whether they will be able to face the future.

Although this fear is sometimes amplified by the media, it is certainly not unfounded. France's unemployment rate is currently over 12 percent, which is roughly the European average. In the European Community, the near future boils down to declining GNP, with one European worker in eight jobless (the Spanish workforce has already reached the one in five mark). Jacques Delors pointed out that "between 1970 and 1990, the United States created 29 million new jobs, Japan, 11 million, and Europe 8.8 million." Analysts in Brussels reckon that to stabilize its unemployment rate, Europe would need to achieve a 3 percent annual growth rate, which currently appears to be quite impossible.

As the economic situation becomes increasingly uncertain and unstable, people begin to seek collective security rather than real freedom. Everyone calls for more solidarity, whether on the part of specific groups or on the part of the government, while loudly insisting on their own independence. The individual thus adopts a psychologically untenable position, in which unbridled selfishness is combined with demands for support from others.

THE FRINGES OF SOCIETY ARE LOCATED LESS AND LESS ON THE FRINGE

The vast movement of individual emancipation that has been under way for two centuries has led people to reject hierarchical power structures and to proclaim a theoretical equality with an ever-growing number of applications, from political, social, and economic equality to racial, sexual, and generational equality (between young and old). While making possible greater upward mobility and social intermixture than ever before, this principle also serves to underscore the increasing gap between haves and have-nots, between the part of the population that is integrated into the system and the part that is left out.

In a sense, new forms of social segregation have developed over the past several years, including outright exclusion. The dividing line may be between those who enjoy stable employment and the long-term unemployed, between a highly qualified, over-educated elite and an intellectual semi-proletariat, between high-technology industries with a bright future and industries requiring assistance (family farming, self-employed tradesmen), or between big cities that absorb a rising population and rural areas that have been essentially deserted.

In any case, the various categories of non-beneficiaries of economic growth now form a mass outcast population, part of which is condemned to experience the decay and the violence of ghetto life. An additional gap with potentially even more serious consequences should also be mentioned, that which separates age groups.

On the one hand, the developed countries are confronted with an aging population, due to the drop in birth rates and improved health conditions, so much so that the non-working population has acquired greater social and economic weight in relation to the working population, as evidenced by new kinds of demands. In Germany, for example, elderly women dubbed the "Gray Panthers" now attempt to exert a political influence in keeping with their actual numbers.

On the other hand, or rather, at the other end of the spectrum, young people are entering the labor market later and later and are having trouble fitting in. The result is not only an age segmentation of society, but also age discrimination. With two billion young people in the world pushed out onto society's fringes, while their elders monopolize wealth, the situation may soon become explosive. Since the haves don't want to share and the have-nots demand solidarity, we are bound to witness outbursts of violence.

In a more general sense, it is hard to escape the impression that our entire planet is totally unbalanced. Some 700 million persons living in relative affluence attempt to preserve an island of prosperity in a sea of distress, although the survival instinct ought to induce them to share what they have and to let others participate in modern consumption. The phenomena of exclusion that we are currently witnessing are not only morally unacceptable, they are also untenable in a period in which the notion of global balance has penetrated the collective subconscious around the world.

SEPARATISM TAKES ROOT PARTICULARLY IN WEALTHY REGIONS

Unfortunately, however, the degree of solidarity in evidence is simply not up to the requirements of our era; in some cases, in fact, it has even declined. In 1989, 40 percent of voters in northern Italy, where income is higher by one-third than the national average (per capita gross domestic product is around 20,000 Ecus in Lombardy, as opposed to 15,000 in the whole country), voted for the Lombard League, which called at the time for no less than the partition of the country into north and south. Changing its name to the Northern League in 1990, this movement, which now advocates a federal structure for Italy that would reduce solidarity with the South, conquered the city government of Milan in June 1993 and has become the leading party in northern Italy. Its supporters want to part company with the Neapolitans and the Sicilians, whom they consider too poor, too uneducated, and too prone to Mafia activities.

Similar phenomena can be observed in the attitude of the Catalans toward the rest of Spain or in that of the Flemish toward the Walloons in Belgium, two examples from the European Community. Somewhat further east as well, the tensions that ultimately gave rise to armed conflict in Yugoslavia originated in the sense of economic superiority in certain regions, especially in Slovenia. As for Russia, currently grappling with serious difficulties, it has drastically reduced its subsidies to the ex-Soviet Muslim republics. China, which has granted a great deal of economic autonomy to its southern provinces, but little political power, will soon be facing vigorous opposition from the fast-growing coastal areas, which will undoubtedly be averse to sharing the fruit of their labor with the rest of the country.

A BIPOLAR WORLD IS LOOMING ON THE HORIZON

The dominant impression today is one of an increasingly polarized world. Between the wealthy countries ("the North"), and the opposite pole, the poor countries ("the South"), economic inequality is rising at an alarming rate. It is estimated that three-quarters of all solvent demand comes from the 700 million inhabitants of the wealthy countries, whereas the remaining quarter is spread out over the more than 4 billion inhabitants of the rest of the world. This gap shows no signs of diminishing, since the debt burden of the poor countries becomes heavier each year. Thus, the entire African continent is in dire straits.

The polarization is not only geographical in nature, for it is gradually extending to all societies, which are more and more divided into privileged and underprivileged. This can be clearly observed in our cities, where some people – the highly educated – have both access to the latest technology and the opportunity to use it, while others, who are often illiterate, get their education on the streets, in basements, in abandoned buildings. The violence that has flared up in London, Paris, and Lyons, while much less intense than the Los Angeles riots, none the less reflects the same kind of social unrest. In some megalopoli in poorer countries, the situation is obviously much worse. Calcutta, and now Mexico City, with its 30 million inhabitants, have become shantytown patchworks where poverty, violence, and pollution constantly reinforce each other.

THE GAP BETWEEN RICH AND POOR HAS DOUBLED

Between 1960 and 1990, the economic gap between the upper fifth and the lower fifth of humanity increased significantly. At the beginning of the period, the wealthier group obtained 70.2 percent of world income, as opposed to 2.3 percent for the poorer group; 30 years later, the corresponding figures were 82.7 percent and 1.4 percent. In relative terms, the gap thus doubled, going from 30 : 1 to 60 : 1.

The slums and shantytowns of cities such as Bangkok, Rio de Janeiro, Lagos, and Los Angeles are overflowing with 700 million desperate people who will never get the chance to live in proper housing, to eat healthy food, to drink clean water, to receive adequate health care or education. Not far away, in the countryside, a peasant population, almost 2.5 billion strong, has not yet succumbed to the enticement of migration to the cities. Although extremely poor by Western economic standards, they have stayed in their traditional villages, drawing sustenance from an ancestral way of life with a specific culture.

The shift toward intensive agriculture requiring a decreasing workforce, combined with the trend toward totally free international trade in both economic and cultural matters, is likely to propel part of this rural population toward the cities, where they will suffer even greater destitution than before. A barely imaginable human disaster will ensue if the developing countries give in to demands from abroad and fully open up their home markets to Western agricultural products (doped up by chemicals, and soon by biotechnologies). Domestic farming will be wiped out, and over a billion people will be compelled to pack their bags and set out for their country's rat-infested shantytowns, all in the name of essentially mythological free-trade theories. Only Middle West farmers will reap the benefits of this kind of "progress."

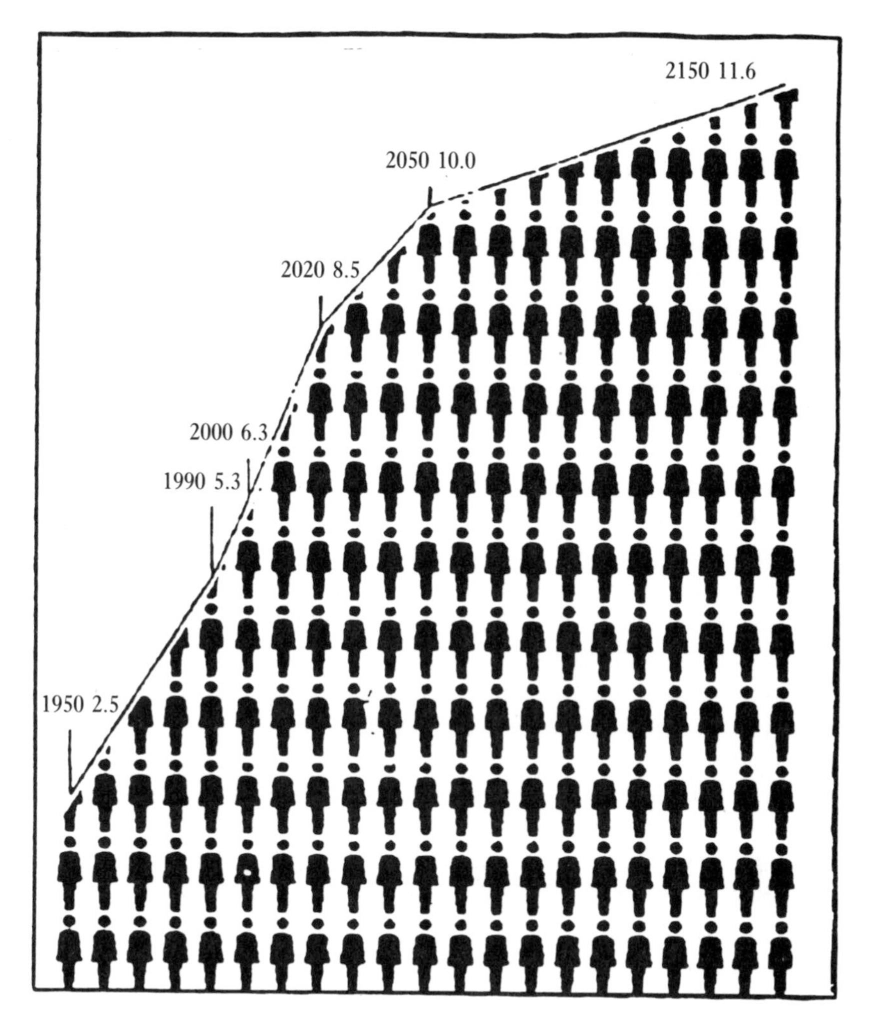

Figure 4.1 Projected world population in billions (*Source*: UN Population Fund)

UNEQUALLY DISTRIBUTED POPULATION GROWTH HAS LED TO MASS MIGRATION

The increasingly rapid growth in world population constitutes a major threat to humanity. The Earth had 2.5 billion inhabitants in 1950, and 5.3 billion in 1990. The figures are expected to rise to 6.3 billion in the year 2000 and to 10 billion in 2050 (figure 4.1). A good many experts agree that, by that time, our planet will no longer be able to absorb the waste products of such a population.

To begin with, the population increase in the poor countries remains impressive (70 percent of world population is concentrated in a mere eight of them), owing to the drop in infant mortality (a relatively recent phenomenon). In addition, declining birth rates and an aging population in the developed countries are now well-established trends. In 30 years, Europe will only represent 4.5 percent of the Earth's inhabitants. In such conditions, international migratory pressure will necessarily mount. Refugees and illegal aliens will pour into wealthy, sparsely populated regions. Whether or not they are there to stay, they will be in competition with the local workforce.

Thus, Europe will increasingly have to deal with the problem of integrating immigrants from the South (and, as of more recently, from the East). Every year, over 700,000 come in, including 100,000 without papers.

In all likelihood, immigration will elicit hostile reactions in Western nations with a stagnating or declining population (such as Germany) and conditions of economic recession, accompanied, as always, by large-scale unemployment. It is easy to imagine that the privileged strata of society will do everything in their power to protect their property, setting up elaborate security systems, while others with a more fanatical bent will wind up resorting to violence and terrorism in order to make their message heard.

THE TIME HAS COME TO AID POORER COUNTRIES, WHILE TAKING THE ECOSYSTEM INTO ACCOUNT

The combined effect of an economy that has run out of steam and demographic explosion in the Third World may well lead us down a blind alley. At present, the world appears to be heading for a division into three major regions or "empires."

- Japan and the ASEAN countries, which may end up including China
- Europe, which will have to absorb the former Eastern-bloc countries – and perhaps Africa as well
- North America, which will take charge of Latin America

According to the "scenario books" put out by the Global Business Network (GBN), these "empires" are confronted with three possible hypothetical situations. At best, a sufficient level of investment and research will enable them to achieve economic growth rates of over 3 percent and thus to pull the poor countries in tow. At worst, with the economy growing at less than 1 percent, the whole world will slide into practically unmanageable chaos. Between the two, i.e. assuming that economic growth is somewhere between 1 and 2.5 percent, Western countries will experience declining prosperity as their working population becomes smaller, whereas the poor countries will one day refuse to accept their desperate living conditions.

The idea that the developed countries could remain islands of prosperity in a sea of poverty is simply unthinkable. We have the obligation to draw all of the Third World into modern economic relations. Specifically, this means setting aside sufficient savings to be able to help those countries with particular difficulties. To do so, we must achieve adequate rates of expansion, i.e. above 3 percent. Such results depend, however, on the percentage of GNP that wealthy nations are willing to invest in basic research, the only road to breakthroughs that can generate new growth opportunities. Thus, a major emphasis on research will provide the basis for the savings that will enable us to give developing countries their share in world consumption.

There are reasonable grounds for assuming that Japan and the Asian "dragons" can reach such a threshold, and that North America, with its great adaptiveness, will also exert a positive influence in this area. One wonders, however, as to the ability of Western European countries to include their neighbors to the east in a common project. Should Europe prove incapable of doing so and of sustaining growth rates of between 2.5 and 3 percent for several years in a row, it will lack the level of savings needed to aid the suffering masses of the Third World. In such a case, acts of desperation are to be expected.

The world population explosion and the emergence of ecological awareness in public opinion raise an extremely serious problem that we will have to face sooner or later: the elimination of domestic and industrial waste. Even assuming total control of salvaging and reprocessing techniques, the costs will be considerable. To make matters worse, the fate of the natural environment in the twenty-first century will be determined first and foremost in the poorest and most populous countries (China, India, Brazil, etc.). What will be financially accessible for companies and citizens in wealthy countries will not be for the already debt-ridden poorer ones.

Yet even among developed countries, energy policies differ much too much, as the contrast between the European Community and the Commonwealth of Independent States clearly shows. The international dialogue required for collectively managing the world's natural resources has yet to materialize.

To varying degrees, all of world public opinion has begun to realize the risks that lack of long-term vision entails for the ecological balance of our planet. And although no international forum or organization has emerged to deal with the situation, the impact of the various forms of pollution produced over the past 30 years and more by the mad race for technological development and energy consumption can be felt around the world. By now, all regions of the globe are faced with problems such as acid rain, radioactive clouds, water pollution, the greenhouse effect, deforestation and the extension of the desert, and the threat to the ozone layer.

THE DOUBLE-TALK OF WEALTHY NATIONS

It seems tolerably clear, however, that we can hardly ask the poorest countries to spend money they don't possess to save our planet. Yet it is precisely in such overpopulated, under-equipped regions that we can expect the worst ecological disasters. Whether we like it or not, we are compelled to take the necessary steps in order to come up with the means to help these countries overcome their problems.

How can we convey to the inhabitants of the Amazon River region the idea that, by destroying thousands of acres of forest land each year, they are endangering the entire planet? The answer is that as long as they are not integrated into the major circuits of the world economy, and as long as the wealthy nations continue to evince their usual selfishness, we simply can't.

The international summit conference held in Rio from June 3 to 14, 1992 made it clear that the North is much more concerned over pressure from environmental movements than over ecological threats to our planet. This meeting, which brought together almost 30,000 persons (including 175 heads of state and 3,000 journalists) raised tremendous hopes of international cooperation for guaranteeing our common future. In practice, however, national interests received top priority, and the Lilliputian commitments made by the developed countries at the end of the conference had the effect of a cold shower. Several wealthy nations displayed great ecological fervor in relation to problems far from home, but revealed their attachment to petty economic calculations as soon as the discussion touched upon their domestic affairs.

AN ASSESSMENT OF THE THREATS TO OUR PLANET

Whatever we may think of the Rio conference, it did make possible an assessment (however bleak) of the damage done over the past 20 years. The following points deserve to be mentioned.

- The United States accounts for 5 percent of world population, India for 16 percent. The United States produces 25 percent of world GNP, India 1 percent, while consuming 25 percent of all energy, as opposed to 3 percent. The United States sends out 22 percent of all the carbon dioxide (CO_2) produced on Earth, India 3 percent. (CO_2 is widely considered responsible for the "greenhouse effect" and thus for global warming.)
- In the past 10 years, the ozone layer in the stratosphere, which protects living organisms against radiation, has apparently been reduced by between 4 and 8 percent in the Northern and Southern hemispheres.
- In the world's coastal regions, population growth (617 million persons in 1980, an estimated 997 million in the year 2000!) is responsible for considerable sea pollution as well as the destruction of traditional coastal habitats. Roughly 6.5 million tons of waste wind up in the seas each year.
- Since 1972, the Earth has been losing 480 million acres of trees per year, the equivalent of one-fifth of United States territory. Every year in the tropical forest, the equivalent of the entire surface of Great Britain is burned down, i.e. the equivalent of a soccer field *every second!* The tropical forest's fauna is also under attack. Over the past two decades, about one million species have disappeared there, and the pace is accelerating. Whereas in the 1970s, about 30,000 species disappeared each year; in the 1980s, the figure jumped to 50,000.
- Traditional subsistence farming has been severely disrupted. In Africa, per capita grain production has dropped by 28 percent since 1967 as a result of drought, soil erosion, and overpopulation. For the tribes living around the Aral Sea in Russia, massive use of

pesticides in agriculture has caused an abnormally high rate of cancer of the esophagus (seven times above average).

Having made this assessment, the authors of *Beyond the Limits*,[2] who also wrote the Meadows Report for the Club of Rome more than 20 years earlier, claim that it is not too late to apply the ideas they expounded at the time, i.e. replacing the notion of growth with the idea of "sustainable development," one that respects the environment, but also means calling into question the level of consumption in the most affluent societies.

SURVIVAL REQUIRES SOLIDARITY

Solidarity can be seen as a moral, ethical imperative, but it is also a precondition for human survival. We must involve the poor countries in modern development. We may not be keen on offering our support, but leaving things as they are would mean taking an even greater risk.

Solidarity is the only way to continue to move forward, and to finance it, the wealthy countries must attain that crucial figure of 3 percent annual growth, as we have seen. The main goal is to forestall the worst, namely that the most hard-hit countries resort to desperate solutions. Let no one minimize the gravity of the matter, for in 50 years, the Earth will have almost 10 billion inhabitants, in all likelihood a near-maximum level.

There is an obvious lack of world institutions capable of carrying on the essential discussions and of managing such transnational problems. Yet sooner or later, the compulsory world solidarity we just mentioned will have to give rise to new tools of international regulation. Our future is at stake.

GETTING AWAY FROM THE CONSUMER MENTALITY

An important question has to do with just how far Western consumers are prepared to go in their desire to protect the environment. Citizens calling themselves "ecologists" who take great pride in their "environmental consciousness" declare their willingness to sort their garbage and drop off their empty bottles in special glass recycling bins – provided, of course, that they can go there by car and continue to eat strawberries all year round. This is the paradox that the industrial nations will have to resolve in the 1990s. Instead of making doomsday statements and practicing sensationalism, the media and governments would be better off trying to convince people that crying wolf is not enough, that the real issue is whether together we can define new rules of self-discipline and imagine ways of doing things on a day-to-day basis that contribute to environmental protection.

Seen in this light, the current slump in demand – no doubt a reflection of an increasingly jaded attitude toward consumption on the part of "the children of the affluent society" – does not have only negative aspects. It points the way toward a new equilibrium in the future, one that would greatly mitigate the unequal distribution of our planet's resources.

Notes

1 Professor Shuishi Kato, the Director of the Tokyo Central Library and a historian of ideas at the University of Tokyo, in an interview published in *Leonardo*, a special issue of the newspaper *Le Monde* devoted to the World Fair in Seville, Paris, May 1992.

2 Donella H. Meadows, Dennis L. Meadows, and Jorgen Randers, *Beyond the Limits* (PO Box 130, Vermont 05058: Chelsea Green Publishing Company, 1992).

5

The Satiated Consumer

Man is a product of desire, not a product of need.

G. Bachelard, *The Psychoanalysis of Fire*

The craving for material things is dying out.

Too much choice, too many options, rapid model turnover, and constant advertising overkill have created the jaded consumer, whose budget is in any case getting smaller.

A feeling for qualitative value, the quality of services provided, authenticity, and the symbolic weight of products currently represent the best possible sales arguments.

The consumer buys a sign more than the product itself; consumption is related to communication.

From the end of World War II until the 1980s, the Western world enjoyed a period of unprecedented economic euphoria. Expansion was consistently rapid, near-full employment was achieved, and average purchasing power rose markedly and regularly. Throughout the period, consumption in all fields increased exponentially.

For obvious reasons, such consumption first involved acquiring the basic durable goods that define modern comfort: refrigerators, home appliances, cars, televisions, record-players, followed by stereo sets, etc. Households in Western countries thereby acquired objects that could both change their life-style and symbolize their entry into modern life.

This modernity took a firm hold everywhere, bringing with it an aura of prestige that was often more illusion than reality, as Jacques Tati's films so well underscored, but that none the less offered undeniable benefits that greatly facilitated daily life. Chief among them were the automobile, which soon became accessible to all, and, in general, the development of all modern means of transportation. Buying a car was a way to make all kinds of dreams come true, such as getting around easily, going on vacation, touring distant regions, and discovering previously unknown leisure activities.

All of a sudden, the world was there to be explored by everyone. Each new technical innovation reinforced the attraction of novelty. Our entire society was swept up in an apparently insatiable buying frenzy that ultimately resulted in what came to be known as the consumer society.

With the development of public and private transport, shopping centers sprang up on the outskirts of cities or in resort areas. Unlike nineteenth-century department stores, which were meant primarily for a clientele of well-to-do city-dwellers, shopping centers were intended for a heterogeneous public. They offered a wide range of items, from household staples to exotic, unconventional products of questionable utility but that people none the less wanted to try. The status of innovation, the magic of technology, and the label of scientific progress induced consumers to desire, discover, and experiment with an ever-growing variety of products and services.

I recall that when we used to go to Japan over 20 years ago, on each trip we came across new gadgets to bring home with us. These objects, which we avidly hunted for, appealed to us for no other reason than that they were more advanced than those we could find in Europe. There was obviously something unsophisticated about our approach, since any given product only remained new until it was replaced by another, "newer" one. With the gradual opening of national borders and the extension of world trade, the novelty effect quickly wore off. After a short time, we in Europe began to see products from Japan, the United States, and other distant countries side by side with European goods on store shelves.

A GLANCE AT CURRENT CONSUMPTION

For several years now, however, unemployment has become a lasting feature of Western countries, one that has produced a considerable shift in the social and economic climate. People no longer seem so concerned with the way in which new wealth gets distributed, but rather with job security and maintaining their living standards. The desire for change has undergone a few changes itself. For many inhabitants of today's large cities, whose economic situation may be precarious, vital needs such as employment, housing, and their children's education clearly take precedence over the wish for more or less essential purchases. The upshot is that consumption is not what it used to be.

In addition, the present situation has little in common with that of the first post-war years, in which we were just emerging from a period of hardship. The urge to accumulate goods in order to be prepared for future shortages no longer weighs so heavily on a society that, for several decades now, has managed to provide a relative degree of comfort and material well-being to the majority of the population. In fact, the over-abundance of goods and services available in the past 20 years tends to lessen the consumer's desire to consume.

Today's supermarkets offer 78,000 different products, as opposed to 21,000 two decades ago. Countless brands of condiments, ready-to-serve dishes, detergents, not to mention shampoo, make-up remover, and face creams line the shelves; so much choice is liable to make your head spin. Even selecting something as simple as a pain reliever becomes a complicated endeavor: do I want it in powdered, soluble, or effervescent form, with or without vitamins added? In a situation of global competition, in which technical and sales performance becomes increasingly similar the world over, companies are compelled to go to great lengths in order to escape the uniformity of equivalent products and to offer a wide variety of models for every taste.

THE WILD SCRAMBLE FOR INNOVATION

Since the advent of the industrial revolution, the major objective of entrepreneurs has been to establish their presence in new markets, which implies a strategy of conquest. Today, all possible markets have been explored, and a vast, interconnected, interdependent global market has come into being. In such a context, it seems doubtful whether technical performance, energetic sales policies, and financial results can still serve to define a business strategy.

As competition becomes more and more international and interconnections are created faster and faster, the competitive advantages that technological innovation once brought begin to lose their significance. Similar discoveries and patents make their appearance at roughly the same time everywhere, while the lead time for them to become operative regularly gets shorter and shorter. Throughout the world, advertising and marketing use the same recipes for winning over customers, thus approaching the saturation point in the long run. It is hardly surprising, then, that as soon as anyone invents or tests a new market opportunity, everyone else quickly follows suit.

Modern technology allows companies to offer multiple options and a practically unlimited product selection. If you want to buy a car, you have 300 models to choose from; if you like beer, you can try up to 400 different brands. More and more, industrialists are using new flexible technologies like CAD-CAM (computer-aided design and manufacturing) that make it possible to customize virtually any product to meet the requirements of each customer, however special they may be. The usual sales promises of giving the customer what he wants, the way he wants it, and when he wants it can now be kept.

Thirty years ago, there was only one telephone receiver on the market (a standard black one); today, you can find as many as 1,000 possible variants (in color, answering systems, various services). In Japan, bicycle manufacturer Kokubu offers a range of custom models involving no less than 11,231,862 different combinations for a mere 10 percent more than the price of standard models, and with just two weeks' delivery time.

Such constantly expanding ranges of possibilities can be mind-boggling. Most people use a mere 10 percent of the functions available on their VCRs and compact disc players, and only two or three of the 10 or more programs on their washing machines and dishwashers. Furthermore, the rising complexity of instruction booklets has discouraged many users from even attempting to understand them. The end result is that consumers no longer rush out to buy the latest gizmo, but confine themselves instead to simpler products that meet a clear-cut need.

ADVERTISING HAS MADE CONSUMERS WARY

Media hype only makes matters worse. Constant advertising and overuse of superlatives induce skepticism, and sometimes even overt psychological rejection. In the United States, it is estimated that consumers are bombarded with between 3,000 and 5,000 advertising messages a day – figures that are apparently still on the rise. The average consumer only retains 2 or 3 percent of those messages, which seem to have a steadily declining impact.

Market research has revealed that the ability of American television viewers to recall the commercials they see has taken a big drop in four years. In 1986, 64 percent of viewers surveyed could remember a commercial presented sometime during the previous four weeks; in 1990, the percentage had gone down to 48 percent. In addition, consumers are losing the capacity to specify what distinguishes a given product from a competing one, and in some cases even to associate the commercial they saw with the right product. Advertising for Eveready batteries is a case in point. The commercial showing a mechanical toy rabbit playing a drum and getting increasingly tired with "wear and tear" (an excellent advertising concept that quite deservedly won a prize) was attributed by 40 percent of all consumers to Eveready's rival Duracell. As a result, Duracell increased its market share to such an extent that it subsequently bought out Eveready!

In fact, too much choice winds up killing off real choice, and advertising loses its credibility. Most people now watch commercials without really paying attention to them, in the same way as one might look at entertainment whose content has little or no importance. Last of all, consumer zapping has its counterpart in TV zapping.

IN SEARCH OF NEW VALUES

In the present context, characterized on the one hand by stagnant growth rates and purchasing power, and, on the other hand, by a relative disaffection for constant advertising, consumers react in increasingly selective fashion. They establish a new order of priorities. Spending and possession as a means of getting full pleasure out of a rising standard of living, or to increase your social status, appear to be on the wane. Yet, although people still give due weight to the minimum of material well-being considered essential, they now seem to focus much more on the need for autonomy. Whereas accumulating objects in order to protect oneself or "just for the fun of it" has lost its power of attraction, those who can afford it spend a rising share of family income on leisure activities and travel. You wonder whether this is mere escapism, or if people are in fact seeking to expand their individual horizons beyond what the latest shopping bargains have to offer.

Whatever the case may be, a large number of our contemporaries prefer not to buy a new car or to replace their TV or refrigerator, which, after many years of use, still work properly, if it means giving up a week of skiing. Some people now save for a vacation abroad that they have been planning for a long time (and from which they hope to come back with lasting memories), rather than looking into a new model of car. The indicators of consumer satisfaction have thus shifted toward "products" that involve qualitative appreciation much more than quantitative accumulation.

At the same time, since staple goods are now subject to constant replacement, consumers spend less freely than before. With everything changing so fast, they are inclined to postpone their purchase until a later, more sophisticated model comes out, rather than rushing to buy the novelty of the day, whatever it may be. And why clutter up a relatively small apartment or house with useless objects when you live in a bustling metropolis where the rapid pace of life makes you want to stick to essentials? First and foremost, consumers are interested in service quality. They would rather have useful, fast, practical, and humanely provided services than sophisticated products that are ill-suited to daily life. Faced with a vast quantity of options, they need help. Service is of vital importance. It even has greater weight than the intrinsic value of the product.

SYMBOLIC INFLATION, SEARCH FOR MEANING

Recently, there has been a lot of talk about "the end of the buying fever" (as a headline in the magazine *Marie-France* proclaimed in April 1992) or the end of the "put-on years" (as the weekly *Le Point* announced in December 1991). After the rage of material possessions, comfortable home furnishings, status symbols, technologically sophisticated gadgets, and the latest styles in clothing, behavior patterns have begun to shift. Flashiness is out; people now tend to spend their money on whatever most contributes to making their daily lives more fulfilling. They have become less wasteful, particularly since purchasing power has ceased its upward climb.

In Italy, for instance, the average consumer would rather buy copies of luxury goods rather than spend too much on the real thing. The "cheap imitation" industry is now a highly profitable one. In any case, the younger generation, which simply can't afford the signs of affluence and success that their parents flaunted, gets along with considerably less. Although this is undoubtedly above all a matter of necessity, it also reflects a shift in taste and dominant values. The currently widespread ecological outlook entails much greater frugality and naturalness, and perhaps common sense as well.

Elsewhere, as in certain poor neighborhoods in Great Britain, the values of consumer society meet with open hostility and violent rejection. Gangs of young people (skinheads, punks, and others) see themselves as total outsiders to mainstream society, cultivating rebellion against a conformist environment.

Yet without going to such extremes, which only involve a tiny minority, large numbers of people now harbor doubts about the widsom of our society's consumer frenzy. Needs and desires that are constantly aroused or created through an ever-growing quantity of increasingly short-lived products ("here today and gone tomorrow") are eventually felt to be artificial. Consumers now know that in any event, given current rates of product turnover, they will never be able to keep up with the latest fad.

When your budget is limited, you have to be careful to select items of real utility, which means determining which of your needs should receive top priority. When the proliferation of equivalent products becomes a source of confusion, you have to decide what ultimately has meaning to you. The days are gone when consumers uncritically accepted whatever advertising told them. The more signs of well-being there are, the less actual suggestive power they have. The new behavior patterns currently emerging revolve around the idea of satisfying immediate, daily needs in a realistic way; then of pursuing whatever furthers your own personal goals (life-style, ethical values, etc.) or corresponds to your ideals (e.g. environmental protection or fighting poverty).

The demand for authenticity is back in full force. Having accumulated the means of existence, our society is discovering more and more that what has always been a truly scarce commodity, what really matters, is to have something to live for. It is therefore in relation to such a goal that new patterns of consumption, and economic and social behavior in general, are currently taking form in the Western world.

ACCUMULATED FRUSTRATION

Nowadays, we have less and less a direct relationship with the basic things of life. Man is separated from his environment by elaborate social structures, machines, commercial networks and hierarchies which make communication a more complex affair, one that usually requires the presence of intermediaries. Thus, postmodern socioeconomic systems combine all-powerful tools of high technology with the powerlessness that comes from a tangled web of interconnections that wind up canceling each other out. Nobody knows who is in charge any more.

In a sense, we are the victims of our civilization's paradoxes. We continually sing the praises of modern means of communication, and design even more efficient ones in order to facilitate exchange between people. In practice, however, we delegate the task of communicating to public relations agencies, advertising experts, and other mediators.

We have call for self-management of our own bodies, as the increase in the number of books on self-medication suggests. We want to take charge of our health and act as if we could dispense with doctors. Yet at the same time, an ultra-technological form of medicine that is inaccessible to common mortals becomes increasingly powerful. There is now a specialist for every organ.

We have experienced a period of sexual liberation: sex is now publicly displayed, contraception has become self-evident, and abortion, now covered by the social security system in France, has lost much of its dramatic character. None the less, we are now subjected to a veritable avalanche of recommendations on sexual practice aimed at stopping AIDS.

FROM CONSUMER SOCIETY TO COMMUNICATION SOCIETY

The rapid evolution of our society over the past decades has led to the disintegration of inherited forms of human solidarity. In today's urban desert of atomized social relations, whose underlying principle is individual autonomy, the shopping center seems to have replaced the village square. It has become the only locus of exchange in which all participate. Thus, consumption, previously vested with a liberating function related to the growing feeling of individual independence and to the tremendous appeal of the modern world's showcase, no longer assumes the same role as before.

The act of consuming is no longer simply a way to assert oneself; it now also expresses a need for communication with others, for "intelligent" relations with one's surroundings. In short, human values and the meaning we attribute to things take on greater importance than the mere fact of possessing them. What people now buy are less material objects than signs of harmony, of balance, of security, of general well-being, and of social interaction. The quantitative thus fits into a qualitative perception, which no longer derives merely from individual needs and desires, but which also reflects, more or less consciously, the demand for a way of being that has holistic coherence.

The only acts that all individuals have in common today are consumption and communication. This explains why communication turns into an act of consumption (skillfully prompted by ubiquitous media stimuli, the "zap" generation zaps from urge to urge in search of as many sensations as possible, with easy, immediate pleasure guaranteed) and consumption into an act of communication that is hoped to be instantaneous yet fulfilling. It has become vital for everyone to perceive the significance of their acts and to communicate as broadly as possible with anyone or anything that gives positive value to existence.

Lastly, following a phase in which people frenetically pursued "having," a new desire related to "being" can now be observed. This is undoubtedly the major psychological revolution of our time, one that all economic players must take into account if they don't want to miss the postmodern boat.

6

The Triumph of Intelligence over Material Factors

Man's future can't be to become the errand boy of tomorrow's robots.
Marvin Minsky, Massachusetts Institute of Technology

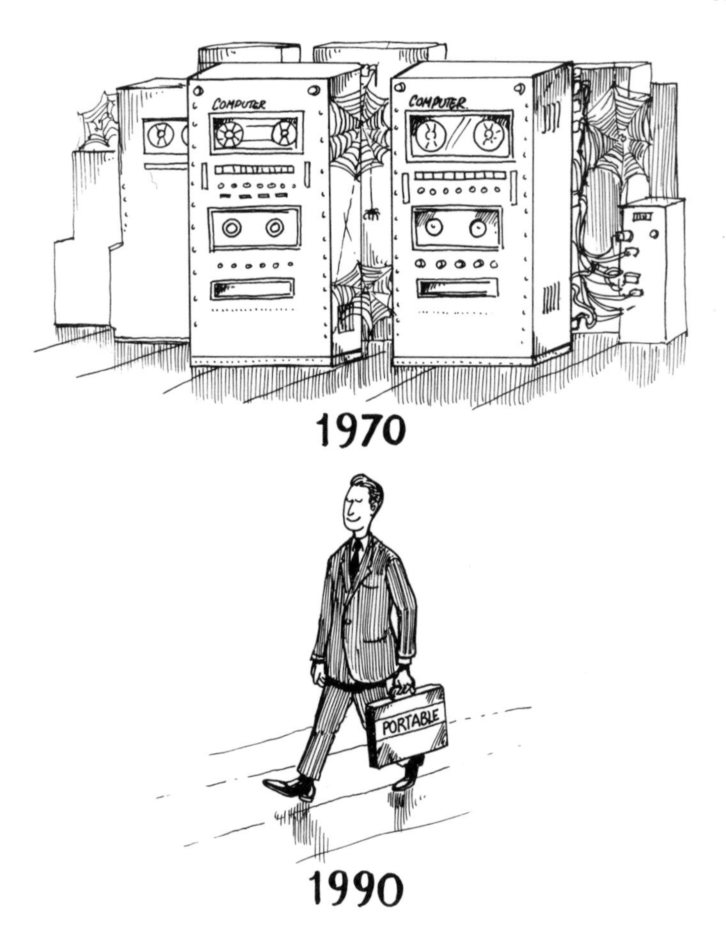

Manufacture no longer has decisive weight; what creates value today is the intelligence of a complete service.

The task at hand is no longer to dominate space, but to dominate time.

"Heavy" has given way to "light"; robots have replaced unskilled workers, and the information society has ousted the industrial society.

The powerful machinery of large organizations has little value compared to the adaptiveness of micro-organisms designed to be like living ones.

In the early 1970s, computers were still uncommon, expensive, bulky machines. In addition to being used for ultra-specialized research, these awe-inspiring creatures also carried out important collective functions with far-reaching strategic implications in the areas of defense and industry. Access to them depended on learning a number of languages with strange codes, comprehensible only to the initiated.

INFORMATION TECHNOLOGY WITHIN EVERYONE'S GRASP

Today, in the world of information technology (as in electronics and video), the languages employed have become transparent to the user, whose technical knowledge need not go beyond icons, menus, and the double clicks of his mouse. Anyone can now work, study, or just have fun on the desktop, and even the smallest companies have at least one computer. Such machines have turned into ordinary work tools. Furthermore, information technology, with its auxiliary branches (credit cards, home servers) has become part of daily life everywhere. Any household can afford it.

In the meantime, the field of electronics has made rapid strides. The advent of the microprocessor constitutes a revolution no less significant than the invention of the transistor.

The rapid progress accomplished lately in miniaturization has reduced the cost of equipment, machinery, and energy to next to nothing. At present, it is estimated that, in the average computer, hardware now represents between 10 and 15 percent of overall cost, software 25 percent, with 60–65 percent going to maintenance and service. A microchip now contains over 100,000 transistors, as opposed to 200 a short time ago.

This technological leap forward has led to an astounding increase in computing power. Computerized systems are so widely distributed throughout the economy and government administration that they now form an integral part of modern society's functioning. Without them, the whole machine would grind to a halt.

Miniaturization techniques have made it possible to build portable devices, and compatible systems facilitate transfer from one language to another. The very concept of computing has thus undergone a major change. What was once a form of expert knowledge for processing confidential data, one that few possessed, today plays a vital role in ordinary book-keeping, mailings, and word-processing.

In addition to storing data, computers enable their users to tap worldwide information sources. Through the rapid expansion of telecommunications, markets on the five continents of the world are now equipped with interconnected terminals that constantly increase the mass of information circulating. The result is that, once again, the power pyramid has been inverted. It is no longer suppliers who run the show in the marketplace, but users.

IBM AND MICROSOFT: FROM MANUFACTURER TO CUSTOMER

In its desire to become the giant of the computer world, IBM initially banked on a heavy-industry strategy with hardware production as its central feature. Although at first the company enjoyed an enviable situation, mass producing equipment and leasing it on a new market, it made the mistake of clinging to its productivistic outlook at a time when consumers were beginning to dictate conditions in the market. This strategy in no way prevented the rise of competitors like Apple, who understood the importance of combining technical performance with a concern for the user's interests.

After a decade of booming business, the major hardware producers all found themselves in serious trouble. Twenty years ago, when there were roughly 50,000 mainframe computers in the world, the leading manufacturers sold their wares at exorbitant prices with exceptionally high margins, owing to the low number of computers in existence and the relative unfamiliarity of most people with the field. At the time, computer companies did a little of everything, rarely dissociating hardware from software. Buying from

IBM or Hewlett-Packard was like signing up for life: once the first purchase was made, you had to continue to use the same supplier. Any company that wanted to switch ran into unimaginable difficulties in transferring data and methods.

Even in the past few years, with some 60 percent of the workforce in industrial nations using computer-related tools in one way or another, computer manufacturers realized only belatedly that the balance of power was shifting and that users would soon be in a position to dictate terms.

Desktop computers were soon to become the most important market. Today, there are apparently over 100 million of them in existence. Increasingly compact and just as powerful as those huge contraptions built two decades ago, they can be easily produced, since the cost of the equipment required has itself dropped to incredibly low levels. Nearly a thousand desktop manufacturers around the world are currently engaged in a price and service war, all to the consumer's benefit.

As the industry moves from gigantic central processing units meant to run an entire company's operations to micro-computers purchased for individual jobs with specific requirements, its products have changed considerably, as have their function and cost. The variety of features demanded – for example, multiple links to networks with electronic mail capacities – ultimately works in the customer's favor. The present-day challenge is to be able to come up with new applications for each kind of machine and to get optimal leverage from a varied range of equipment.

With the rapid, many-sided spread of desktop computing, the software industry has freed itself from its previously heavy dependence on hardware. In 1981, IBM chose the Microsoft operating system for its first PCs. It was from this point on that software houses began to receive the lion's share of the industry's profits. Today, 17-year-old Microsoft has a market value of $22 billion, i.e. about the same as that of General Motors, the world's largest industrial corporation.

It seems absurd that a company that sells floppy disks in plastic wrappers, employs 10,000 people, and has annual sales of just $1.8 billion should be as highly rated as a company with 766,000 employees. Yet this anomaly reflects the predictions of millions of investors, who are confident about the future profits that the exponential development of the software market will bring.

By offering more flexible, modular systems, second-generation computer companies demonstrated their awareness of the shifting sources of added value. Microsoft, however, went even further, since it understood that manufacturing computers would be infinitely less lucrative than levying value at a point located between production and consumption.

CONQUERING TIME RATHER THAN SPACE

Technological evolution over the past 20 years has generated opportunities for armchair travel and exploration such as on-line data services, home computers, and fax machines. These electronic instruments have given rise to instantaneous information, "virtual" meetings, and flexible work schedules that are rapidly making timeclocks obsolete, as actual results become the essential basis for evaluating an individual's work. All these improvements now make it possible to reintegrate the sphere of work into private life and to conceive of work at home, or at least to create smaller, decentralized workshops that can be located outside major urban areas.

This trend runs counter to the reflexes of entrepreneurs who are still imbued with the values of traditional industrial society. In the nineteenth century, the main task was to conquer markets in order to secure an outlet for mass production. This required appropriating and exploiting sources of raw materials and energy supplies, which boiled down to extending one's influence over space and winning out through sheer machine power. In other words, the logic of success implied domination by force and territorial occupation. Europe's colonial expansion can to a large extent be explained by this dynamic of conquering markets and raw material supplies.

Today, however, the economy no longer operates on the same basis. It draws its strength from the ability to master time, i.e. to innovate, to anticipate the evolution of technology and trade, and to adjust to new needs, perhaps even stimulating them. Contemporary production processes make increasing use of light-weight, often synthetic materials that require relatively little energy, and reflect current concern for preserving the environment. Changes in both attitudes and cost structures have encouraged the shift of "heavy" production facilities abroad.

The classical industrial model was exemplified by the automobile, a hallmark of modern society. Through the highway network that it called forth, the automobile has remodeled our living space and transformed our landscape. It has greatly contributed to a spatial segmentation that separates work zones (factories and offices), housing (dormitory towns), and shopping or recreation areas. The economic and ecological cost of adapting cars to the urban environment, a process that obviously leaves much to be desired, has turned out to be disturbingly high. Exhaust fumes now constitute the primary factor in urban air pollution, so much so that under anticyclonic weather conditions, the authorities are sometimes compelled temporarily to prohibit the use of cars within city limits, as has occurred a number of times in Italy. One wonders whether the time saved by motorists and the pleasure they derive from driving really make up for such problems. It seems doubtful, particularly if we judge by their growing discontent, which brought about a decline in the number of new car registrations in 1993 (–18.3 percent in France). The gap is enormous between the ever-increasing technical possibilities of cars, especially engine performance, and average speeds actually attained in big cities. Although the gap is somewhat narrower outside urban areas (on super-highways, for example), it should be stressed that speed limits are essential and are likely to be enforced with rising severity in the future.

Thus, everything that the automobile represents as a form of social and economic organization currently appears to be running out of steam and breaking down, but we only make veiled allusions to it, as if the subject were somehow taboo.

Be that as it may, there is little chance of renewed economic growth as long as we fail to work out alternative models of development that take the current changes in values into account. We have absolutely nothing to gain from maintaining the status quo.

ECONOMIC CHANGES REFLECT A REVOLUTION IN VALUES

It used to be that muscle-bound paratroopers, macho tough-guys, and IBM engineers with manly crew-cuts were the latest rage. They were efficient and they operated at fever pitch. Europe received this belief in Superman from the United States, seemingly a nation of Herculean warriors.

Against the grain at first, then in increasing numbers, anti-heroes have begun to appear. Sensitive and understanding, they go in for child care, platonic relationships, non-violence, and spiritualism. "New Age" is with us. Relaxation cures and sea-water therapy are replacing body-building; affinity, power relations; consensus, confrontation. In the Age of Aquarius, psychology and behavior patterns are changing. Communist materialism has imploded, America seems to have lost its soul, and, in the business world, a number of triumphant Goliaths like ITT and IBM have been worsted by resourceful, friendly looking Davids who speak a totally different language, one based on affinity and easy-going relations.

The fact that a number of brands operating in the same universe, in the same competitive environment, with less elaborate product offers (or even less efficient ones) none the less manage to thrive in spectacular fashion indicates that they know how to stimulate the consumer's desire. They find the right tone, and they elicit an irresistible feeling of community. All this means that our cult of performance and excellence is sorely in need of revision, for it represents a necessary, but not sufficient, condition for winning over consumers in an evolving market.

THE TWILIGHT OF THE INDUSTRIAL ERA

Since the nineteenth century, economic organization has rested on the idea that value came from the mechanization of labor and the high output that it allowed. Today, however, this is clearly no longer the case. Cybernetics, electronics, and diverse forms of artificial intelligence now contribute significantly to the majority of production circuits. What gives value to a product is that intangible bit of brain power, service, and the inventiveness that it incorporates.

A product's material structure has much less importance than in the past, as cost indexes in all industries show (from computers to the food industry). The "hard" side of a product has become a mere residual element that plays a subordinate role in defining its value. The price of any given item currently depends above all on the intelligence required to produce and distribute it (design, preparation, service, packaging, and display).

Initially, Taylorism made possible an extraordinary jump in production at reduced cost. The problem, however, with such a system was that it judged individuals solely in relation to their labor power, as if they were blue-collar or white-collar robots. At present, real robots, which make fewer mistakes in repetitive operations, are starting to replace them. Legitimate concern over man's future in the world of production is heard more and more often. As Marvin Minsky prophesied, "We will be lucky if robots accept us as pets."

Industrial concentration and the trend toward building gigantic, perfectly coordinated production facilities, as in America, proved their efficiency for many long years. After World War II, however, when the Japanese had to reconstruct their economy, they simply could not afford to set up such vast integrated structures. They were thus compelled to reconsider production methods. They were confronted by a starkly simple choice: either disappear entirely as an industrial power, or come up with methods other than those employed in the West. Motivated by necessity, they decided to emphasize human potential and the community spirit associated with teamwork, a spirit to which their national culture predisposed them, of course, but on which they by no means had a monopoly. These new methods, arrived at essentially through trial and error, have recently proved to be formidably effective.

THE NINETEENTH-CENTURY FACTORY IS DEAD AND BURIED

We can no longer reproduce the model of giant industrial complexes that emerged in a mythical, nineteenth-century working-class world of steel mills and coal mines. Factories topped with huge smokestacks and filled with thousands of workers in grimy overalls barely exist any more, and even if they did, they would have trouble attracting a workforce. Increasingly clean, ventilated, and bright, today's factories are often located in pleasant surroundings. The "hard" world of the "Rustbelt" has given way to the "soft" world of the "Sunbelt."

This shift in the industrial and technical landscape has brought in its wake a radical change in attitudes. With the passage from classical industrial society to an economy based on information and communication, an inversion in values has taken place. The logic of the market has shaken up all bureaucracies; centralized, clearly defined organizations focused on production tend to be supplanted by decentralized, service-oriented structures whose contours continue to evolve.

As a result of this shift from a producer logic to a consumer logic, the imperatives of economic efficiency have changed in nature.

- Standardization loses ground with the demand for diversity and specialization.
- The strict division of labor into repetitive functions has proved to be less effective than the synergy of creative capacities (admittedly a more complex undertaking).
- Assembly-line production in interchangeable segments with fixed schedules has given way to individualized job descriptions and modular scheduling.
- Where technical means and decision-making were once concentrated in highly integrated, hierarchical industrial complexes, we now find activities decentralized in small production units in which broad participation is the rule.
- Emphasis on quantitative maximization, which involves constantly increasing output with ever-greater efficiency, has proved to be counter-productive in comparison with a focus on qualitative improvements that conform to market flows.
- Engineers and managers, whose power was previously unchallenged, must now work together with innovators (research personnel, designers, and teachers) and take their cue from those who possess an aggregate view of the goals to be reached, one that is in keeping with conditions prevailing in the field and in society at the time.

FROM MASS STRUCTURES TO MICRO-ORGANISMS

Mere manufacturing potential no longer offers any guarantee of profits. The main challenge today is to position the company so as to integrate technological innovation directly and to use it in the customers' interests. Not surprisingly, large equipment producers are rapidly losing ground to companies that focus on software development, systems integration, marketing, ongoing training, research, and mobilizing people.

The number of square feet in a factory no longer makes much of a difference. What matters today is the ability to come up with ingenious, outstanding technical solutions that meet the user's specific needs. Production capacity is merely one of a number of possible assets in a business strategy predicated entirely on service to the customer. This means that the competitive edge depends less on the mass of plant and equipment you have than on your ability to innovate before everyone else and to create constantly updated models. In spite of all appearances to the contrary, we are no longer living in a world dominated by vast, top-heavy institutions, but one characterized by the efficiency of light-weight, highly mobile "micro-organisms."

A useful analogy is with the field of modern physics, which explained the constitution of matter first in terms of particles, and subsequently in terms of waves. In parallel with this shift in perspective, the paradigms governing the business world have moved from heavy to light, from tangible to intangible. More than machine power, it is organizational intelligence that will be of prime importance tomorrow. A cluttered, polluted environment will give way to one in which miniaturization and the concern for health and cleanliness are essential.

7

The Future: as Ominous as Predicted?

We are shaping the world faster than we can change ourselves and we are applying to the present the habits of the past.

Winston Churchill

We have all been pleasantly surprised by the recent past.

Since we will get the future we deserve, we would do well to become its active builders, rather than be its passive victims.

Although globalization is irreversible, uniformity is not inevitable.

To get out of the current impasse, we must move from having to being.

In the past several years, the current events newsreel has been spinning so fast that the viewer may well begin to fear that if she takes her eyes off the TV screen for only a few minutes, she will miss some major event that could change the course of history.

Let's imagine ourselves back in 1988. If any soothsayer had announced at the time, "Communism's day is over; Eastern Europe will soon get its freedom back; Germany will be reunited in a few months; the USSR will be broken up from within into a set of more or less rival states; Leningrad will be renamed Saint Petersburg; the pre-1917 Russian flag will replace the red flag; Yugoslavia will divide up into several states that will plunge into a cruel civil war; Czechoslovakia will undergo partition by mutual agreement" who would have believed him? Most people would probably have dismissed him as a raving lunatic. This idea is clearly illustrated by the remarks of author-president Vaclav Havel, who was asked during a visit to the United States how he felt about the 1989 events in Eastern Europe. He answered, "It is such a moving and absurd drama that no one on Earth could possibly have written it."

THE FUTURE DOES NOT BELONG TO THE WORLD'S PROPHETS OF DOOM

Our society is drifting off into a state of anxiety (more than justified by unemployment, drugs crime, AIDS, and environmental disaster) that tends to paralyze all initiative. Yet we tend to forget that we have recently witnessed a series of events with extremely positive outcomes. The fall of the Communist dicatorships, the historic mutual recognition between Israelis and Palestinians, peace in Cambodia, and the end of apartheid in South Africa are among the encouraging upheavals that came in rapid succession.

Although the crisis in collective identity caused by such an acceleration of history should not be underestimated, the fact remains that over and above the sensational images broadcast around the world by the media, a new planetary consciousness and a worldwide public opinion are being forged. Even if the need for security, for clinging to familiar references, sometimes leads to fanatical forms of withdrawal, whether religious or nationalistic, such reactions are unlikely to hold back the current sweeping trend toward elimination of traditional barriers. This trend is preparing the way for a new openmindedness and an explosion of creativity that the decision-makers and businessmen of today must take into account.

Despite our growing awareness of the various threats we face (or perhaps because of such awareness), it is important to give greater thought to the considerable grounds for hope that the present period presents. We may just have the opportunity to build a new, more harmonious world order, one based more on consensus than in the past, and to establish new rules that safeguard a set of basic values. A precondition for such a reconstruction, however, is the realization that the economy is not an end in itself, that its ultimate purpose is to further the cause of human happiness. It might also be pointed out that drugs, crime, and malnutrition were not the product of the recession period; on the contrary, they emerged on a large scale in the preceding years of prosperity.

In all likelihood, the crisis of confidence generated by rising unemployment in Western countries should diminish somewhat as time goes by. After all, someone currently receiving the RMI (guaranteed minimum income) in France enjoys a higher standard of living than the average worker in 1900! What serves to amplify the current crisis is widespread pessimism. For example, everyone appears to agree that unemployment will continue even after the return to economic growth. Of course, Umberto Eco quite rightly warned that "imagining the worst is the only way to be optimistic in the long run." The trouble is that you always get the future you deserve, particularly the one that you prepared. Georges Bernanos said, "The future isn't something that happens to you, but something you make happen."

THE IMPORTANCE OF GLOBAL VISION

Taking expected technological breakthroughs as a starting point and imagining that they have the capacity to change the world instantly is usually a recipe for making excessively optimistic predictions. Yet even when erroneous, such conceptions have at least traditionally had one thing in their favor: they encourage dynamic activity.

Having to face an unforeseeable future is a serious handicap. We need to be able to imagine what tomorrow will look like if we are to take creative action. As long as the future remains impenetrable, creativity is inhibited. Accepting events as they come, while reacting more or less intelligently to them, can only cause lasting uneasiness. One of the chief problems we currently face is finding a way to overcome this uneasiness, for it necessarily leads to conservative inertia and regression.

In a constantly changing world, there are few challenges more formidable than guessing what tomorrow may bring. It makes little sense to count on the continuation of those past trends that produced the present situation, supposing that such a forecasting procedure ever had anything to recommend it. In general, everyone makes the same predictions at the same time – which doesn't guarantee that everyone won't be mistaken.

Since we have no assurances as to the accuracy of our predictions, we might as well work out the scenarios that we would most like to see come to pass. We should attempt to formulate a shared vision of the future to which we aspire, while stressing the dangers we face in the event that we don't succeed in bringing it about. In this connection, I would like to make use of elements provided in the Global Business Network's scenario books in order to help us to imagine in rough terms our world at the beginning of the third millennium.

FROM CHAOS TO MOSAIC: CHOOSING OUR SOCIETY

Depending on the rate of growth and the degree of social cohesion that we achieve tomorrow, three possible portraits suggest themselves. Let's start with the worst one, and then work upwards.

- *The chaotic society.* Pervasive egoism has become the rule. Every country attempts to export its unemployment and social problems to other nations. International harmonization is impossible. The economy stagnates (with growth rates of at best 1 percent) and social conflict becomes rife. The notion of a general interest gives way to sectorial demands that often take on a violent form. Corsica, Flanders, and Catalonia are a prey to nationalist or separatist forces. The struggles of farmers create a climate of hostility to the European Community; the "Euroskeptics" dominate public opinion. Germany, now bogged down in the difficulties of reunification, does virtually nothing to reverse this trend, judging that European unity no longer takes top priority. Meanwhile, the rest of Europe is getting poorer and poorer. Russia is sinking into anarchy. The United States has returned to isolationism. Confrontation increases between China and Japan. Deficits and debt burdens reach astronomical proportions. Protectionism is inevitable. Countries around the world begin rearmament.

- *The fortress society.* A ruthless, worldwide economic war rages, driven by Anglo-American *laissez-faire* ideology. There is widespread encouragement for innovation and risk-taking. In high-tech sectors, economic growth has picked up, whereas the slump continues in the more traditional industries. The application of free-trade principles does not produce the desired results (growth stagnates at a mere 2 percent), since it winds up reducing employment levels and destroying social cohesion. Deflation continues. Fear of unemployment inhibits demands for wage increases. Workers in high-growth industries balk more and more at the idea of paying taxes that finance aid to the underprivileged, whose ranks continue to swell. Once again, the US economy is booming, but this is achieved through cynical policies that demand free trade abroad, while applying barely concealed protectionist measures to the domestic market. As a result, American world leadership is discredited. Japan retreats into its regional sphere of influence. Germany also enjoys a return to prosperity, but prefers to go it alone. The idea of European unity, to which everyone still pays lip service, is in fact devoid of any real content. The development of a dual society wreaks tremendous damage, as the privileged strata of society invest heavily in veritable electronic fortresses in order to protect themselves against the hordes of the poor.
- *The mosaic society.* Everyone cultivates his distinctive features, and the tendency toward uniformity seems to have reached its limits. Ethnic and cultural minorities are protected. None of the three "empires" manages to dictate conditions to the others. Europe can turn to account its culture of universality and further develop its know-how in fostering cooperative relations between other nations. A new form of collaboration, rather than deregulation, has made possible greater harmonization between countries. Farmers are encouraged to continue to work the land. There is no longer a premium placed on economic specialization: high-growth industries help to finance the survival of less profitable ones. New, more balanced social structures with a greater concern for justice make for a more peaceful society. Europe becomes increasingly unified, while contributing to the development of its neighbors to the east. The United States invests heavily in the development of

Mexico, and eventually of all Latin America. In Germany and Japan, economic slump is little more than a bad memory. China, now united to Hong Kong, has moved in the direction of true democracy and is busy solving the serious environmental problems attending its rapid development. The world economy has found its way back to economic growth (at least 3 percent) and relative prosperity.

THREE COMPETING FORMS OF CAPITALISM

The above scenarios are based on the assumption that three major poles will determine world economic growth.[1] Each of these regional empires (America, Europe, and Asia) takes its inspiration from a dominant model of capitalism. Anglo-Saxon *laissez-faire*, Rhineland social liberalism, and Asian government interventionism, in spite of their common support for the values of free enterprise, all possess a number of particularities, and thus specific strengths capable of stimulating world economic recovery.

- *America*, through its creative capacity, can return to the top level if it combines economic leadership with political leadership. It must, however, incorporate the lessons of Japanese experience and raise its standards of quality, while making full use of its traditional strong points such as being market-directed, aggressive, and inventive.
- *Greater Europe*, assuming it actually comes into being, can take over from the United States – in the event that American influence should go into decline – by creating an even larger, more dynamic market than before. The continent faces the same strategic demands as America: higher quality and greater creativity. For welfare entitlements to be preserved, the workforce must develop expert know-how and aim for zero defects. German influence will help Europe to succeed in this endeavor. In contrast to American-style unrestrained capitalism, the European system will emphasize cooperation at all levels of economic and social life rather than competition.
- *Japan*, provided it gains control over the Chinese dragon by means of technological assistance, can unify the Asiatic pole, turning it into the world's economic center of gravity (it already holds 41 percent of world bank reserves). Japan alone now has two-thirds of the economic

weight of the United States and twice the weight of Germany. Compared to Western countries, it is certainly not lacking in assets. The Japanese give greater importance to the long term than to the short term, think globally rather than locally, prefer gaining market share to maximizing profits, and explore any and all possibilities. Asians know better than Westerners how to cooperate. Owing to their mastery of many of the most promising technologies, they currently occupy a strategic position on the international playing field.

It is to be hoped that these three forms of capitalism, instead of embarking on a collision course in pursuit of world leadership, will work out new means of collaborating and of influencing each other, without having to give up the qualities that distinguish them.

THE NEED TO MOVE FROM HAVING TO BEING

We used to dream of small, coherent, smoothly running entities, with every country being self-sufficient. Today, as national borders lose their relevance and a global society emerges, people around the world can experience the Los Angeles riots "live." Finding ourselves in the midst of a terrifying spectacle that comes from anywhere and everywhere, we sometimes feel like onlookers who are incapable of comprehending or of assimilating the endless flood of images they see.

The continuous proliferation of goods and services and the spectacular technical breakthroughs accomplished by our society have led us at times to believe, like Prometheus, that we could storm the heavens. We took it for granted that things would continue indefinitely to get better. The insane process that began a century and a half ago has resulted in today's post-industrial society, in which everyone lives in his own private sphere and pursues his own selfish, hedonistic happiness, albeit haunted by insecurity, while showing no interest in self-awareness.

By devoting all our efforts to accumulating practical knowledge, we have managed, through science and technology, to produce goods and services on a hitherto unimaginable scale. Although such a system has undeniably made life much easier, it has also drawn humanity into a sort of vortex in which discoveries, technological advances, and tangible consumer goods spring up like magic formulas that are supposed to provide solutions to all problems. What is lost in the process is a sense of what really matters in life.

Even in the most affluent countries, people don't appear to be any happier than they were in the past; in fact, the opposite often seems to be true. Modern civilization has created a huge number of artificial needs and, as a consequence, opportunities for dissatisfaction. The relentless pursuit of the quantitative has gone hand in hand with the destruction of the qualitative. Today, as the system of quantitative logic reaches its ultimate conclusion, we rediscover, through a sort of inversion of polarity, that only the qualitative gives meaning to life. Hyperconsumption leaves a bad taste in ours mouths; widespread discontent is eating away at our society.

At long last, certain contemporary currents point the way toward a return to a kind of logic of voluntary deprivation, to an eternal truth of the Gospel, namely that only after giving up the superfluous, artificial things – the world of having – can we get back to essentials, to the real joys of living and being.

Note

1 Information derived from the *GBN Scenario Book*, "The Crisis of Fragmentation," 1992–1993.

PART II

Beacons in the Storm

8

Living with Uncertainty

The medieval world believed in a supernatural but comprehensible order. The Newtonian model believed in an order that was part of nature and that could be apprehended by reason ... The Heisenbergian paradigm seems to deprive us of any protection against the threat of an unknown future and an unknowable reality.

Walter Weisskopf, "Reflection on uncertainty in economics"[1]

Experimental science cannot explain everything, nor can the world be cut up into slices.

The whole takes precedence over the parts.

A link between chance and determinism, chaos governs processes of adaptation, and even the functioning of the brain.

Our vision of the world and our values have drastically changed as a result.

In present-day Western society, the conception of the world that shapes attitudes does not draw its inspiration from religion, as in times past, or from philosophy, as is still the case in other civilizations. Since the late eighteenth century, experimental science has provided the basis for collective beliefs, or rather has served as the criterion of certainty. This means that we only consider valid or real that which can immediately be verified by observation and tangibly submitted to experiment.

In the past few decades, however, it has become apparent that the very act of observing, say, a physical phenomenon can modify its initial components. We thus have the famous paradox of Heisenberg, which postulates that reality is a field of possibilities that cannot be reduced to what is perceptible to the observer.

NEW DEVELOPMENTS IN SCIENCE ARE PROFOUNDLY ALTERING OUR OUTLOOK

As a mortal creature, man is doomed to live with uncertainty. Since time immemorial, however, he has constantly sought to limit, or even to eliminate, the area of uncertainty that surrounds him. Nineteenth-century Westerners, steeped as they were in positivistic ideas and fascinated by the rapid development of experimental science and technological invention, labored under the delusion that man could attain absolute knowledge by exploring the outer reaches of the physical world. By working out increasingly sophisticated methods of analysis, it was thought, we could discover the laws governing material phenomena, and in so doing, explain the way in which both the entire universe and living things were structured.

Experimental science was supposed to offer the key to all fields, from physics and chemistry to medicine, and the technical progress to which it led was expected to make it possible to influence and transform the world. According to this deterministic, mechanistic conception, man had only to demonstrate the inner workings of the great clock of the universe in order to be able to achieve total mastery of nature through his "positive" knowledge and his technical ingenuity.

THE WORLD IS NOT ONE BIG CLOCK

Yet from one discovery to the next, physicists began to realize that everything did not boil down to arrangements of material particles and that the laws of mechanical causality were not universally applicable.

Underneath molecules and atoms, there exists the irreducible mystery of a reality more complex than the workings of a clock. The findings of quantum theory, for example, imply a radical shift in perspective. From the standpoint of traditional science, the universe was composed of particles of matter linked together by gravitation and magnetic fields. These particles were, in a sense, autonomous, just as the observer was separate from the phenomenon he studied. This Cartesian, mechanistic vision has completely collapsed. We now know, for instance, that the electrons in a beam of light behave both like waves and like bodies, and that what determines the form in which they manifest themselves is the influence exerted by the observer. Like the bat in the fable, a particle can thus say at one point, "I am a mouse: look at my paws!", and at another, "I am a bird: look at my wings!" The solution to the riddle may be inaccessible to the modes of perception of which our measurement instruments are capable.

Once opened up, this breach in our certainties has been getting larger and larger. Science, while essential to our comprehension of the universe in which we live, thus loses its privileged status and becomes a mere tool. Since physics, a "hard science" that seemed best qualified for dissecting the mechanisms that rule the world, began to admit its own limits, other disciplines have gone even further, teaching us the virtues of humility. Scientists no longer try to project an image of omnipotence. They now assert that we must accept an irreducible amount of uncertainty in our environment. The universe they describe has little in common with a system of building blocks. It is rather an aggregate of interacting interconnections in which man directly participates. It no longer makes sense to reduce reality to tangible phenomena that can be measured within a given space or time. Reality in fact possesses a holistic character that goes well beyond the mere analysis of its component parts.

Likewise, the complexity of life cannot be accounted for by the simplistic mechanisms of Darwinian theory. Recent work in biology has questioned the validity of such a linear vision of evolution and highlighted the existence of infinitely more subtle correlations and interplays. Whereas it used to be believed that human consciousness resulted merely from the sum total of the chemical operations in the brain, contemporary science has discovered that man is not a "neuronal" creature. Recent progress accomplished in the field of artificial intelligence reveals precisely those aspects of the human mind which no mechanical logic can grasp: man alone can have access to meaning; he is the only one able to understand what he does.

THE AGE OF OPEN-ENDED KNOWLEDGE

Carlo Rubbia, director of CERN and Nobel prize-winner for physics in 1984, recently stated, "We now have a good understanding of visible matter, but unfortunately, it only represents about 20 percent of the universe, and we don't know what the remaining 80 percent is made of . . . The complexity of vacuum continues to elude us. The question of mass is one of the most tenacious riddles in the universe."[2]

Now that the conquest of matter has been taken to its logical conclusion, we are witnessing a dramatic shift in emphasis. What appears to us are not the simplest components of matter nor the "elementary corpuscles" so often looked for, but the extremely complex nebula of the infinitesimal. What is more, after studying matter, we discover laws that contradict its principles (such as anti-matter) or that are simply different in nature, laws that give new relevance to the question of an organizing consciousness underlying perceptible forms and energies.

CHAOS: THE CONNECTING LINK BETWEEN DETERMINISM AND CHANCE

In a brilliant demonstration that has by now become a classic, French mathematician René Thom set out the idea that any organization, system, or living organism follows a logical growth curve until reaching the limits of its developmental potential. At that point, there occurs a break (or "catastrophe") that causes the entity involved to come apart or dissolve. Another form then arises that could not be foreseen on the basis of the previously observed conditions and that organizes itself according to new laws, producing a different pattern of development. This thesis offers a highly relevant description of living matter, which is much less often marked by linear progression than by radical breaks and crises stemming from the passage from one state to another.

In much the same vein, Nobel prize-winner Ilya Prigogine demonstrated, with his famous termitarium image,[3] that an instable state of unorganization and fluctuation ruled by what we call chance, i.e. unpredictable, uncontrollable data, sooner or later gives rise to a new structuring order. According to Prigogine, this phenomenon characterizes all life and creation, and leads to higher forms of organization.[4]

Only in appearance is chaos nothing but disorder. If we analyze a large number of orbits, each one absolutely unpredictable, in an unstable system governed by chaos (e.g. a pendulum or a "chaotic laser"),[5] what emerges is a figure denoting a "strange attractor" (the terms used by David Ruelle and Floris Takens, who discovered the phenomenon some 20 years ago). Some orbits turn out to be more common, more "typical," than others, and experiments conducted in 1990 at the University of Maryland (Ott, Grebogi, and Yorke) show that it is possible to control the evolution of a chaotic system toward greater stability by introducing minute corrections so as to force the system to repeat such trajectories.

Mathematical models for analyzing and characterizing chaos are by now well known, and Agnessa Babloyantz of the Free University of Brussels has made use of them to highlight chaotic phases in the functioning of the human brain. The most interesting thing about the concept of chaos is that it invalidates the famous alternative between determinism and chance that has traditionally divided philosophers and theologians. It can now be said that random, "unpredictable," yet organized systems do exist, albeit "far from equilibrium." Jean Chaline and his colleagues at the University of Burgundy came upon them in 1992 in their research on the evolution of species of small rodents over 5 million years.[6] According to their findings, the model that best accounts for this evolution is neither the pure chance nor the pure determinism of external factors, but – once again – chaos. In this conception, chaos serves to optimize the variety of the species on Earth at any given time by contributing to their adaptability and limiting the "bursts" of collective extinction generated by such external factors.

TOWARD A NEW CAUSAL LOGIC

Such recent findings show us in fact that any system of causal laws valid at a given level and conditioning a given state of matter depends on other, higher, more general laws of causality that can only be identified following a qualitative leap to another state. The idea that change occurs in sudden breaks, which ancient wisdom recognized, is now reconfirmed by the most advanced scientific research. The universe can thus be characterized as an open system, a series of worlds within worlds in which the unpredictable (i.e. higher, unknown laws) and necessity (i.e. the principle of sequential, logical organization) constantly interact.

In practical terms, this implies that there is no single road to truth and to decoding reality, but several possible explanations that account for the same phenomenon at different levels, or even an infinite number of fields and discovery methods. We can no longer believe in the absolute pre-eminence of experimental science, as our grandparents did. For although the spectacular technological achievements of the past 50 years may reassure us as to the ability of science to provide the practical means for controlling the world, scientists themselves upset such convictions by claiming that as their work advances, they encounter more and more unknowns, which makes it impossible for them to formulate explanatory theories on how the world functions.

Basic research has produced a profound conceptual shift. From notions such as uncertainty, indeterminacy, and non-reductionism, a new, holistic paradigm has emerged, positing that "everything is part of everything." Our vision of the world has been all the more shaken up since some contemporary scientists, in their attempts to define matter itself, have ended up conceiving of it as "energy," or even "spirit," according to its state of organization.

RELATIVITY IMPLIES GLOBAL INTERRELATIONS

According to this new scientific logic, the universe takes on the appearance of a fabric of interconnections between interwoven, interdependent forces that "gravitate" around each other, without our being able to determine which ones are causes and which ones are effects. Consequently, the subtler research becomes, the more it reveals that the whole, i.e. the aggregate unity of these interactions and the organic forms of cohesion that result from them, is greater than its parts, and even that the whole precedes the parts, in the same way that an architect's blueprint arranges in advance the layout and functioning of the various elements in a building.

The emerging holistic view of reality must therefore integrate all these dimensions simultaneously, without separating the logic of one element from the overall logic that conditions it. Global knowledge of interactive relations has become a leading priority. It reinforces the idea of dismantling artificial, sectorial barriers and of conducting interdisciplinary scientific work. Contemporary science demonstrates that the world is not composed solely of bodies of solid matter or of energy masses, but rather of *information*, in the sense of genetic cell programs, of *communications* circulating between forms, of continuous *interactions* between observer and observed, and of *intersolidarity* (i.e. global interdependence) among all the pieces of the puzzle.

FROM MENTAL CHANGE TO SOCIAL CHANGE

The spread of this new scientific paradigm lies in part behind the new values that our society currently emphasizes such as communication, interaction, individual responsibility, and a sense of global, shared fate. After the predominance of hierarchical, machine-like organizational forms, as epitomized by the Tayloristic assembly line, which were thought to maximize quantitative output, we are turning increasingly toward more flexible network structures designed to encourage creativity and qualitative achievement.

At present, innovation is more a matter of intelligence and information than of sequential equations and imposing machines. With new fields of possibility (and of the unknown) constantly opening up, acquiring the ability to learn continually and to expand our knowledge has become the primary task today. An engineer now requires retraining every five years. We can no longer reason as we did in the past. According to Umberto Eco, "As our century draws to a close, the two main characteristics of an intellectual are wanting the impossible and being sure of nothing."

After a prolonged, centrifugal struggle to dominate matter, we are relearning that "everything is a part of everything" and that, as ancient wisdom teaches us, the visible appearance of things conceals an essential mystery. The point is no longer to accumulate fragmentary, rapidly outdated bits of knowledge, but to be able to learn at each stage with a fresh outlook. This requires making ample use not only of practical, technical know-how, but also of imagination, intuition, and all the creative resources that the mind and the soul possess.

Notes

1 Walter Weisskopf, "Reflection on uncertainty in economics," Seventh Annual Conference of the Geneva Association, *The Geneva Papers on Risk and Insurance* (Geneva 1984), quoted in Orio Giarini and Walter R. Stahel, *Les limites du certain* (Lausanne: Presses polytechniques et universitaires romandes, 1990, p. 169).
2 Interview in *Leonardo*, a special issue of the newspaper *Le Monde* devoted to the Seville World Fair (Paris, May 1992).
3 The construction of a termitarium begins with a chaotic process. Each termite drops off his clump of earth more or less at random, but he mixes into it a hormone designed to attract his fellow termites. After a while, another termite deposits his clump at the same spot, then another and another. This cumulative process produces an entirely unpredictable outcome.
4 Ilya Prigogine and Isabelle Stengers, *La Nouvelle Alliance* (Paris: Gallimard, 1979).
5 See issue no. 914 of *Science et Vie* (November 1993) for a description of the experiments conducted by Lefranc and Glorieux at the University of Lille.
6 J. Dubois, J. Chaline, and P. Brunet-Lecomte, *Comptes rendus de l'Académie de Paris*, vol. 315, 1992.

9

Ethics as a Foundation for Consensus

The churches are empty; the only places we know how to fill on Sunday mornings are the supermarkets. Science has failed to say what good is and history to give meaning. The only thing left is reality, and reality makes no judgments. Something more is thus required: values, principles, commandments, in other words, morality.

André Comte-Sponville, *L'Expansion*[1]

Once he is "liberated," the individual experiences more anguish and a greater need for solidarity than before.

The new powers of technology generate a rising demand for ethics.

A higher order is needed to regulate economic and scientific evolution.

The free-market company is the only remaining collective structure still capable of elaborating an ethical consensus that could serve as a basis for human action.

Since there is no longer any religious or ideological model that can create shared beliefs, our contemporaries are disoriented; they are in search of new ideals. With the collapse of deterministic doctrines (Marxist ideology or various scientistic myths), demands related to identity take on renewed vigor. It is as if people hoped that by appealing to memories of the past, they could give the present meaning and substance. Yet we can hardly expect to build a more human future merely by restoring a sense of cultural, ethnic, linguistic, or religious identity, with the obvious attendant risk of cutting ourselves off from the rest of the world.

In any case, it is impossible to return to traditional forms of society. Those who attempt such a restoration (like Iran under Ayatollah Khomeini) encounter tremendous difficulties and sink into totalitarian fanaticism. The question is this: how can we invent a new force capable of mobilizing people that is not dogmatic and that constitutes a common denominator accepted by all? The answer is unlikely to be found in mere pragmatic regulation of the imperatives that characterize our society. In the meantime, we are all groping our way toward the appropriate rules and values.

FROM THE NEED TO BELONG TO THE NEW RELIGIOUSNESS

The need to find one's place within a larger whole, to belong to a group with a more or less pronounced community character, expresses itself in a large number of forms. From "underground" groupings to charity and volunteer organizations, from leisure activity clubs to cultural associations, people are trying to escape the loneliness of city life and to rediscover a shared identity and a meaning to existence.

The need for religion (i.e. joining together in a meaningful whole) is quite widely felt at present. Cultural, national, or ethnic background is currently asserted as a source of identity, one that the participants generally experience as a means of setting themselves apart from a drab, anonymous modern society.

The desire to commune in the service of noble causes sometimes leads to sectarianism and to religious fundamentalism. The dominant trend, however, is rather one of a vague kind of religiousness. Proceeding from its most structured to its least structured manifestations, we can observe the revival of certain pilgrimages, whether within mainstream churches or around less open "chapels"; the flourishing activity of sects; the New Age phenomenon, a vaguely defined set of mixed aspirations toward experimenting with alternative forms of rationality, communicating with other "worlds," immersing oneself in a vast cosmic totality, or simply practicing group relaxation techniques; and the popularity of personal development methods aimed at liberating the potential of the individual, at stripping down his protective armor. Last of all, when none of these approaches seems to offer a credible solution to the problem of anxiety, some engage in forms of transgression that enable them to float off into an informal dream world (drugs, or more or less suicidal paroxystic experiences).

The pursuit of ideals is also often reflected in participation in humanitarian causes. The individual hopes to deal with this problem by actively committing himself to the fight against epidemics, malnutrition, or natural disasters. Former French government official Bernard Kouchner represents a prime example of this phenomenon. The basic idea is that by sending food and medication to the troubled areas of the world, you can assuage your conscience. Although such actions are useful and the sentiments that motivate these volunteer movements are certainly lofty, humanitarian involvement can sometimes have perverse effects. As we have seen, it can serve as an excuse for doing nothing, as in Bosnia, or as a means of launching a mass media operation strongly reminiscent of colonialism, as in Somalia. Beneath the surface of the current humanitarian vogue, we can also detect a certain fear of insecurity and the desire to feel good about oneself.

THE DECLINE OF HEDONISM

We all aspire to be shielded from want, and material possessions give a strong feeling of security. However, when faced with a nearly dizzying choice of goods and services, we end up "losing our appetite." We then begin to wonder whether continued consumer frenzy is really such a good thing. And as the taste for accumulating objects wanes, the notion of value once again becomes of central importance.

We are looking for an underlying meaning to our contemporary world, one that responds to the growing concerns it prompts regarding environmental deterioration, social breakdown, media brainwashing, and other similar problems. By focusing on material development, our possession-oriented civilization has destroyed age-old forms of equilibrium or wrenched man from his traditionally harmonious relationship with his environment (the notion of harmony captured by the Japanese word *wa*).

As soon as modern science made its Promethean breakthrough, Westerners were carried away by the feeling that they could at last free themselves from all existing constraints. More recently, yet in a similar fashion, former colonial countries also got the impression that they could have everything when they achieved their independence. Meanwhile, in Western countries, this feeling of liberation did not so much affect whole social groups as individuals, who set about doing away with established moral codes and traditional fetters of all sorts. Mores became freer in every area of life, from material consumption to relations between people. Conventional family patterns faded away as people began forming non-married couples, living singly, indulging in hedonism, and generally doing whatever appeared to enhance individual autonomy. Yet emancipation sooner or later raises serious questions, for the cult of the ego can hardly be an end in itself. And in any case, it comes up against natural limits.

When you have the opportunity to do whatever you want, you wind up not wanting much of anything. Likewise, when economic and financial power can proceed unchecked, in the long run, it destroys forests (the Amazonian forest following many others), depletes the fish population of the oceans through uncontrolled fishing, and devastates not only landscapes, but also the entire ecosystem. Nor can the need for higher productivity justify all the damage done.

Images of malnutrition, of growing poverty, of pollution, and of ecological disaster now put pressure on consumers' behavior, creating widespread awareness that we can no longer do whatever we please. If humanity is to survive, freedom must be placed under control.

IN PURSUIT OF NEW VALUES

In reaching the limits of such freedom, the previously sacrosanct individual discovers that he or she is obliged to offer solidarity to his or her fellow beings as well as to the environment. The individual begins to feel that the world's fate is very much his or her business. This is a new, highly significant phenomenon. Maximal autonomy has shown itself to be synonymous with solitude, fragility, and insecurity. Furthermore, the current context of declining economic prosperity has rekindled the need for meaning and mutual support.

This vision comes across clearly in *The City of Joy* by Dominique Lapierre, which shows that the worst extremes of illness and destitution in the slums of Calcutta also generate an incredible outpouring of solidarity.[2] Albeit for different reasons, the wealthy countries, threatened at present by new forms of social and economic distress, are in turn rediscovering the value of this natural feeling for others.

It should be stressed, however, that moral values are closely linked to the value we attribute to objects, meaning the degree to which we consider them necessary. In previous centuries, when humanity was confronted with immediate needs such as food, clothing, and shelter, the relative importance of things was dictated in the last analysis by the challenges at hand and by scarcity. It is perhaps in our society of abundance, in which almost everything appears to be within reach, that the question of choice becomes a pressing one for the first time. How, and by virtue of what principles, can we determine what takes priority, given the huge selection available? It seems essential to impose limits on certain forces that could turn out to be dangerous if left to develop unhampered.

The more technology progresses, the greater its impact on the world and on people. From nuclear energy to molecular biology, we know that every new "means" discovered has increasingly profound, complex implications for humanity. There is no such thing as a truly neutral technology, particularly since the new scientific paradigm has invalidated the idea of an absolute dichotomy between mind and matter.

Confining our discussion to recent findings in genetics, a whole series of questions arises. Should we allow systematic detection of genetic deficiencies? The improvement of genetic inheritance? The use of biological evidence for identifying criminals? The tracking down of an abandoned child's "natural" father? Prenatal diagnosis as a possible instrument of eugenics? Increasingly aware of such moral and social implications, a number of governments are busy setting up ethics committees composed of modern-day "sages."

WHAT SHOULD BE THE BASIS FOR ETHICS? THE OPINION OF A PHILOSOPHER

French philosopher André Comte-Sponville has cogently demonstrated that expecting self-regulation of the business world and the scientific community is simply unrealistic.[3] "There is no morality in the techno-scientific order," he claims. "It is an order based on facts, one in which all facts are on par with each other. Such an order distinguishes between truth and falsehood, much in the way a company president distinguishes between what will allow him to increase profits and what won't. These are, however, factual considerations in which moral judgment plays no part. There exist no valid scientific reasons for holding back scientific progress, nor any sound technical ones for limiting technological development. This means that if we leave this order to its own spontaneous devices, everything technically possible will in fact be done . . . There are no economic grounds for limiting the interplay of economic forces, the very essence of the market and its famous laws. Yet can anyone possibly believe that we need nothing further to make a world? In the nineteenth century, child labor was also subjected to the laws of the market. Should society have simply resigned itself to the situation?"

A different order is clearly needed in order to control these areas; yet it would be wrong to see it in juridical or political terms. "If the people have unrestricted rights," Comte-Sponville goes on to say, "there is no guarantee that they won't vote anti-Semitic laws, eugenics measures, or wars of extermination. We thus face the risk of a barbaric democracy. We forget all too easily that Hitler came to power by legal means . . . We therefore need another kind of order able to impose limits on the democratic functioning (which is democratic only in the best of cases) of the juridico-political order. Needless to say, we are talking about the moral order." This order is structured around the contrast between duty and prohibition. Yet it is hard to believe that that is sufficient. Imagine an individual who confines himself to doing his duty, and nothing more. Although no one would dream of calling him a rotten bastard, you might be tempted to describe him as a pious hypocrite.

Comte-Sponville concludes by saying, "A higher order is required, one that I would call *the ethical order*, an order based on love. To my way of thinking, it is the ultimate order (others might subordinate it to a supernatural order) and the only one that requires no limits. After all, infinite love does not exactly constitute a major threat to humanity, and even if it did, what more could one ask for?"

WHO IS TO SET NEW STANDARDS OF BEHAVIOR?

As we have seen, the leading institutions that are in charge of providing a general normative framework are rapidly losing ground before the onslaught of free-market individualism. The very notion of an established morality binding on all no longer holds water. In these conditions, people are seeking principles, values, and rules of conduct that enjoy the broadest possible consensus. The word "ethics" best covers this aspiration, which is both individual and collective in nature.

Empirically speaking, such a new ethical system might be based on what society judges acceptable and, by way of contrast, unacceptable. Instead of appealing to notions of good and evil that remain indefinable in the absence of shared beliefs, be they religious or secular, we are moving toward a pragmatic approach to demands for humanity and solidarity, one involving an increasingly global perspective. In short, the point is to identify a code of good conduct, a contractual form of ethics, rather than to decree ten new commandments.

THE COMPANY BECOMES THE FOCAL POINT OF THE NEW CONCERN FOR ETHICS

Just as when the father dies, the traditional family group is reconstituted around the mother, who assumes surrogate authority, perhaps along with the eldest son, the gradual extinction of previously sacred forms of authority, whether religious or political, should induce companies to take their place and to fulfill their functions.

In actuality, the company is the only collective cell left that possesses a real capacity to provide structure and whose function gives it the ability to keep pace with social and technological change. In this respect, it currently receives the credit once given to the family, the village community, or even to church and state. A company is a modern point of social convergence and congregation. In order to make people eager to work, it should give them a sense of purpose, laying down ethical standards able to mobilize their energy – in place of those that have disappeared. The isolated individual needs to recreate a social framework providing meaning, solidarity, and security.

For however surprising the idea may seem today, it will be clear tomorrow that the competitiveness of companies depends more and more on intangible factors, especially on their ability to constitute a frame of reference that helps people to confront a barely tolerable world. They will thus have to replace the forms of assurance that traditional normative institutions used to provide. In order to succeed, a company can no longer confine its efforts to achieving economic results. It must also imbue its acts with a strong ethical content, both in the eyes of its employees and from the standpoint of consumers and the general public.

In the future, the quest for personal and business success will no longer be an adequate excuse for any and all acts. The predator philosophy of the "golden boys" or of a number of particularly rapacious entrepreneurs has increasingly fewer admirers. There are good grounds for believing that the demand for ethics will become one of the leading challenges facing the business world, with growing importance in relation to mere quantitative parameters such as technological or financial efficiency.

It will be up to the humanistic managers of tomorrow to find a proper balance between the three images that late twentieth-century society holds in high esteem: *capitalistic values* of free enterprise (the market, competition, the mystique of the entrepreneur, financial success); *technocratic values* (the technical achievements and mathematical logic of "scientifically" programmed organizations); and *democratic, moral, and ethical values.* Negotiation over this last category of values takes place within a framework that postulates that all individuals are by right both free and equal, that *common rules* depend on contractual agreement, while what is *good and right* is everyone's business, is determined by their choices and conceptions, and reflects their own degree of commitment.

At the junction of the contradictory aspirations of our contemporaries, these new humanistic managers will rediscover that solidarity and social responsibility serve as a bridge linking security to freedom.

Notes

1 André Comte-Sponville, "Le capitalisme est-il moral?", *L'Expansion*, January 9–22, 1992.
2 Dominique Lapierre, *The City of Joy* (Warner Books, 1988).
3 Comte-Sponville, "Le capitalisme est-il moral?"

10

Social Responsibility for All

Democracy derives its strength from the rise in individual aspirations, but . . . also brings in its wake a correlated withdrawal from any institution (family, church, or trade union) responsible for providing solidarity. Ultimately, we end up with a perfectly altruistic community made up of individuals cultivating an unalloyed selfishness with no qualms whatsoever.

"Essai sur l'avenir de l'identité française"[1]

Once the individual has won his freedom, he longs for lost security.

An ill-conceived social security system has made Europe sluggish.

When government decides on economic programs without calculating their impact on employment, it shows itself to be penny wise and pound foolish.

We have to choose between low prices and a generous welfare state.

The thankless role assigned to women in both family and work life makes it difficult to reconcile the two.

We can no longer ignore the repercussions of our own choices upon the lives of those around us.

Everyone should feel responsible for the direction that society takes.

In the twentieth century, democracy has made impressive advances in a world previously dominated by feudal or authoritarian structures. From East to West and North to South, rising aspirations toward greater individual autonomy and political, social, and economic freedom have demonstrated their ability to sweep away the majority of existing models based on rigid constraint, even producing the implosion of one of the leading ones, the Stalinist empire. This oft-demanded liberty involves first and foremost the elimination of everything that kept people under tight control, and thus the possibility of depending only on oneself or on voluntary agreement between individuals.

A GROWING NEED FOR SECURITY

The struggle for freedom was experienced as a fundamental need. However, with the growing number of democratic conquests that have made it possible to achieve this much yearned-for aim, people around the world immediately began to feel another need: the need for security. Yet freedom necessarily diminishes security. A field that is free cannot at the same time be guarded. Under feudalism, the nobles had duties as well as rights. A lord was expected to look after his community, ensure the safety of his vassals, wage war to defend them, dispense justice, and aid the needy. Freedom implies a weakening of such obligations.

Paradoxically, once we achieve liberation, we gradually alienate part of our precious freedom in exchange for security. This dual movement can be observed everywhere. Countries that have recently established democratic systems all tend to waver between the risks that their new-found liberty entails and the reassuring effect of powerful collective institutions.

Although in the East, the Communist economic system has collapsed, values and behavior patterns have not changed to a notable extent. The citizens want higher living standards, but with the same security, and even the same parasitical practices as in the past. Four years after coming to power in Poland, former Solidarity activists lost the elections to the ex-Communists, born again under the name of "Social Democrats." In spite of their successful, yet socially painful economic policies, the first Polish democratic governments were punished, whereas the former power-holders, who bore responsibility for the state of siege and the country's economic disaster, were suddenly exonerated when they promised more comprehensive welfare measures.

FREEDOM MEANS ACCEPTING RISKS

In economic matters, the English-speaking countries are wont to say that free competition and initiative include four indissociable characteristics: "high commitment, high speed, high risk, high profit."[2]

Obviously, the majority of the population has no desire for perilous adventures and would rather make moderate commitments involving minimal risk. This holds true both in economic affairs and in social life in general.

In 1981, Faith Popcorn announced the advent of the "cocooning" years. Twelve years later, the trend has become even more pronounced, so much so that the new term employed is "burrowing," whose main connotation is one of digging a hole in the ground in order to hide from a hostile environment.

No one wants to go out on a limb – unless, of course, there is a solid safety net down below. Acquiring one is by no means a luxury, since those still willing to take risks are immediately accused if things don't turn out as planned. We seem to need to have someone to blame. One wonders whether Europe is going to follow the same path as the United States, a country in which the number of lawsuits has undergone exponential growth and the latest trick for getting rich quick is to sue someone in court for astronomical damages, seizing upon the slightest pretext. While this trend certainly means excellent business for lawyers, it unquestionably impoverishes society in general. Involvement is shunned, time and energy are wasted, and stress continues to mount, all of which hinder creativity. Many American surgeons today prefer not to operate (thus relinquishing a possible means of curing the patient) if they feel that there may be a risk – of legal action if the operation fails.

IN AN INCREASINGLY THREATENING ENVIRONMENT, THE IDEAL OF FREEDOM IS LOSING GROUND

In the words of Paul Valéry, "Freedom is a state of mind." A person is only free to the extent that he or she is motivated by a revelation coming from deep within that no external power can weaken, whether by force or by indirect influence. The feeling of freedom is thus one of the most advanced states of which the human soul is capable.

Western society is currently being worn down by an undercurrent of insecurity. Everyone expects a worsening of living conditions or some new ecological catastrophe. Technological progress now signifies little more than rising unemployment and disregard for humanistic ethics. Trust in the predictions of leaders has reached an all-time low. Illnesses associated with stress and anxiety are steadily gaining ground. Boredom and loneliness play into the hands of drug dealers and merchants of other, equally perverse, forms of dependence. Our culture conveys images of cynicism and despair much more frequently than manifestations of optimism and self-confidence. And since the latter qualities are precisely those that give sustenance to creativity, it is hardly surprising that we observe so little creative achievement around us.

In such a situation, a growing number of dysfunctions now hinder the exercise of freedom, which also applies in those countries enjoying considerable economic and political freedom. In this light, let's consider two major phenomena that can be seen as unexpected byproducts of society's progression toward greater freedom and equality and that may well create tremendous social tension. The first one is the rise in structural unemployment, which, in conjunction with other factors, inexorably results from the combined effect of an ill-conceived welfare system and an ideological attachment to free market principles. The second one is the intolerable situation of women with children, who are all too often compelled to chose between career and family, with the weakening of family ties that ensues.

PUSHED TO EXTREMES, THE WELFARE STATE ENDS UP HINDERING THE SYSTEM

At the end of World War II, the United States accounted for 57 percent of world GNP, and average American wages were three times higher than in Europe. During the three decades of prosperity that followed, however, European purchasing power caught up with the American standard of living. Western Europe went even further: in the course of this period of vigorous growth, it set up a system of social welfare that was without parallel in the world.

For the past 20 years, however, an increasingly anemic economy no longer creates new jobs; in fact, the opposite is true. Owing to automation, factories now produce more with about two-thirds or even half the previous workforce. In offices, widespread use of computer systems has also nearly halved the number of employees needed. And, even today, some observers maintain that companies still employ between 20 and 30 percent too many white-collar workers.

During the 1980s, whereas purchasing power in the United States declined slowly but inexorably, pushed downward in particular by high defense spending, Western European countries managed to maintain both welfare entitlements and wage levels, although, as it turned out, with disastrous consequences for employment.

Today, shifting from production to consumption, the considerable financial burden imposed by retirement schemes, health care, and unemployment benefits seems to me to be of the utmost urgency. The recent extension of the social security system, in France and elsewhere, has validated the idea that every citizen, whether employed or not, has a right to at least a modicum of economic protection, which may take the form of health care, a pension, or even a guaranteed income (in France, the RMI). It should, however, be recalled that while everyone doesn't produce, everyone certainly consumes. Seen in this light, it is both unfair and uneconomical to force only the producers to pay for something that benefits the entire national community. Having consumers cover this expense amounts to spreading it over the whole population covered by social security, rather than by only part of it. This would clearly offer a more equitable solution.

At each purchase and according to a modular scale, the consumer might be required to pay a social contribution that would be withheld at source and transferred to the relevant funds, much in the same way that VAT is collected on behalf of the Treasury. Wage and salary earners would certainly be paying a higher price for products, but at least their earnings would not be so heavily taxed, and they might even receive a sort of compensation bonus from the company employing them, which would also be exempt from the previous social security taxes. Such a system would have no effect on the consumer price index, since it would eliminate contribution payments, which amount to a transfer of savings. It would also place on an equal footing countries with highly developed welfare systems and countries where production costs are significantly lower as a result of the lack of such social protection.

It is indeed paradoxical that, in the present system, a company that agrees to hire additional personnel should pay even higher contributions to unemployment funds, while a company that decides to lay workers off is rewarded through a reduction in the rates it has to pay. It seems even more nonsensical that the price of a product still manufactured in France should be affected by deductions that rise continually because of the growing number of jobless to be supported, whereas a similar product made in Thailand (and thus indirectly to blame for French unemployment) can be sold at a much lower price. This kind of economic absurdity, to which the advocates of unrestrained free trade discreetly turn a blind eye, amounts to whipping an innocent man while crowning the guilty party with a laurel wreath. To remain on such a course, Europeans would have to be either mindless or masochistic.

BUT SO DOES THE FREE MARKET

If we bear in mind that today, an hour of labor time for a skilled worker, all taxes included, comes to $10.50 in France, while the equivalent cost is only $2.50 in Hungary, $1 in Poland, and 50c in Romania, we should have no trouble understanding the pressures leading to shifting production abroad.

Up until a few years ago, these pressures remained limited to a few industries such as textiles, shoes, or steel. At present, however, if the current trend continues, no industry can expect to escape this process. French telephone directories are already typeset in the Philippines (where an hour of skilled labor is worth 80c), and several major European companies leave their data processing work to Indian engineers, thus reducing costs by one-tenth.

Even Japan, a nation with cost structures comparable to ours but with only one-fifth the percentage of jobless workers, has had to shift its production facilities offshore, either to Western countries for institutional reasons, or to its neighbors for economic ones. Formosa pays its skilled workers half as much as Japan (i.e. only $4.60), and the gap grows wider in relation to China (under $2), Thailand ($1.10), the Philippines (80c), and the record-holder in Asia, Vietnam (30c).

EUROPE ENVIES THE SOCIAL COHESION OF JAPAN

Compared to its leading competitors in America or Japan, Western Europe represents a daring combination of the *laissez-faire* typical of the English-speaking world and the continent's traditions of social welfare, the direct consequence being that Europe has set a number of records in job destruction. As a result, the European market is the most severely exposed to foreign competition, whereas the United States and Japan are quick to "forget" their theories as soon as their interests are at stake.

Of the three mega-regions, Japan is the least affected by the process. A veritable symbiosis between the business community and government, based on a shared concern for maintaining social cohesion, has generated a rigid pattern of state intervention as well as an unavowed protectionism. Westerners are only familiar with those 15 percent of Japanese companies like Sony, Sanyo, Mitsubishi, and Toyota that have truly global presence. These leading-edge corporations – as far as modernity, performance, and productivity are concerned – have contributed in part to the West's misfortunes. The $120 billion trade surplus they make possible for their country have in all likelihood cost three million jobs in the Western world since the late 1980s.

In addition to what could be termed the spearhead of Japanese industry, we find two other sectors. One of them comprises traditional industries, including a vast network of subcontractors (90 percent of all Japanese companies are small or medium-sized), which must often struggle to break even but whose activities and markets are more or less guaranteed owing to their close ties to larger corporations. The other one, including rice-growing and certain public services, is archaic; its survival depends entirely on massive subsidies, which the profitability of the most dynamic industries makes possible. The effect of this government-directed system of redistribution is reinforced by the fact that a large number of companies are linked together inside consortiums called *keiretsus*. Thus, it makes little difference if a few of them are in the red as long as the others make enough money to keep the whole group profitable.

The ultimate justification for this three-tier arrangement lies in the survival and flourishing of a society and culture for which companies actively mobilize. For example, Mitsubishi takes part in hospital management or creates joint ventures with universities. In Japan, art is not, as in the West, cut off from the world of production. On the contrary, the aesthetic dimension of any work environment is treated much more seriously. All through its incessant changes, the land of the Rising Sun applies a philosophical concept that goes back nine centuries: *ukiyo*, i.e. the floating world, whose main feature is "impermanence." The impressive flexibility and adaptability that characterizes Japan reflects in fact its desire to preserve its traditions.

Thus, the essential values that structure Japanese life are sociocultural in nature, contrary to what can be observed in the Western world, where democracy and free enterprise are mere ends in themselves that incorporate neither the preservation of certain trades nor the will to maintain social cohesion into their minute calculations.

AND THE FREE-ENTERPRISE FLEXIBILITY OF THE UNITED STATES

America, while sharing democratic and free-enterprise values with Europe, is not confronted with difficulties as extensive as Europe's. American world leadership, which gives the country practically free rein to lay down trade rules, is not the sole reason for this difference. That the United States managed to integrate almost 20 million Asians and Latin Americans in the past decade without generating too much unemployment can be explained by the low level of social security contributions as well as by the high mobility of the average American, who doesn't balk at the idea of changing regions or of accepting a low-skilled, low-paid job if it can't be avoided.

Europe thus appears to be miles away from both American free-market efficiency – because it refuses any significant reduction of welfare entitlements – and from Japanese social cohesion – because it stubbornly clings to monetarist policies that give virtually no weight to social cost. In order to get its message across to its trading partners, Europe should adopt a united stance. In such a case, as the exclusion of audiovisual production from the December 1993 GATT agreement showed, it has the means to protect endangered sectors like farming or film. Of course, such policies should be applied with a view to reaching a broad international consensus, but the negotiations that led to the agreement on import quotas for Japanese cars already indicated the general direction to be taken.

Nobel prize-winning economist Maurice Allais has emphasized this point. "The EEC," he writes, "is by now large enough that intra-Community competition should be able to produce all progress currently made possible by technological development. International trade can only be considered truly advantageous to the EEC in so far as it provides products that Europe is unable to produce itself." He concludes by saying, "EEC trade policy must be based on the dual principle of Community preference and *reasonable* protection against imports that are economically pointless, that destabilize society, and that exacerbate unemployment."[3]

CHOOSING BETWEEN CUT-RATE PRICES AND A GENEROUS WELFARE STATE

It makes no sense whatsoever to try to cut prices and maintain a generous welfare system at the same time. By attempting to sit on two stools at once, Europe's political leaders are in danger of finding themselves on the floor – and of driving their countries into a nightmarish spiral in which production is increasingly relocated offshore, recessions become deeper and deeper, and above all, unemployment rises inexorably.

To be sure, that part of the population still employed enjoys rising purchasing power as a result of declining prices, dumping, or company reorganizations following bankruptcy. Yet even these people are condemned to pay ever higher social security contributions because of the rising number of jobless workers. Their apparent advantage could well be wiped out in the process.

Jean Arthuis, a senator from Mayenne, in Normandy, and author of a report on the tendency toward offshore production, stresses an "unbearable contradiction. On the one hand, we demand high wages and a first-rate social security system, while on the other hand, we buy goods produced by an underpaid workforce with no social protection at all. We want to have our cake and eat it too, but we can't go on for long that way."[4]

French consumers are beginning to show their awareness of the problem, as the recent success achieved by electrical appliance retailer Boulanger demonstrates (a chain of around 40 stores associated with the large distributor Auchan). Through an alliance with some 15 industrialists, Boulanger has managed to offer products "made in France" at competitive prices. The sales promotion labels clearly indicate where each item was manufactured as if it were an exceptional vintage. This experiment has led to the following conclusion: at comparable quality, 56 percent of all buyers claim to be willing to pay 10 percent more for French products, for they feel that they are thereby contributing to preserving living standards in the country – and thus their own.

INTEGRATING THE SOCIAL COST OF UNEMPLOYMENT INTO ALL ECONOMIC CALCULATIONS

Decision-makers in France are sometimes less aware than consumers are of their shared responsibility for our economy's health. In his report, Senator Arthuis mentions, among many equally enlightening examples, a contract for 90,000 sweat suits for the French army won by a French company producing offshore in Mauritius at a unit cost of 107 francs, as opposed to 113 francs in the case of the two other competitors tendering, who continued to produce in France. The Defense Ministry thus saved 540,000 francs (i.e. nearly $110,000), although the unemployment caused by this shift abroad cost the French economy 6.2 million francs, with the net loss amounting to 5.7 million. In other words, this is what the entire nation has to pay for failing to incorporate into economic calculations the social cost of unemployment generated by decisions involving relocation abroad, automation, and company reorganization.

Public opinion knows, and politicians loudly proclaim, that the war against joblessness must be the government's top priority in economic matters. To be sure, the deep structural crisis that Europe is facing on the employment front results from a wide range of factors that should be taken simultaneously into account. The job-reducing effect of technological progress is amplified to a notable extent by the inordinately high level of social security taxes, by immigration, by the free-trade dogmatism evinced by the European Commission in Brussels, by currency disorder (strikingly illustrated by the sudden, thoughtless depreciation of the lira, and then of the peseta in 1993). Yet a number of factors involved lie entirely within the province of national responsibility. In particular, they include a system of unemployment benefits that in some cases ends up discouraging the jobless from looking for work, and, as was pointed out in chapter 3, an educational system for young people that is woefully out of step with the demands of the business world.

Contrary to what monetarist spokesmen would have us believe, however, a drop in interest rates will bring no salvation. An excessively steep decline would even have a harmful effect on employment, since in certain borderline cases (and therefore with scant justification), it would encourage the tendency toward automation, which would have seemed unprofitable in the case of higher interest rates. A solution will only be forthcoming when all major economic participants concern themselves with the repercussions of their choices on all of their partners, on the entire branch of the economy, on the national community, and beyond that, on the whole human race. In a nutshell, everyone must feel "co-responsible" for the fate of humanity.

INCOMPLETE SEXUAL EQUALITY HAS LOOSENED FAMILY TIES

Another major accomplishment of our century with respect to freedom and equality is the growing number of women who work outside the home, an irreversible fact that, in spite of the wishes of some people, will not be affected by rising unemployment. Nevertheless, women's liberation is still far from complete. It should be recalled that this social phenonemon appeared only in relatively recent times. In France, for example, women have enjoyed the right to vote for a mere half-century, and it was not until 1965 that a woman could possess a checkbook without her husband's permission. Lastly, whereas women represent 53 percent of all voters, they rarely hold more than 5 percent of the seats in parliament.

Although women make up a large part of the workforce, the labor market has until now done little to accommodate them. Admittedly, they have begun to make considerable progress in the business world. As far as education is concerned, while only 3 percent of all students in France were female at the turn of the century, this proportion has since risen to half the student population, and even higher if we consider the number of women who now possess the *baccalauréat* diploma required for admission to a French university. This trend has gone so far that, albeit informally, the leading business schools have instituted quotas in order to stem the massive influx of women – a policy adopted quite officially by the École nationale de la magistrature (in charge of training the country's judges and prosecutors). It would seem that certain professions must at all costs remain predominantly male.

The educational system favors the "second sex." Participants in parent–teacher associations are generally mothers, the vast majority of all teachers are women, and girls, who are at this stage less turbulent and more mature than boys, often achieve better academic results than boys do. In this area, it is important for men to take on new responsibility, sharing the task of education and upbringing with women. And yet most of them seem to leave the entire job to their wives or companions, together with housework. This ongoing inequality in the sexual division of roles will weigh heavily on married life in the twenty-first century, for growing numbers of women are already turning their backs on a family structure that offers them so few benefits.

Some observers claim that by the year 2000, no family structure will be compatible with the hectic life of tomorrow. Others conceive of the home environment as a leading place of refuge for those confronted with demanding jobs that leave little room for emotion. Still others maintain that the number of children will continue its downward curve. Those French households that still reach the three-children mark do so in general because the first two children where of the same sex and the parents wanted one of the opposite sex. In light, however, of current strides made in our knowledge of the life of a fetus, we can assume that it won't be long before the mystery of sexual determination will be uncovered. The number of children as well as their sex may soon become a matter of conscious choice.

The rise in the number of unmarried persons and individuals living alone will continue, a trend already apparent in major urban areas. Studies indicate that in Paris, 33 percent of the population falls into this category. There now exists a "Singles' Exhibition," just as we have an Ideal Home Exhibition. Such a phenomenon is characteristic of the modern world. From a statistical point of view, a society cannot exceed a limit generally fixed at 6 percent of the female population of a marriageable age that remains single. Among American women over 25, however, this percentage has climbed to 25 percent. As for men, 5 million of them are listed as single in the European Community and over 4 million in the United States.

It seems relatively clear that the coming century will not be marked by passionate romance. Powerful emotions demand too much energy and run counter to qualities like availability and openness that the world of tomorrow will require. Couples concerned with building a lasting relationship will tend more toward a club-style pattern of family life based on consensus, compromise, and mutual support, a flexible arrangement suited to solving individual problems. Considering the unfair burden that the current family structure places upon women, a new model remains to be created.

BETWEEN CHILD-REARING AND WORK: WOMEN'S DAILY RACE AGAINST THE CLOCK

Greek mythology personifies the three major female roles in Hera (the mother), Aphrodite (love), and Athena (intelligence). Women could achieve much richer lives if our society were to strike a harmonious balance between what these three goddesses represent. The trouble is that such a balance has never existed and does not appear to be in the offing.

"Closed" societies (i.e. traditional, agrarian, religious ones) give the leading part to Hera, leave Aphrodite backstage, and deny Athena. In its obsession with Athena, supposedly "open" contemporary Western society relegates Hera to the sphere of private life and winds up denying Aphrodite, albeit unwittingly. It used to be heresy to claim that women had souls; nowadays, "sexual harassment" (whether overt or assumed) gives rise to lawsuits. As for Hera, she is accepted in the office provided that she copes with her child-rearing responsibilities without making too much fuss about it.

The conflict between Athena and Hera is no less evident. There is little problem with equality between male and female colleagues at work as long as the latter have no children; but can we legitimately recommend not having any to a human being eager for success? A mere 7 percent of French girls today claim their willingness to sacrifice Hera on the altar of Athena.[5] Conversely, however, they refuse just as strongly to give up on work, the only area in which they can "show what they are capable of."[6] Thirty-one percent of them judge it normal to interrupt their careers in order to raise their children, provided that the interruption is temporary.

The working woman who is also head of a single-parent household (either following a separation or through deliberate choice) is an increasingly common figure in our society. Yet she is less available at work than she might otherwise have been and she suffers an enormous handicap in terms of pay and responsibility in the company, unless, of course, she was earning enough right from the start to be able to afford a maid.

It can hardly be said, however, that a woman living with a man enjoys a more enviable situation. In most cases, a non-egalitarian division of labor within the couple merely gives the man greater leisure time. Leaving his wife or companion to fend for herself with the children and the housework, he is free to commit himself fully to his career or to developing networks outside the workplace. He can attend dinners and join clubs, whereas his wife, compelled as she is to stick to a tight schedule, must rise to considerable heights of efficiency and speed (not to mention irresistible charm) just to avoid having to sacrifice sociability to family obligations.

Despite technological progress, women have gained only 10 minutes more free time a day over the past 15 years. When both members of the couple have jobs, the woman still spends three more hours a day than the man doing housework in the broadest sense. In addition to washing and ironing, chores that are never shared, she devotes more time to keeping up on the children's schoolwork, imparting values to them, taking care of them, and in many cases also looking after aging relatives.

The injustice implied in this condition appears most strikingly when a woman reaches her forties. Adolescents become harder to live with and take up more time and energy than before, while the father hesitates to wield his authority and spends more and more time away from home. Although the woman knows how to respond to the emotional demands of her environment, her natural charm begins to wane and she experiences what is perhaps her first real frustrations after giving so much and getting so little in return. She does her utmost in order to remain elegant and seductive, an obligation to which her male colleagues with graying temples and drab, standardized suits are obviously not subjected.

Once she is over 50 and the children have become independent, the woman realizes, sometimes with considerable bitterness, that she has "missed the boat." Having failed to build social networks, she has been granted only limited responsibilities; her inequality with her male colleagues has reached its peak. This is the age at which more men than women file for divorce.

These findings give many women the feeling that they have been had.[7] In the first place, they believed that competence alone was enough to gain access to power, whereas in fact "playing politics" remains essential. Yet had they known, how would they have found the time to do so? In the second place, they had to win forgiveness for what little power they did possess, since men demand of women that they be constantly above reproach. Former Prime Minister Edith Cresson, who noted that "power makes men more appealing, while making women less appealing," speaks from experience when she asserts that a female politician "who fails to dress in a more austere, inconspicuous fashion runs the risk of losing her authority."[8] According to Françoise Chandernagor, "female ministers all have a reputation for dissolute ways, but actually live like Carmelite nuns."

Many women now conclude bitterly that when you come down to it, "we are allowed to do everything our fathers did as long as we keep on doing everything our mothers did."

COMPANIES MUST BECOME OPEN-MINDED ENOUGH TO GRANT WOMEN THE STATUS THEY DESERVE

We are obviously still a far cry from full sexual equality in the world of work, particularly since the professions that women have massively chosen, such as teaching, medicine, and the law, have lost much of their former prestige.

The social and cultural status of women is the best index of the stage of development reached by a country. A simple comparison between the position of women in Islamic countries and that of women in Christian ones immediately makes this abundantly clear. Although we may not know what role will fall to women as the third millennium begins, it is incumbent upon every active participant in social and economic life to take an interest in the issue.

At present, our society's economic and structural crisis works against women, even though their presence would be beneficial in any number of respects. First, it is important to have women at the workplace in order to gain insight into the behavior of female consumers. Secondly, the qualities that we most readily associate with women are those that tomorrow's world will most need: interiority, sensitivity, harmony, a sense of conciliation, respect for the environment and for biological rhythms. Lastly, women engaged in scientific research generally obtain more pragmatic, more useable results than their male counterparts, who are more inclined to come up with elaborate theories and offbeat ideas. A correlation has been observed between periods of technological revolution and a growing proportion of women in the relevant occupations.

Employers should reconsider work schedules, consulting women as to the most desirable arrangements. On executive boards, 95 percent of all members are men. Indeed, management timetables often put women executives at a disadvantage, with meetings called for 7 p.m., and business lunches and dinners that create de facto segregation. Furthermore, women tend to shun meetings in which speakers take the floor for no other reason than to satisfy their egos or to reinforce their power. Most women express themselves less often because they only do so when they have something to say.

Yet one need not be a genius to imagine more flexible forms of incentive, reward, and building of loyalty that would not be limited to mere financial advantages and from which everyone, especially women, would benefit. A workday without interruption and "flextime" would make life much easier for a great many women workers. It appears ill-advised, however, to encourage more of them to work at home, where family life would probably interfere with their jobs. In fact, the government should take concrete steps in favor of nearby employment opportunities and day-care facilities so that mothers can both save time and take a greater part in the company where they work. And, as we have already seen, parental roles must also undergo a cultural change involving shared involvement in housework and child-rearing.

TOWARD CO-RESPONSIBILITY FOR ALL

A society that forces its young people to pay for its contradictions deserves the strongest of criticism. How, indeed, can we justify to our school-age children that they must come home in the afternoon to an empty house because their parents both work, that they must none the less do their homework – alone – and that once they have finished their education, they will be confronted with an unemployment that singles out young people? Claiming that we can't do anything about the situation, while at the same time purporting to inculcate values in our children, is a bit absurd.

Companies can no longer confine themselves to producing and selling goods and services; this primary objective does not give them licence to behave like Attila the Hun in total disregard of their natural and human environment. Dreams of glorious conquest that leave ruin and devastation in their wake have little to recommend them. The future of our society can only be forged through the concerted efforts and synergy of all its vital elements, working to realize an all-encompassing vision.

With the widening of a number of rifts that threaten to undermine social cohesion, whether between workers with stable, or even guaranteed employment and the jobless, between men and women, or between young and old, there is nothing more urgent than inventing new social and cultural models that are open, flexible, and capable of integrating individuals. Such models should enable everyone to feel that in his own modest way, he is one of many contributors to his environment and, as such, he bears responsibility for it. However, we can only move in this direction if two basic conditions are fulfilled.

- "Hard-core" radical groups that reject the dominant social and cultural values and cultivate a form of revolt that at times verges on subversive terrorism must not gain ground. The Mediterranean countries, where a certain cultural adaptation occurs, are less affected by this phenomenon than the English-speaking or Northern European countries, where rebels against material or psychological hardship express fundamental rejection of the prevailing social structure.
- The gap between government institutions and civil society must be reduced. A new conception of public service should be developed that combines the flexibility and the creativity of private initiative (particularly that of the business world) with the stability offered by public administration (whether at national, regional, or local level). This could give rise to a new sense of citizenship, one based on co-responsibility.

Contrary to the message conveyed by an adage frequently heard in the 1980s – "It's not my problem!" – we cannot remain indifferent to the consequences of our choices and ignore "what happens at the neighbors'." Only a new sense of shared responsibility will enable us to achieve a more harmonious world and to reverse the trend toward autonomy and differentiation that has developed over the past three decades, creating more and more divisions, both within single countries and between North and South.

While all traditional frameworks have fallen apart, paradoxically, a new one has rapidly emerged: the global framework. Today, our planet is increasingly seen as an interdependent whole, both with reference to the ecosystem and as regards the expansion of human awareness. In the post-industrial era, a business enterprise can be conceived of as the center of this fabric of world interdependence, which involves not only economic movements as such, but also social currents, cultural references, the information and media world, and ecology. Tomorrow's companies must shift from a fragmented vision to a systemic one that takes into account the global nature of the interrelations that characterize the environment in which they operate. This outlook of co-responsibility, which moves from local to world scale and from quantitative to qualitative, is not merely some vague appeal to philanthropy. It is in fact the only strategy that can make it possible to master the complexity of postmodern society.

Notes

1 "Essai sur l'avenir de l'identité française," an analysis presented by the General Secretary's Office for Planning of the French government in *Le XXIe siècle*.
2 M. Yukawa, the director of the Mitsubishi Corporation, in private conversation.
3 The emphasis is mine. It is obviously unthinkable to go back to protectionist practices that would be dangerous for world peace and stability. Maurice Allais also suggests that, in the framework of negotiated trade regulations, "quota barriers in any regional bloc [should] not exceed a given percentage of domestic consumption." What is paradoxical about this situation, however, is that an anarchic globalization of world trade, which takes little interest in the social upheavals that it can't fail to generate, runs the risk in the long run of sparking the creation of regional forms of protectionism that will be far more formidable than those that are denounced at present (the passages quoted are taken from an article in *Le Figaro*, July 5, 1993).
4 In a statement made to the magazine *L'Entreprise*, issue 94, July–August 1993.

5 According to a survey I commissioned in 1992.

6 Increasingly devalued, housework accomplished by women in the home cannot be quantified, since "you only notice it when it hasn't been done."

7 These conclusions were presented by Ms F. Chandernagor (writer and counsel of the Conseil d'Etat) and Ms G. Rolland (Vice-President of the European Leadership Institute) during a round table discussion held by L'Oréal in April 1993. The scope of this book has made it possible to offer only a rough outline of what they said.

8 Quoted from an interview with the *Nouvel Observateur*, January 6–12, 1994.

11

Reconciling Economy and Ecology

[T]he nineties are a critical decade, characterized by a profound change from a mechanistic world view to an ecological view, from a value system based on domination to one based on partnership.

Ernest Callenbach, Fritjof Capra, and Sandra Marburg, *The Elmwood Guide to Eco-auditing and Ecologically Conscious Management*

Ecology is not a fad, but a necessary guide for reorienting production.

In the long run, an economy without ecology is unrealistic and unprofitable.

The negative costs of progress must be assessed.

Intangible ecological values condition health, the future, and our happiness.

It is time we adopted a global vision that considers the entire world as one big ecosystem.

Nowadays, there is no lack of doomsday warnings about the long-term risks of pollution or the fate of this or that endangered species. Just as common are announcements of new "green" products that have just come on the market. Ecology has taken public opinion by storm. It now constitutes a dominant tendency in contemporary thinking, one that can not be ingored. Everyone feels bound to take a stand on the ecology issue, particularly because it offers the major advantage of attracting support. Needless to say, nobody is opposed to protecting nature and saving the Earth from destruction.

A MAJOR SHIFT IN PERSPECTIVE

"We have not inherited the Earth of our parents; we are borrowing the Earth of our children." This phrase of Saint-Exupéry fairly summarizes the current concern for environmental protection. This new desire to safeguard natural balance has led to a partial change in behavior, and even to a major shift in perspective. It reflects something of a "conversion" in relation to the credo of the industrial age. As pointed out earlier, although man believed for a long time that he could achieve mastery of the universe, he has recently come to recognize limits to this urge to dominate. Starting gradually in the late 1960s (the Club of Rome was founded in 1968), the Western world has become aware of its obligations in relation to nature, simultaneously discovering the global dimension to the problems facing it.

First and foremost, the movement was prompted by a fear reflex. In practice, the predominant attitude in our society toward defending the environment proves to be more reactive than proactive. Everyone can visualize what awaits us if we don't do something soon.

A CHAIN OF BRUTAL AWAKENINGS: HISTORY OF THE BIRTH OF ECOLOGICAL CONSCIOUSNESS

The protection of nature is no passing fad. Although awareness of it has only recently come to the surface of consciousness, both individual and collective, the notion itself goes back a long way. In the writings of certain Greek and Latin authors, then in the New Testament (Paul's Epistle to the Romans, viii, 19–22), we find a call to save nature, and much later, in the Romantic period, numerous hymns in praise of nature's beauty.

However, while the debate between nature and society thus began at the dawn of our civilization, the idea of a serious threat to the environment that could spell irreparable damage appeared much more recently. In 1908, American President Theodore Roosevelt issued an alarming warning. "We have enriched ourselves through the prodigal use of our natural resources and we have every reason to be proud of our progress," he said. "Yet the time has come to contemplate seriously what will happen when our forests will no longer be there, when our coal, iron, and oil will have run out, when the soil will be impoverished and washed away into our rivers, polluting the waters, depleting the land." If we put this appeal into historical perspective, it is easy to see why it was quickly forgotten.

The Judeo-Christian tradition allows Western society to feel that it has every right to take as much of the Earth's resources as it sees fit. As the Bible says, "Be fruitful, and multiply, and fill the waters in the seas, and let fowl multiply in the earth" (Genesis i, 28–9).

In the 1960s, scientists like Jean Dorst began to raise their voices. Dorst warned that "the age-old pact uniting man to nature has been broken, for man now believes that he has sufficient power to break free from the vast biological complex to which he belonged since he was on Earth."

Both the public and society's leaders were becoming increasingly aware as a result of two major preoccupations: the need to slow population growth and the need to protect endangered species. Little by little, a latent anxiety took form in the collective unconscious. Far from being inexhaustible, the Earth was now seen to be in danger because of humanity's selfish behavior. Well before their leaders, citizens realized this, even if their awareness didn't always lead them to take appropriate action.

Created in 1968, the Club of Rome issued its famous call for a "halt to growth." At the same time, societies for the protection of nature sprang up in most of the developed countries. Some participants looked back longingly to a golden age in which people lived in harmony with nature, rising with the sun. There were a number of excessive reactions such as the hippies and the back-to-the-land movement.

By the 1970s, environmental protection had entered the political arena (with the creation of environmental protection agencies, the founding of "green" parties, the Stockholm Conference, and anti-nuclear demonstrations). The 1973 oil crisis forced society into the realization that unlimited exploitation of "black" energy is an illusion.

In 1976, the year of multiple disasters, ecological dramas made headlines. Everyone recalls the huge oil spill in Brittany, the sinking of the *Torrey Canyon* oil tanker, the accident at Seveso in Italy, and dioxin leaks. The year 1978 was marked by the *Amoco Cadiz* accident, but also by rising unemployment and economic slump, which had the temporary effect of making environmental protection seem less urgent.

In the 1980s, public opinion was profoundly disturbed by two major accidents: first in 1984, Bhopal in India (2,000 deaths), then in 1986, Chernobyl in the Soviet Union. In both cases, it was no longer simply flora and fauna that were destroyed, but human lives. Environmental organizations mushroomed everywhere, consumers showed growing vigilance, and the desire to stay in good health became one of the public's leading preoccupations.

After their initial breakthrough in Germany, the greens imposed their presence in the European Parliament. This success undeniably reflects a new political maturity, both in France and in the rest of Europe. Countless declarations have been made, conferences on the subject have become commonplace, and the Twelve agreed on setting up a European Environmental Agency.[1] By now amplified by the mass media, ecological awareness has continued to spread. Even Pope John Paul II has claimed for the first time that ecology is a "precondition for peace with our Creator," while emphasizing our collective responsibility for "maintaining humanity's common heritage."

PRODUCTION PROCESSES INTEGRATING ECOLOGY

The growing need to take the question of salvaging and reprocessing waste into account in the production cycle will increasingly affect industry, including at the level of packaging design and the choice of materials used.

Leaving aside the excesses of certain manufacturers, who are ready to go overboard in order to cash in on the "green" wave, the notion of waste and consumption has changed in people's thinking. Consumers are no longer content with practical or attractive goods; they now want them to be clean, ecological. It is not only the finished product that counts, but also the materials used to make it. In addition, the question arises as to what will become of it once it is no longer used. This implies that the product must be thought through from A to Z.

Tomorrow's running shoes may well be made out of recycled waste such as sawdust, plastic, rubber from worn tires, cardboard boxes, and coffee filters. This is already the case for Dejashoes, made in California from salvaged materials.

One of the leading computer companies, NEC, explains in its advertising inserts in the United States that it recycles paper even though the process remains expensive (since the company's machines only work with high-quality paper). NEC proudly proclaims, "We are able to invest in something much more meaningful than company profits. That being the future of our environment." Such a statement on the part of a manufacturer would have been unimaginable just a few years ago.

Dow Chemical offers a further astonishing example. For fear of polluting with toxic fumes and waste a small town near one of its plants in Louisiana, the company moved the entire village out, housing its 300 inhabitants in much better accommodation than before, and created a "green belt" on the abandoned property. The operation cost 10 million dollars. Dow claimed that it lost no money in doing so, and, in any case, it won new respect and established a brand image that is the envy of many a competitor.

In addition, respect for the environment can be a factor that brings members of a company closer together. Everyone takes action at his own level for a common cause. This new attitude can be observed in the eagerness with which many office employees go about collecting and recycling old paper.

POINTS OF AMBIGUITY AND EXCESSIVE CLAIMS

Ecological awareness is everywhere around us. The problem is that everyone defines it in the way that best suits them. Protecting nature offers a means to ease a troubled conscience, or to retrieve a lost moral framework and a clear line of conduct.

Under the pretense of ecology, two risks suggest themselves. The first one involves the possible emergence of a "scientistic" ecology that would be part and parcel of a general trend toward artificial manipulation of life (e.g. genetic engineering, the patenting of genes, the production of bubble-protected, sterilized "chunks" of nature ready for consumption in leisure activities, control from outer space over environmental damage wreaked by humanity, particularly for keeping track of the hole in the ozone layer). The second one is that ecology could become the basis for a movement which, appealing to the idea of tradition, would struggle to defend "purity," and subsequently, a local identity and a territory that would be rid of things foreign. Such a drift to the right might go hand in hand with the rise of authoritarian nationalism, xenophobia, and racism.

It should, however, be possible for us to steer a middle course between a mythical attachment to the land that those who experienced the Vichy regime would rather forget and being wrenched away from the Earth by modern technoscience.[2] It is highly regrettable that ecology currently attracts interests that have nothing to do with its fundamental purpose. As a result, what began as a science has been corrupted. Even the word "ecology" has been debased.

ECO-BUSINESS: TRYING TO OUTDO COMPETITORS

A good many industrialists have jumped on the environmental bandwagon in the hope of thereby gaining an advantage over their competitors. Some of them, who dream of winning the largest share of what promises to be a highly lucrative market, have had no qualms about putting an artificially colored "green" icing on an otherwise tasteless cake.

To be sure, we should consider the creation of environmentally safe products as a positive step. Yet there are legitimate grounds for concern, as a glance at department store shelves makes clear. Manufacturers eager to carve out a niche for themselves are churning out eco-products of dubious quality at a great rate – and often at premium prices. A certain amount of false advertising can be detected. Sometimes it is deliberate, as in the case of so-called biodegradable detergents. At times, however, it is involuntary or indirect, as when it turns out that the process used for recycling paper pollutes the environment or that glass recycling is an extremely expensive undertaking.

Consumers do not passively accept all this. Many of them have a good idea of what constitutes appropriate advertising and are not easily hoodwinked. Customers have begun denouncing products that have nothing "green" about them other than their label. In this area, as in the area of blood transfusion or charities, consumers want to be able to trust others to attend to problems for which they themselves have neither the time nor the know-how required.

By going all out just to keep up with the latest trend, companies run the risk of generating hostility. People are not so easily fooled, and they rarely appreciate the excessive character of certain ads (for example, the two-page ad promotion for Audi showing Indians from the Amazon). They reject the product, giving its creator a slap in the face proportional to the absurdity of his claims.

THE VITAL NEED TO REDUCE WASTE

"Green" fever has caused great confusion and polluted people's minds, much to the detriment of ecology itself. We now have "environmento-mania," a prime example of which is the "clean" car. The auto manufacturers are competing with each other to come out with non-polluting vehicles. "If all the countries in the world would declare war on pollution, they might stop waging it against each other," suggested Philippe Saint-Marc. He is undoubtedly right, but such competition, however praiseworthy it may be, should not obscure the fact that a good many Western households have two cars. What needs to be reconsidered is therefore how we use cars rather than what exhaust pipe we equip them with.

Traffic and the speed at which it moves clearly rank among the leading forces of aggression against the natural environment and housing conditions. Increasing air traffic has accelerated the phenomenon by which modern patterns of living have taken us further and further from our traditional integration into our natural surroundings. Without denying the benefits we draw from economic and technological progress, we must begin to reflect on alternative patterns of development that do less damage to the environment, especially since the wave of expansion we have experienced appears to be subsiding, having reached saturation point.

Finding replacements for automobile and aeronautic transportation clearly represents one of the major challenges facing the developed countries in the years to come, not only for their own benefit, but for that of countries that remain largely outside consumer society. New developments in information technology, biotechnology, and medicine should, it can be hoped, open up new avenues of prosperity that are less wasteful of natural resources and energy.

GROWTH IS MERELY ONE ASPECT OF LARGER DEVELOPMENT

Progress as we have thus far conceived of it entails a negative cost that has not been taken into account. Landscapes are blighted with shopping centers, and today's individuals feel compelled to consume increasing quantities of anti-anxiety drugs in order to be able to hold out in a cruel, lonely world.

In several studies, American author Willis Harman has underscored the absurdity of a classical, purely quantitative vision of development centered on immediate productivity. He points out that treating agriculture as if it were an industry leads in the long run to rising costs in the form of impoverished soil and pollution. To this should be added the negative consequences for our health of ingesting the meat of incubator-bred animals fed a steady stream of antibiotics, and even hormones. This industrially produced meat is exceptionally rich in saturated fats, which are probably carcinogenic, while containing low levels of polyunsaturated fats, which are vital to maintaining the nervous system's balance. It makes no sense to accept such ills in the name of economic necessity, even less so because the farmers rendered superfluous by these intensive methods are currently swelling the ranks of the unemployed.

If developing a country means devastating its vegetation and paving it over with asphalt, increasing production and consumption at the expense of natural resource reserves and ecological balance, and even destroying traditional communities so as to force their members to live in crowded urban jungles, where psychological and sometimes physical stress leads to rising health and welfare expenses, then we should conclude that focusing on short-term profits generates disasters that cost a fortune to society.

Quantitative growth cannot be an end in itself; it can only be a means to furthering the overall well-being of individuals and societies. Seen from this standpoint, capitalism and socialism have both failed to offer a solution. Motivated by a productivist industrial logic, both systems have done tremendous damage by seeking short-term gains that make the long term unlivable.

A crucial question thus arises. Can we continue to measure and to judge the health of nations solely in terms of gross national product, since we know that there is a close correlation between the scarcity of resources and environmental destruction? Such forms of evaluation in no way reflect the degree of well-being of the population; in fact, they don't even reflect its standard of living, but merely its level of economic activity. Thus, the more ecological accidents there are to repair, the higher this value will go. If ever France has the misfortune to experience its own Chernobyl (a purely hypothetical example, of course, since all our leaders assure us that it can't happen here), the ensuing catastrophe would contribute directly to raising our gross national product. Just imagine the sophisticated health care radiation victims will receive, the new equipment hospitals will have to acquire, and the elaborate means of decontamination that will be employed on a vast scale! Yet our general well-being would not improve in the slightest; it would instead take a serious turn for the worse.

As long as we drive people to obtain quantitative results and we judge them on this basis, we are keeping an unrealistic dynamic alive, one that is incompatible with a comprehensive vision of social needs, with a satisfactory approach to helping the poorest among us (the "fourth world") out of their desperate situation, with the restructuring of the former Eastern-bloc countries, and with closing the gap some day between rich and poor countries.

TOWARD A NEW ECONOMIC LOGIC

The notion of ecological value should be reconsidered so that we cease to assess the real wealth of a country merely on the basis of its GNP. To commodities, we must now add non-monetary values such as air, water, and space; social services (solidarity, family structures, health, education); and housing and landscape. Yet we must also include in our calculations the other side of the coin: the cost of waste disposal, pollution, stress, etc.

Only a comprehensive approach will enable us to grasp the way in which the economy is but a subordinate part of overall ecology and to gauge its impact on health, education, and housing. Production is a component in a more vast systemic whole. "Value added will be less related to the existence of a tool or product than to the functioning of a complex system."[3]

During the prehistory of our ecological age, "environmental problems" were viewed as tangible drawbacks of economic growth that needed to be corrected. This involved reducing disturbances and pollution, reprocessing waste products, and saving energy. Thus, over the past 20 years, efforts have been made to limit wastefulness and to avoid rapid depletion of energy sources. Technological advances in the direction of dematerialization and miniaturization offer new opportunities in this regard. Alternative solutions (solar energy, biomass, etc.) have received occasional encouragement. Yet we are now beginning to realize that policies aimed at limiting risk are simply inadequate and that the task at hand is to consider ecology from here on in within the context of an ecosystem, and thus as a genuine goal of economic policy-making, rather than as a mere accessory parameter.

Economy and environment are related in the same way as light and electricity are. The point is to work out a comprehensive approach to the question that is both balanced and lasting.[4] This means recognizing that infinite economic growth on a finite planet is an illusion that can only lead to catastrophe, and that economic development is not an end in itself. As Jean-Marie Pelt put it, "According to its own current concepts, the economy is mortal."[5]

TOWARD A NEW MORALITY OF THE INHABITABLE EARTH

From now on, the strictly economic balance sheet of a company (productivity, profits, etc.) should be supplemented by both a social balance sheet (employment and human resources) and, inevitably, an ecological one. Senior managers must acquire the ability to assess the impact of the ecological balance sheet on their company's environment.

The shift in mental models that we will have to carry out implies the idea that life takes precedence over machines and that the whole, which is organic, is greater than the parts. We must trade in the demand for "more" in exchange for a demand for "enough," as the authors of *Beyond the Limits* rightly stress, and therefore reconsider our "rich people's" values, think globally, regard the world as one vast ecosystem and individuals as the world's citizens.[6] A number of simple principles follow from this that should limit needs and prevent humanity from destroying itself, chief among which is the regulation of fertility.

The ultimate question is how we can shift "from a merciless economic world war that has transformed the world into a giant powder keg to ecological wisdom." Up until now, attempts at reaching international consensus on specific matters have fallen flat, and unfortunately, the World Trade Organization, which has been in gestation since the most recent GATT agreement, includes no ecological preoccupations, in spite of European requests for such an emphasis.

No one suggests that we give up electricity and go back to candle light. Yet we must rediscover those values of our ancestors that made nature an ally, a sister, instead of a subject to be exploited with no scruples, and we must do so with all due haste. We simply cannot afford to wait for a world government to come into being that would presumably define a number of ground rules. Starting right now, we must induce everyone involved to adopt the appropriate tone, with leaders taking the lead in establishing a more harmonious relationship between man and nature. Otherwise, the universe will become increasingly unlivable. Only a genuine morality of the inhabitable Earth, one that has yet to be worked out, can provide the foundations for a new alliance between man and nature and a change in the way our society is organized. Such a perspective presupposes that we set radically new priorities that emphasize being rather than having, and love instead of possession.

Notes

1 Cf. *L'Homme face à la science* (Paris: Critérion, 1992), p. 59.
2 See Pierre Alfandéry, *L'Equivoque écologique* (Paris: La Découvete, 1991).
3 Orio Giarini and Walter R. Stahel, *Les limites du certain* (Lausanne: Presses polytechniques et universitaires romandes, 1990), p. 169.
4 In 1987, the World Commission on Environment and Development stated in the Brundtland Report, "The world economy and world ecology are now inextricably bound together. For some time now, we have focused on the effects of economic growth on the environment. At present, however, we must concern ourselves with the attacks of the environment . . . on our economic perspectives." As for the 1992 edition of the Annual World Bank Report, entitled "Development and Environment," it lays down three new principles that make economic growth and ecological balance indissociable. "An increase in income is not a source of well-being when it entails additional health-care expenses as a result of worsening pollution. Although it

makes for immediate gains, damage to the environment jeopardizes future productivity and the inheritance of generations to come . . . The experts consider that in reality, policies favorable to the environment can be economically profitable provided they involve reduced consumption of raw materials, lower waste production, and increased technological innovation" (Eric Fottorino, "L'Ecologie pour le développement," *Le Monde*, May 19, 1992).

5 In *L'Homme face à la science*, p. 199.

6 Donella H. Meadows, Dennis L. Meadows, and Jorgen Randers, *Beyond the Limits* (PO Box 130, Vermont 05058: Chelsea Green Publishing Company, 1992).

12

Controlling and Sharing Information

Imperceptibly, we were heading for an information-based society in which the problem of processing data would take precedence over all else. Industrial society was one of artificial muscle. Information society was to be one of artificial memory, and subsequently to a lesser extent, one of artificial brains.

Robert Lattès, *L'Apprenti et le Sorcier*[1]

The number of computer applications is growing more rapidly than our ability to conceive of an optimal use for them.

Organizing the power of knowledge has become the primary source of competitive advantage.

Distribution networks possess a gold mine of information that they could share.

Interconnections between computer networks will eventually lead to interconnections between companies themselves.

The appropriate use of computers does not merely involve obtaining the rapid execution of a given function in a purely linear pattern. There now exists an impressive spectrum of operational capacities that is getting wider every day.

President Bill Clinton's first step, upon taking office in Washington, to boost American high-tech industry was highly symbolic. He launched the construction of a vast optical-fiber network designed to link up "nerve centers" in the entire country as well as to improve and accelerate information distribution and access to data banks. This program, somewhat pompously christened "information superhighways," will create a high-level communications network that will facilitate cooperation between companies in technologically advanced industries. Although the new system is meant particularly for Silicon Valley laboratories, it will also greatly benefit universities, hospitals, schools, and public services.

KNOWING HOW TO ORGANIZE KNOWLEDGE: A DECISIVE COMPETITIVE ADVANTAGE

At a time when products absorb immense quantities of brain power, their value depends increasingly on the knowledge they incorporate. This implies the need to set up genuinely strategic information channels. In the upcoming information network war, all participants will have to keep constantly abreast of developments in their particular field.

Doing so in this rapidly evolving situation will above all require unfailing mobility – and mobilization of organizations as well as a capacity for immediately integrating and utilizing new data. The main challenge facing today's companies lies in perceiving technological trends and in defining functions within the organization so that they fit in with the emerging technical solutions. Organizational superiority has become a decisive competitive advantage. As Alvin Toffler has pointed out, "Of all the strategic instruments [of power], there is none more important than organizational superiority, particularly as regards organizing knowledge itself."[2]

The trouble is that equipment is undergoing such accelerated technical development that organizational choices become more and more crucial and complex. The power of machines has increased faster than our ability to imagine optimal uses for them. Technological evolution advances more rapidly than our capacity for absorbing it, and thus for adapting to it. This situation has a disturbing side to it, even though computers themselves can help us understand and design new applications. The Japanese in particular are conducting thorough-going studies on this sensitive subject.

KEEPING UP IN AN INCREASINGLY DIGITAL WORLD

There is apparently no limit to the current expansion of computer use. Yet, whereas the younger generation already learns how to play around on a keyboard in school, thus acquiring a frame of mind appropriate to this new kind of tool, older people remain somewhat uncomfortable with it, since they are accustomed to pencil and paper rather than to dialogue with a screen.

Although systems of voice recognition have not yet become a reality, the time is not far off when we will be able to enter handwriting directly into a computer, thus eliminating the need for actual keyboard operations. It seems obvious that a technical leap of this magnitude will greatly expand the market for desktop computers.

The multi-media revolution will bring yet another imminent extension of this field. In the near future, work stations combining the advantages of different means of communication are likely to develop on a mass scale. In fact, computers that are not hooked up to a screen or a telecommunications network already come across as extremely "cold" tools. The publishing industry will be radically altered by future interactive encyclopedias that will make possible the simultaneous use of sound and image, owing to video disks and high-definition screens. The user will thereby gain access to vast documentary sources that save valuable time that would otherwise be spent in searching for the information required.

Multi-media tools will ultimately pose a threat to the major computer manufacturers, who will find themselves in direct competition with the top audiovisual, communications, and consumer electronics firms. The growing digitization of all forms of expression (audio, visual, etc.) will lead these different industries to overlap more and more. If we take telecommunications, television, and computers together, the number of players is on the rise, and the problems involved are increasingly complex.

The digital revolution is only the first stage, after which it will be necessary to expand the capacity of digitized networks to accommodate the daunting volume of information implied by widespread exchange of files or animated images.

LEARNING TO DISTINGUISH BETWEEN USEFUL INFORMATION AND "FATAL" INFORMATION

We are constantly accumulating new means of gathering material and information, and the tremendous technological progress accomplished over the past several years raises the question of just how to make rational use of all these data. In a world in which we are overrun with information in every shape and form, the main problem is figuring out a way to pick out the essential elements and to integrate them. Amidst a plethora of information that could have fatal consequences for us, we have to distinguish what is truly useful.

Since sources will be gathered in an increasingly exhaustive fashion and made accessible to just about everyone, the only people able to single out useful, significant data and to interpret them will be those who have received adequate training in information retrieval. It thus turns out that, although the development of computer technology unquestionably makes information more accessible than before, it also heightens the need for training in the art of handling knowledge.

"The tools [computer systems, data banks, etc.] exist, and people do possess a computer culture, but they lack an information culture," points out Peter Drucker with some concern. "All too few of them ask themselves: What information do I need? From whom should I receive it, in what form, and when? What information should I provide, to whom, in what form, and when?"[3]

We are in fact witnessing no less than a change in function. Initially, computer science was a form of *knowledge* that mainly involved storing data and carrying out complex calculations at high speed. What subsequently emerged could be termed *specialized knowledge*, i.e. techniques for processing and utilizing information as well as for programming computers with the greatest possible efficiency. Next came the wave of compatibility and of local area networks, which made storage as such less vital and gave priority to interconnections and data exchange. *Knowledge power* had become the key element. Today, with the development of expert systems and the growing body of research on artificial intelligence, we have reached the stage of *organizing knowledge power* and of controlling the processes used to design information-processing programs.

The long-term trend is for machine manipulation to give way to communication, communication to information programming, and information programming to organization of information systems. "Gray matter" has become essential, not only in terms of memory, but also in terms of intelligence. The inescapable conclusion to be drawn is that leadership in the field of technological performance, and thus economic power, will depend directly on an ability to organize technologies related to learning.

THE STRATEGIC IMPORTANCE OF THE "INTELLIGENT" ORGANIZATION

Management of information flows should be viewed in strategic terms. It is not merely a matter of running computer systems. The goal is to provide the company with an overall mode of organization able to regulate information in a coherent flow that penetrates the entire chain of the company's functions (its value chain), while fitting in with the firm's culture and its working atmosphere. In a large number of today's organizations, there are too many small orchestras playing independent symphonies. The danger is that in developing their own culture instead of that of the whole company, they wind up producing sheer cacophony. In such a case, it becomes impossible to harmonize information from different company units or departments.

In addition to the need for internal company cohesion and consistency of the available data, the problem arises of interconnecting the information possessed by manufacturers and that possessed by distributors. Confronted with sluggish sales, the leading distributors (by now equipped with a formidable electronic weapon: bar codes and cash registers linked up to a mainframe computer) have chosen to organize as tightly as possible their inventory turnover and the selection of goods they offer. They now know almost immediately which products consumers choose and which ones they ignore, and they have masses of statistics on customers' buying patterns which enable them to rationalize their management decisions.

In mega-store chains minute after minute, hour after hour, every sale is recorded and the central processing unit automatically sends out orders for restocking. In such a context, the struggle to organize information takes on primary importance. It is vital for suppliers and distributors to combine their data on an interactive basis in order to gain greater control over their respective management choices. This alliance for the rationalization of decision-making will necessarily save both parties time and money, and as a result work to the advantage of consumers too.

DISTRIBUTORS: A GOLD MINE OF INFORMATION

In a world where money takes the form of information and information the form of money, consumers who shop in a store with directly memorized bar codes pay twice for each purchase: by giving money and by providing information that is worth money.[4] Banks, retailers, and manufacturers would probably sell their souls in order to get hold of such information, provided free of charge. And since sharing it is not all that easy, the major distributors have everything to gain from branching out into banking.

Even when a buyer pays cash for certain day-to-day purchases (e.g. food, magazines), the information gathered remains considerable. Besides data on the shelf space that his purchase just cleared out, the store enters into the computer what kind of products he uses, in what quantities, whether he prefers cut-rate items or known brand names, at what time he does his shopping, and the kind of magazine through which advertising is most likely to reach him.

If the same customer goes shopping for the entire week and takes home a shopping cart full of different products, the retailer can then analyze these purchases over time and thereby derive a distinct behavior pattern, the customer's personal "signature," in a manner of speaking, which may subsequently help to define a market group. Marui, one of Japan's leading sales networks, which even has its own credit card, uses a system called M-Tops that allows the company to target those families that have just moved. The procedure involves identifying purchases that one would normally associate with fitting out a new home. By acting on the assumption that a couple that buys an air conditioner or kitchen furniture may also be in need of new beds, Marui has managed to obtain surprisingly high numbers of mail orders for its products.

This logic can be taken even further. If the consumer pays with the store's own credit card, the distributor possesses her name, address, and zip code (particularly useful for delimiting catchment areas), and even has the means to assess her creditworthiness or her family income. And when the distribution company and the bank are one and the same entity, nothing escapes it. By combining all the information in its possession, the firm will have no trouble drawing an astoundingly accurate portrait of the buyer's life-style, including her habits, her travel, leisure, and reading preferences, how often she eats out, what kinds of alcoholic drinks she likes, even what form of contraception she uses and the charities to which she donates.

Obviously, the existence of such multiple cross-references can pose an extremely serious threat to privacy and give rise to all kinds of sordid bargaining and shady deals about which the consumer remains entirely in the dark. The economic value of such information (which can be sold or exchanged) is colossal, so much so that companies might well be inclined to evade whatever regulations the government has laid down (in France, there is the Commission on Data Processing and Freedom).

Even if ethical considerations lead to effective protection of consumer anonymity, utilizing all data gathered on customers during their shopping none the less remains a considerable source of competitive advantage. Thus, among major American distributors, Wal-Mart, although starting out as a minor challenger, managed to outrun industry leader Kmart (by several miles, in fact) by investing heavily in communications in order to implement just-in-time distribution. All its stores are equipped with sales outlet terminals (which make it possible to keep track of the evolution of sales, item by item) and interconnected with each other through a private network of communications by satellite. There is thus instantaneous feedback on sales that enables Wal-Mart to restock its stores without having to build up inventory.

The system offers yet another advantage. The compiled information is accessible in every store of the chain, and a department manager can consult the figures for the same department in another outlet. Real-time feedback can also be established between company headquarters, stores, and warehouses.

By setting up an unprecedented data bank on sales, Wal-Mart stimulated great interest on the part of its leading suppliers like Procter & Gamble, which sent out a team to the distributors in order to arrange for regular collaboration on logistics and computerized order handling. Electronic data exchange thus became a powerful tool for economic forecasting, sales planning, and cost optimization, one that is based on an analysis of the direct profit that each product yields.

INTERACTIVE COMMUNICATIONS NETWORKS THAT PRODUCE SYNERGY

Electronic data processing and its byproducts (office automation, desktop publishing, etc.) have already proved irreplaceable when it comes to rationalizing routine tasks, sharing time and work stations through the use of desktop computers, decentralizing units with the help of network connections in space, or developing the learning tree in order to get maximum leverage out of existing brain power. They also give rise to more efficient tools for avoiding storage problems and ensuring the smooth flow of information from end to end of the economic circuit, from producer to vendor, thus eliminating any number of traditional bottlenecks.

In this connection, a typical example is provided by a program designed to manage airplane parking for American airline companies. Previously, it took over eight hours just to find adequate space on the ground for all the planes of a given company. Fortunately, a computer scientist from India invented a mathematical model making it possible to reduce this time to *five minutes*. The two airlines that first had access to this system thus obtained a significant competitive advantage.

As Mr Bundo Yamada, the President of the Fujitsu Research Institute, points out:

> Computer networks have become the key infrastructure in the business and industrial worlds . . . because they have created electronic communications that facilitate the transmission of information. The flow of people, goods, and services requires the use of computer networks . . . Networks in which information is at the heart of systemization strategies aimed at vitalizing a company and its members, at achieving harmonious relations of interdependence between several firms, at establishing strong ties between a company, its suppliers, and its customers, etc., have led to a consolidation of resources, both inside and outside the company, and to the emergence of a synergy-producing phenomenon.[5]

In 1993, six of the leading telecommunications companies set about constructing a world cable network using submarine optical fibers. This represents the first stage in the development of a new system of interactive tele-video (the Global Networking Project) for which tens of billions of dollars have already been invested. It can be expected that this "federation" of companies (including AT&T, Deutsche Bundespost Telecom, Sony, Time Warner, BBC, Motorola, and NEC) will succeed in the next ten years in revolutionizing the way in which we receive information and education by merging together data processing, telephony, and imaging capacities.

Building the infrastructures of our "informational global village" clearly involves such high stakes that no single corporation, however multinational it may be, can hope to meet the challenge on its own. This task thus opens up the perspective of a new brand of "relationship company" based on the interplay of strategic alliances. Such "multi-domestic" groupings set the pattern for a more powerful sort of company, one that is better suited to the global scale than those we have seen up until now. This is what Cyrus Freidheim has termed "the trillion-dollar scale corporation."[6]

Notes

1 Robert Lattès, *L'Apprenti et le Sorcier* (Paris: Plon, 1988), p. 105.
2 Alvin Toffler, *The Third Wave* (New York: William Morrow and Company, 1980).
3 Quoted from an interview with *L'Expansion*, December 6–19, 1992.
4 See Alvin Toffler, *Powershift* (New York: Bantam Books, 1990).
5 "In search of creative harmony in a company with intelligent EDP systems," a talk given at the 35th CIES Congress in Amsterdam, June 7–9, 1992.
6 Vice-President of the Chicago consulting firm Booz-Allen.

13

Human Progress: the Sole Justification for Technological Change

Any major invention or discovery brings forth what might be called a "crisis," i.e. a complex process of innovation, change, imbalance, and then at last readjustment.

Robert Lattès, *L'Apprenti et le Sorcier*

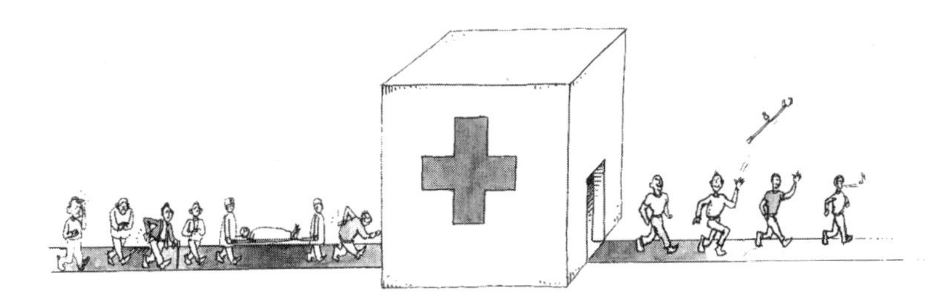

Since the tendency is toward the rapid levelling of technical performances, only a focus on improved service can make a long-term difference.

Innovation requires a fresh outlook unencumbered by images of past success.

Man must be the beneficiary of new technology, not its slave.

Citius, Altius, Fortius. This motto thought up by Pierre de Coubertin to characterize the spirit of modern Olympics applies quite well to the current wave of technological development. Technologies change faster and faster, their range steadily increases, and their effect on our way of life is more and more powerful. And the volumes they can handle are more and more colossal every day.

Change has accelerated to such an extent that it has been claimed that a mere 1 percent of the technologies we use today will still be in use in the year 2050.

TECHNOLOGICAL PROGRESS: FROM COARSE TO FINE

Throughout history, energy sources have become more complex and sophisticated. After the obsolescence of the water mill, then of the steam engine and coal combustion, the supremacy of fossil fuels is presently coming to an end. The future belongs to solar energy, geothermal science, the use of biomass or synthetic fuels, and perhaps nuclear power, provided we solve the problem of storing radioactive waste products with extremely long half-lives.

As for the materials employed, they are now both more sophisticated and lighter than before. Metal has given way to plastics, to polymers and composite materials, and even to ceramics. The tendency is towards increasingly "pure" products modeled on the molecular structures of living organisms. Indeed, it has become increasingly clear that the "cutting edge" of current technology is to be found in "gray matter" industries like computers, electronics, and telecommunications, and in the study of living matter, as demonstrated by biotechnology and its diverse applications in agriculture, food products, medicine, and even cosmetics.

BELIEVING IN THE GOD OF TECHNOLOGY AND THE MIRACLE OF MEDICINE

State-of-the-art electronics, robots, computers, CAD-CAM, computer-aided production management, desktop publishing, and their multiple future offshoots will continue to modify our living conditions. With the development of expert systems, by the year 2000, artificial intelligence will be an essential government, administrative, and management tool for tracking down and solving problems. Expert systems will be intensively used in a wide variety of areas, including prospecting for energy resources, designing new products and manufacturing processes, automatic diagnosis of machine failure, not to mention illness, management of insurance systems, setting of official standards, and reinforcing and codifying legal and regulatory measures.

The marketing of superconductors controlled at normal temperatures will enable us to construct electrical motors much lighter and more compact than ever before (with a 75 percent reduction in relation to current volume). As a result, high-speed trains like the

French TGV will be able to run along magnetic bearings at over 200 miles per hour.

Needless to say, all possible forms of wireless communication will undergo rapid development. Increasingly easy to handle terminals will be readily transported, instead of remaining stuck on a desk. All these developments will have cumulative effects. Mass media as well as satellite or cable communications will soon make it possible to publicize ideas and inventions instantaneously throughout the world.

In the field of health, medicine, and biotechnologies as well, considerable progress can be expected. Every year, some $100 billion are devoted to research on genetics, artificial blood, immunization, hormones for increasing longevity, maintaining memory, or carrying out transplants. New medication, artificial organs, and microsurgery will be of considerable use, while the exploration of immune systems will open up the way to a cure for cancer, and computer diagnosis will eliminate a number of exploratory surgical operations. And through bloodless laser surgery, more patients will be treated at home, which will help to reduce overcrowding in hospitals.

Research on brain cells will make it possible to repair certain shocks through tissue transplants. For the heart, similar techniques will be employed. Pacemakers and defibrillators will greatly contribute to the treatment of cardiovascular ailments. Lastly, with the help of new means of detection and analysis, preventive medicine will make gigantic strides. (It is estimated that by the year 2000, 53 percent of all medication will be sold over the counter.)

The more technology progresses, the more it produces repercussions that go beyond questions of mere practical utility and imply political options (for example, nuclear power) and ethical choices (artificial procreation and genetic selection) that have consequences for all of society. Furthermore, as technical means become increasingly subtle and sophisticated, they acquire a power that turns them into a source of additional upheavals.

Every major innovation thus leads to increasingly thorny questions and choices. Everything that is technically possible is not necessarily economically profitable, nor socially desirable, nor even politically acceptable, not to mention morally and ethically admissible. In this respect, "the faster you drive, the further your headlights must shine and the wider they must sweep."

TRYING TO ANTICIPATE CHANGE

At present, it takes little time, once ideas, inventions, and innovations hatch, for imitations to appear. The rush is on to turn new technologies into immediately saleable, successful products. The time during which new patents can be effectively utilized is rapidly dwindling, particularly since product life-cycles have gotten shorter and consumers' tastes change faster than in the past.

Information and new ideas now make it around the globe in just a few brief seconds, and business deals are concluded at the same speed. Inevitably, the leading industrial concerns all tend to work in similar lines of business and to employ roughly the same research and development methods. As a result, the advantages to be derived from technological breakthroughs are less and less lasting, and, in any case, competitors are just a few steps behind and quickly catching up.

In these conditions, of course, every company has an interest in benchmarking its competitors. We have seen how Japanese examples have stimulated the United States to surpass previous performances, and vice versa. Yet benchmarking is not enough if all it leads to are strategies that take their inspiration from what others are doing. To remain competitive, an industrialist must take the lead in technological innovation. Maintaining and developing the business potential of his firm means giving priority to research and development, avoiding the trap of being tied to a single kind of technology, and knowing constantly how to anticipate the future, instead of simply adjusting to it once it is here.

THE NEED TO FORGET IN ORDER TO INNOVATE

A company that holds a leadership position in its industry has little trouble adapting to new situations; it recruits intelligent people who are able to bring competitive products to market quickly; it can even afford to launch new products, in spite of the risk of failure. However, although this attitude allows the company to keep up, it also presents two related dangers: turning out numerous new products that are too much alike, thus confusing consumers, and above all letting other companies gain ground.

A small firm eager to succeed targets cultural niches ignored by larger companies and thereby manages to make a strength out of the weakness of its powerful competitors. Any number of examples show that major innovations started out as marginal initiatives. The minitel was designed outside France Télécom's orbit, Polaroid was rejected by Kodak, and the memory card was invented by an engineer working in isolation. In the United States today, the number of these tiny, innovative start-ups is mushrooming (some 233,000 of them have been counted!), and they are destabilizing leading companies.

The frequent reactions of rejection that radical innovations often meet are signs of a psychological block that André-Yves Portnoff has aptly described. "We are inclined to see only that with which we are already familiar, which corresponds to some stereotype in our culture, and not what is actually in front of us. We are also terrified by the unknown, which we prefer to deny, reducing everything to what we know and control."[1]

In order to innovate, we have to know how to forget and, once again, to take a fresh look at the world around us. This is clearly more difficult than learning how to adapt. Yet sometimes we are better off not taking our past experience into account, even if it was associated with great success, if we wish to find new, creative ideas. Admittedly, it is a lot easier to produce roughly the same thing twice than to come up with a radical innovation.

QUANTITATIVE PERFORMANCE AND QUALITATIVE EFFICIENCY

Since competing companies tend increasingly to achieve similar quantifiable results, differences in value will have to be assessed in terms of service quality, and even the quality of life. It is this extra bit of well-being, rational or irrational, that is provided to the end user, after a thorough analysis of his motivation and behavior, which makes it possible to add value.

To face up to new challenges, companies should emphasize research and development policies geared to long-term profit rather than to spectacular, but short-lived returns. Following their defeat in 1945, Japan and Germany managed to rise again only by mobilizing collective energy behind ideals of reconstruction implying the solidarity and cooperation of all of society. Paradoxically, this enabled them to develop long-term visions and strategies. They organized and planned their reconstruction along these lines by giving priority to collective rather than individual accomplishment.

To both countries, money was not an end in itself, but merely a means to achieve other goals. In both Germany and Japan, traditional culture and social patterns tended to favor patient, long-range strategies. This example demonstrates how important it is to put forward a coherent model, a clear vision of the product and its strong points, and to know how to organize production and marketing efforts in synergistic fashion.

The quality of a company's internal and external organization thus takes on primary importance. This is not simply a matter of getting information systems under control. The company must also introduce flexibility into its production methods in order to be able to adjust to market fluctuations, and to enrich jobs by developing smaller, decentralized units that operate like *ad hoc* teams capable of modifying production set-ups as needs shift. Micro-technologies now make it increasingly possible to transform mass production into production of customized models. And it is the direction that technological change has taken that has paved the way for the emergence of new needs and a change on the supply side of things.

TECHNICAL PROWESS AND SOCIAL MODELS

The more technology progresses, the more it comes to dominate the economy and shape social behavior. Its decisive role requires that, at the same time, human beings know how to master it, instead of becoming its slaves. The technological gap between developed countries and developing countries will continue to grow. The former already possess ten times more engineers per capita than the latter, and research capacities are obviously proportional to these numbers.

On the other hand, we are currently witnessing a powerful trend toward integration and standardization, for the world economy is increasingly interdependent. For example, 39 percent of all components used in the United States are manufactured elsewhere. This tendency toward interconnection will continue as the world moves harmoniously toward the easing of economic restrictions. At every step along the way, it is important to take stock of the cross-effects produced by technological innovation.

We cannot separate technical progress from the evolution of society and daily life. Values and attitudes undoubtedly change more slowly than technology does. Extremist reactions such as those of fundamentalist movements or of people like Lanza del Vasto, who wove his own linen cloak, are simply unrealistic.[2] Yet whatever contributes to achieving greater balance between technological development and individual well-being is a step in the right direction.

THE LOGIC OF CUSTOMIZING

In a world dominated by consumption and the mass media, everyone directs his attention to himself, in search of his own particular truth and well-being. The Socratic imperative "Know thyself" takes on renewed vigor in a new context.

In a society of abundance that is saturated with vast quantities of technically and commercially equivalent products, the only way to make a difference is to offer the consumer the greatest possible satisfaction. What she buys now is an increasingly personalized, complete service. Besides usefulness, she is looking for security, enjoyment, creativity, and a feeling of human contact.

Post-industrial society is not merely a service society, but also a self-service society based on seduction and attraction. Under the combined effect of modernism and mass consumption, our culture is now centered on ego gratification, spontaneity, and pleasure. Communication has replaced coercion, enjoyment has replaced prohibition, and the custom-made has replaced the anonymous. People are now eager to experience everything, see everything, taste everything, feel everything, discover everything. Feeling and individual freedom dominate postmodern culture, the culture of narcissism.

We have gone from a productivist logic characterized by bulk or mass to a service logic oriented toward customer satisfaction. This logic requires adaptation, segmentation, and fragmentation of product lines, in other words, the flexibility that new computer-aided systems now make possible. As Giarini and Stahel put it, "Whereas the main question in the industrial economy was 'What is the monetary value of a product?', in a service economy, very different questions arise like 'What is the use value of a product? What functions does it fulfill? How, and for how long?'"[3]

THE ACID TEST: ACTUAL SERVICE

But let's not get carried away. All too often, discussion of new projects is conducted in a vacuum, in laboratories or boards of directors cut off from reality. In many cases, this process generates sophisticated research that none the less fails miserably in the marketplace, for in spite of its unquestionable intellectual merits, it focuses much too little on the underlying expectations of potential users.

Truly modern technical objects are those that were most intelligently thought out and designed, even if the solutions adopted were surprisingly simple and devoid of any high-tech features.

When all is said and done, what enables new technology to prove itself in practice is the perceived value of the service in the eyes of the consumer or citizen. For this reason, the more technological potential develops, the more we would do well to chose those technologies that reduce the feeling of complexity. As André-Yves Portnoff stresses, "The essential point is not to make use of the most advanced solutions, but of those that are best suited to meeting the user's needs."[4]

Notes

1 André-Yves Portnoff, "La révolution de l'intelligence ou la libération du bon sens," working paper written for the review *Science et Technologie*, 1992.

2 A French advocate of non-violence as Gandhi preached it, this ecumenical spiritualist was active in the resistance of farmers on the Larzac plateau to confiscation of their land for military use. He also founded the Arch Communities, which rejects mechanization and looks askance at technological change.

3 Orio Giarini and Walter R. Stahel, *Les limites du certain* (Lausanne: Presses polytechniques et universitaires romandes, 1990), p. 169.

4 André-Yves Portnoff, "La révolution de l'intelligence."

14

Today's Changes, Tomorrow's Products

Man constructs objects, but it is emptiness that gives them meaning. Only what is lacking can justify things.

Lao-tse

1990 PERSONAL COMPUTER

1960 TELEVISION

1910 RADIO

We need new goods and services that are faster, more functional, more diversified, more meaningful.

These products should take factors into account such as more fragmented life-styles, the aging of the population, new sources of value, and the need for a personalized relationship with the customer.

Current economic difficulties are not merely due to insufficient demand, for, as it turns out, the deflation we are experiencing is accompanied by a rise in the savings of upper-income households. It is therefore high time that we invented goods and services of a different kind.

Jacques Barraux has deplored the Western world's reluctance to carry out ground-breaking innovations, an area in which it generally excels. He considers this quality the best possible antidote to a situation of low economic growth that can be explained above all by a failure to innovate. "In the developed countries, most of the workforce is involved in satisfying dulled needs," writes Barraux. It is therefore important to review our society's shortcomings, with which we are by now almost too familiar. "We have to be on the lookout for new needs. Urban decay, the aging of the population, increasing leisure time, environmental protection, concern for physical fitness, fear of loneliness, the desire for culture and communication . . . At no other time have the press, movies, and literature expressed as clearly as now the expectations harbored by the children of the affluent society. Why is the market taking so long to respond to them?"[1]

Without claiming to have an answer to this question, I will none the less attempt, in the next few pages, to sum up ten new criteria that underlie the current changes in consumer behavior: speed, convenience, the aging of the population, product diversity, life-style, discounts, value-adding, customer service, technological innovation, and quality.[2]

SPEED

High-speed trains, planes, fax machines, snapshots, and microwave ovens are obvious bestsellers because they save time. Faced with demanding jobs, tight schedules, family responsibilities, and expanding leisure activities, we all have to move faster and faster. Work has become more complex and information more abundant; operations are getting more intricate and networks are burgeoning.

Far from diminishing, labor time tends to increase. If we include meetings, seminars, business trips, and reports to be read, it becomes apparent that French managers spend an average of 50 hours a week working. To this calculation, we should of course add transportation time, shopping, waiting around for the plumber, and driving one of the kids to the dentist. All this leaves just about enough time for a cup of instant coffee, a Big Mac, and five minutes of TV news watching. As for female executives, they have no more than a few seconds to put their makeup on before running to catch the train or starting the car.

This acceleration of the modern world in every area profoundly affects consumer behavior. Companies are having trouble speeding up their internal functioning, which depends on human, technological, and organizational factors. This problem is fraught with consequences, since it affects all company departments, from marketing, production, and shipping to research and development. Yet increasing speed remains essential to success. One of the key ideas of the 1990s, time-saving increasingly marks the business world in the following ways.

- *Time-saving products.* This is the marketing basis for a large number of day-to-day products. Such products respond to the consumer's need for more time, more than ever a coveted object. Fast food restaurants are an obvious example, although in France, most observers predicted that they would never take hold. TGV trains, fax machines, and microwaves for heating up frozen foods all fall into the same category, as do the various "two-in-one" products such as shampoo with hair conditioner, powder makeup base, automatic mascara, and various aerosol products. The same trend can be observed in the area of food products, where prepared salad dressing, pre-sliced vegetables, and fresh fruit juice have become increasingly common.
- *Luxury speed.* Consumers are prepared to pay more and more for immediate satisfaction, for "everything here and now." This can well be termed luxury consumption, since the consumer pays more than the average market price for an otherwise equivalent service. The product itself does not save time; accelerated service is the value involved. An internationally known example is 30-minute pizza delivery. The company's slogan is: You get your money back if the pizza ordered by telephone is not on your table half an hour later. This arrangement enjoys tremendous popularity, particularly among young people, who don't like planning ahead, but who can't stand waiting when they get hungry or want to have a snack with friends. The same concept is behind the

success of large rapid-delivery companies like Federal Express, which prides itself on being able to deliver anything anywhere in the world in under 24 hours. A similar logic can be seen in any number of one-hour services such as instant photo developing, dry cleaning, express shoe repair, or even shampoo, cut, and blow-dry in less than 45 minutes.

- *Rapid reaction to perceived desires.* Rapid creation and marketing of products that meet customers' expectations is vital for today's companies. Those that "get there first" have a clear head-start in a given market (even though the competition may subsequently catch up). Japanese automobile companies design and manufacture a new model in three and a half years, whereas in Detroit, the same cycle takes five years (i.e. 62 months as opposed to 42 months). As far as rapid development is concerned, the Twingo marks the shift of Renault to a Japanese-style efficiency. As the chronicler of this adventure points out, "A company starts to get old as soon as it freezes its products. If development takes longer than in rival companies, the product is in danger of already being outdated when it finally comes out on the market."[3]
- *Rapid service.* If one of two suppliers promises one-month delivery time, as opposed to three months for the other one, it clearly enjoys an immediate competitive advantage. Internal speed is just as important. You have to scratch your head in perplexity upon discovering that once a customer places an order with the European Community, the whole process of handling, preparation, shipment, and at last arrival on the buyer's premises can take anywhere from 25 to 50 days.

CONVENIENCE

In an increasingly competitive world, consumers make their choices on the basis of the relative convenience or functionality that a given product has to offer. Theirs is an all-encompassing view that reflects the power of individual desires, urges, whims, and demands much more than the imperatives of the manufacturer himself. Functionality combines several characteristics.

- *The satisfaction of a need* or the ability of a product to meet the consumer's expectations. In this category, we find, in addition to the Walkman and the fax or answering machine, the mini-backpack that young people have enthusiastically adopted, and exceptionally comfortable footwear by Nike, Reebok, and Adidas.

- *The practical aspect of the product.* Possible examples are easy-to-carry mini detergent drums, packaging that facilitates storage at home, and products whose shape and design make them easy to grasp or to handle (such as lids and caps).
- *Simplicity.* Mini-stereos and automatic focus cameras are objects that can be immediately understood, often due to clear instructions or buttons with explanatory symbols on them.

Conversely, hairspray cans that are too tall to fit inside the medicine chest, washer-dryers that can wash ten pounds of clothing at one time, while drying only half of it, and generally any form of packaging that is at odds with the limited storage space in most modern apartments are all exemplary of non-functional design.

The point is that it is possible to innovate merely by offering greater functionality and simplicity of use. Just to hook up a TV set, a VCR, or a portable telephone, 80 percent of all adults, in their bewilderment, turn to a young person for help. This has led companies to work toward making their technically sophisticated products less complicated for the user. Philips has launched a new line of products called "Easy Line" (no more superfluous buttons), and Sony has come out with a new stereo set whose advertising slogan can be summarized in three words: sound, style, simplicity. Less important buttons are concealed; only the essential functions start/stop/volume are clearly in view.

The combination of simplicity and convenience corresponds increasingly to the expectations of consumers, who often suffer mild stress because of the excessive sophistication of certain products. In brief, someone who is dying to film his baby's very first steps has no desire whatsoever to become a programmer in order to do so. Cold, impersonal video cameras can render images but not emotions. This explains the consumer's unconscious vexation, for it is precisely this extra bit of emotion that he is looking for. Although advertising has done its utmost to offset this shortcoming, the results attained leave the consumer disappointed, for they seem so artificial. What gives certain products a plus nowadays is their harmonious integration into daily life.

For the same price, service quality, and satisfaction of needs, consumers will make their choice based on the more or less conscious relation they sense between the product's use and all the material and immaterial functions that allow them to find their bearings, to satisfy their desires, and to achieve fulfillment.

AN AGING POPULATION

Ten years from now in France, men and women over 65 will represent the equivalent of the Paris metropolitan area's current population: nine million people. In the European Community, this same age group will reach the 50 million figure by the year 2000, i.e. nine-tenths of the present population of countries like France, Great Britain, or Italy. The era of the "grandpa boom" will soon be with us, threatening those who hadn't reckoned with it.

In the United States, there are now some 30 million "senior citizens" (a less demeaning term than "old people"), whose numbers should increase by another million over the next ten years. As for the Japanese, they and, to a lesser extent, the Germans are the slowest aging people we know of: 20 million of the 121 million Japanese are senior citizens.

Over a period of two decades, from 1964 to 1984, birth rates in the European Community registered an annual decline of nearly two million. At present, 3,800,000 children are born each year in Western Europe, as opposed to 5,600,000 some 20 years ago.

It thus follows that population growth and market expansion no longer occur among young people, but among the elderly. In France, the average life expectancy for a woman is 80.1 years (the European average being 79.4). Men do not fare nearly as well, since on average, they only make it as far 72.9 (72.8 in all of Europe).

Market specialists will have to focus increasingly on an aging population, which rising longevity and declining birth rates make inevitable. Product design, including the bulkiness of products and the physical force required to use them, should be revamped to meet the needs of the elderly. The content of messages should also be modified. The older generation still likes to read – providing that written matter is readable for someone whose eyesight is probably no longer what it once was. And products must be made more readily accessible through methods like direct marketing and reply cards. The French bank Société générale has taken stock of these new needs, as is shown by the popularity of its Senior Convention, which includes home assistance and help in dealing with administrative formalities, services that have little to do with banking.

PRODUCT DIVERSITY

There was a time when engines had to be made of steel, furniture of wood, and bottles of glass. Today, there are virtually no technical limits to the conceivable solutions. Designers have a vast array of possibilities available to them. A given cream can now come in a glass, metal, or plastic container, in tube, aerosol, or stick form.

Some options, however, just don't work for cultural reasons. Consumers buy not only goods and services, but also atmosphere and ambience. To a Frenchman, for example, drinking wine in plastic bottles is tantamount to an error of taste. And although few people turn up their noses at plastic car bumpers any more, the use of plastic for automotive body work still comes across as cheap, poor, and ersatz. The Renault Espace minivan initially had trouble winning over customers precisely because its monocoque body is made of plastic. The fact is that sociocultural aspirations and technical possibilities must converge.

Consumers now demand customized, de-standardized products. Contrary to what occurred during the "melting pot" period, people today assert their diversity, whether it pertains to race, age, or life-style. Increasingly aware of the market segmentation that results from this new trend, companies have begun offering more and more variety to consumers, sometimes going to absurd lengths in the process. The best-known example is that of the thousands of different options that you can order for the same basic car model. The rising number of options is of course a response to the demand for greater choice. Yet it should be borne in mind that although constant innovation is certainly a plus, the options proposed must really bring some tangible, distinguishing advantage. Otherwise, they amount to little more than new packaging, gadgets, and in some cases additional complications for the user.

LIFE-STYLES

Constant probing of the social and cultural currents underlying new patterns of behavior is essential. In the Western world, the past two decades have been marked by a series of major upheavals. Women have massively entered the workforce, society has become increasingly atomized, the marriage rate has plunged, with many couples simply living together out of wedlock, the divorce rate has risen sharply (one in every three marriages), and single-parent households are increasing in number.

In virtually all Western countries, children living in urban areas have a 50 percent chance of growing up totally or partially outside classical family norms (i.e. living under the same roof with their married parents).

Today's children are often sole children, whom their parents pamper to a considerable degree, spending vast sums of money on them (for high-priced clothing, or even cosmetics and health products specially made for children).

The society of tomorrow will be more complex and perhaps more fragile as a result of growing solitude. More educated than in the past, young women want to travel, have careers, achieve financial independence, and be open to change. In France and the United States, 65 percent of all adult women work. A young woman often shares an apartment with a girlfriend. Although this does not prevent her from having a steady relationship with a man, she doesn't necessarily move in with him, and in any event, she conserves her freedom. Marriage is less common and takes place later than in the past; young people are more inclined simply to live together. As for having children, they tend to do it much, much later in life, when they really feel the urge to, when it no longer stands in the way of career opportunities, and when they have sufficient means to do so. Medical progress has to a great extent diminished fears regarding pregnancy after the age of 40.

Even marriage no longer seems to prevent both partners from pursuing their careers. In 1985, 50 percent of married women worked outside the home, a figure that should rise to 75 percent by the year 2000. Taking this phenomenon into account, a number of American companies have set up programs to assist the spouses of managers transferred to another region in finding employment. Needless to say, women who have to juggle career, household, and child-rearing greatly appreciate functional, high-quality, and above all time-saving products.

Men witness the evolution of women's condition without fully comprehending it, for they have yet to work out a new paradigm. A surprising new trend has thus become perceptible among boys: staying at mom and dad's place until the age of 25 or 30. Whereas girls learn quickly how to fend for themselves, boys seem to have trouble leaving the parental nest. The explanation for this is not economic, since young women are three times more exposed to unemployment than young men, while they generally earn less at work. Out of pragmatism, boys have realized that remaining within the nuclear family turns out to be easier – and cheaper. In this way, they can set aside much more money for free-time activities or clothes than if they were on their own. This late cohabitation between generations usually runs smoothly, since the relationship between parents and grown-up children has fundamentally changed. It is no longer based on patriarchal authoritarianism, but on balance and compromise implying mutual acceptance. What guides such a relationship is consensus.

The life-styles that emerge from this situation represent an unambiguous break with past practice. Today, age, sex, housing, and income have infinitely less significance than living arrangements such as being single, married, or divorced, with or without children, living with your parents, with friends, or with a lover. Several factors thus influence the choice of goods and services within a given household.

DISCOUNTS

Discount practices are the most dangerous of all forces of change, because they disrupt entire branches of the economy. There are both winners and losers. When discount prices affect staple goods, distribution circuits get shorter, middlemen disappear, and companies have no other choice than to work directly with discounters. Traditional retail establishments, now unprotected, are compelled to mark up their prices to stay in business. Lumped together with other products, increasingly vulnerable brand names have a hard time distinguishing themselves.

Today's consumers find everything too expensive. Wages and salaries stagnate or at best rise slowly. And even though unemployment creates fear among people, it in no way cancels out their desires and aspirations. So they feel that they have to "stay on their toes." Refusing to pay normal prices, consumers wait for special sales, which start earlier and earlier and last longer and longer each year. People bargain with each other, offering to exchange products their company makes ("I can get you shoes at wholesale prices if you can get me a sizeable discount on books, records, or perfume."). All prices have become negotiable, even for cars (which amounts to a covert discount offered by dealers). You have to haggle and swap "hot tips" with others if you want to avoid paying top prices. The goal is to get a good deal, to be a smart customer.

Some companies like Virgin Megastore, the Fnac bookstore, the supermarket chains Leclerc and Auchan, and even toy discounter Toys 'R' Us have made fortunes as a result of this consumer rebellion. All Paris perfume retailers engage more or less overtly in the discount trade (through loyalty cards, or discounts for large purchases).

A number of Japanese hi-fi manufacturers, such as Hitachi and Toshiba, sell directly at a 10 percent discount to consumers willing to pick up the product of their choice at company headquarters (even the Japanese newsletter in Paris runs ads to this effect). There are also innumerable discount shops offering clothing, household linen, and merchandise supposedly confiscated by customs officials.

The success of retailers like Leroy-Merlin, Ikea, or Lapeyre can be explained by their awareness of another major trend: the desire for do-it-yourself materials. At a pinch, consumers still call a plumber or an electrician, but they avoid labor charges on tiling or bathroom appliances.

Whenever possible, people bypass middlemen. They sell their homes themselves in order to save on realtor's commissions. The same holds true for selling cars. As for health care, people now buy kits at the pharmacy for pregnancy tests, blood tests, urine, diabetes, and cholesterol tests in order to avoid high laboratory costs.

When two products have similar characteristics and value, only price conditions choice. However, between two discounters charging the same price, differentiation will depend on intangible factors.

VALUE ADDING

Creating real value is the alternative to engaging in price wars. Value added is that little extra something that customers find in a product or service and that competitors don't offer. Yet this cannot be achieved simply by staging short-lived advertising stunts. A company adds value to its products and services by giving distributors the following advantages.

- Rapid product turnover guaranteed (pre-sold goods).
- Electronic data exchange, including terminals on the customer's premises, as a means of automatic ordering, confirmation, specification of delivery date, and stock taking.
- Easy payment terms.
- Staggered, just-in-time shipment of merchandise, which remains in the manufacturer's warehouses and is shipped according to need.
- Express service.
- Advertising material made available at all sales outlets.
- A training program for sales demonstration personnel and retailers.
- Layout and equipment assistance to retailers (a service akin to that provided by franchise chains).

This added value makes it possible to win distributors' loyalty. In order to accomplish this, companies should regularly sound out both distributors and consumers regarding what competitors are up to, then benchmark the value they offer.

As for consumers, what they pay money for is not merely a product, but also a set of cultural references (naturalness, environmental consciousness, atmosphere, pleasure, harmony). In a way, products must represent the continuation of a captivating story.

CUSTOMER SERVICE

The customer is not only always right – he is the Lord Almighty! The idea may not be particularly novel, but it still manages to give companies headaches, including new ones. Throughout the postwar boom, we were accustomed to constantly expanding mass markets. Only products and distribution mattered at the time.

At present, however, this is obviously no longer the case. Companies must now coax and entice customers. More demanding because they are better educated than their parents were, today's customers wield tremendous power. For this reason, it is important to establish direct links between the consumer and the brand name. This is the function of advertising, of course, but also of customer service departments, toll-free numbers, and post office boxes.

The goal is to integrate consumers into the company, to enable them to engage in dialogue with it. By measuring their satisfaction and getting feedback on their desires, the company is in a better position to create new products or to improve existing ones.

TECHNOLOGICAL INNOVATION

According to predictions, 99 percent of currently used technologies will have disappeared or profoundly changed by the year 2050. We can also reasonably assert that within five years, expert systems and artificial intelligence will be a part of daily life.

As the time between conception, invention, and production of a new product gets shorter, retaining a technological lead on competitors becomes increasingly difficult. All companies in a given line of business make similar investments and wind up with the same tools. Since the advent of CAD-CAM (computer-aided design and manufacturing), all automobiles tend to turn out alike. However, it should be stressed at the same time that anyone who fails to join in soon gets permanently left behind.

In industry, fully robotized workshops already exist. Computer-aided production management, CAD-CAM, and expert systems (which co-ordinate production lines) are revolutionizing manufacturing. All these innovations offer greater production flexibility, which makes it possible both to keep up with renewal orders and to organize batch production in order to satisfy consumer demand for custom-made products without extra cost.

QUALITY

The concept of quality is often defined in all too reductionist terms. In our culture, quality is synonymous with perfect products and flawless production (zero defect, quality circles, etc.). Although quality should certainly include these virtues, it is not limited to them, for it involves both the tangible and the intangible, the rational and the subjective, reality and fantasy.

Total quality means reinforcing the company's brand credibility, its image, and the "vibes" it gives off. In particular, this implies focusing on human relations and communication with the media, while publicizing successful alliances and impressive financial results. A certain amount of charisma and Messianic appeal are also in order. A company must present a world view, a philosophy that helps people to take the changes that await us in their stride.

THE TRIPOD OF INTEGRATED DEVELOPMENT

We have thus reached the end of the second part of this work, which set itself the task of identifying a number of values that could serve as beacons to guide corporate efforts. It should be stressed in conclusion that profit-seeking can no longer be considered the sole objective of business. As the just reward for responses suited to consumers' needs, profit certainly remains a necessity without which nothing else would be possible. Yet instead of forming the backbone of the organization, as it used to, it should now be viewed merely as one leg of the tripod on which the company's long-term survival rests. The other two are comprehensive awareness of the ecosystem to which the company belongs and the primacy of human over technological considerations.

In a situation of global interdependence between markets and economic circuits and of increasing interconnection between natural factors, technology, social behavior, information, education, and human resources, economic growth is no longer paramount. The society of tomorrow will only achieve development if it takes the following three imperatives into account.

- We must invent new, more comprehensive forms of economic measurement that take the growing scarcity of natural resources and environmental destruction into cost analysis.
- We must view solidarity with poorer countries as both the means to integrated development and its goal.
- We must give priority to people. Since brain power and creative potential have become the primary raw materials of our time, it is clearly by making the most of them that we can obtain new competitive advantages.

Notes

1 In a *L'Expansion* editorial, November 4–24, 1993.
2 Robert B. Tucker, *Managing the Future* (New York: G. P. Putnam and Sons, 1991).
3 Christophe Midler, *L'auto qui n'existait pas* (Paris: InterEditions, 1993).

PART III

Basing Strategies on People

15

Cultivating Systemic Thinking

In a machine, the structure of the product depends first and foremost on the strictly predetermined operation of the parts, while in a living system, the structure of the whole determines the operation of the parts.

Weiss, *Beyond Reductionism*

Taking a comprehensive view of the future requires a synthetic rather than an analytical frame of mind.

Intuition and imagination are the basis of creation.

We must change our mental models and develop new forms of intelligence.

> *Group education relying on learning processes rather than on cramming for exams should become the rule, thus sending the current ossification of education back where it belongs – in prehistoric times.*

The discovery of intelligible causes in the universe cannot be equated merely with a world of mathematical logic, economic modeling, classical physics, or statistics. It obviously includes these disciplines, but much more as well. In order to probe further, the human mind must open up to all possible manifestations of meaning that we perceive through the different forms of knowledge we possess and the various conceptual and symbolic languages contained in art, play, dreams, contemplation, silence, intuition, basic gestures of life, and even biological instinct.

THE DECLINE OF ANALYTICAL REASONING

The more we expand our knowledge, the less we can reduce the phenomena we perceive to the laws of analytical reasoning as defined by modern philosophy since Descartes. We now know that "there are things hidden behind things," as Marcel Carné put it.

Contemporary science teaches us that living systems cannot be accounted for by a mechanistic determinism, but rather reveal great complexity and unpredictability that make it impossible to understand them by applying Cartesian analysis. In order to do full justice to this complexity, we must acquire a variety of viewpoints, use alternative conceptual tools, and even enlarge the realm of human consciousness.

THE FUTURE REQUIRES CREATIVE INTUITION AND IMAGINATION

An analysis of present data informs us at best as to what might change current trends or reality. Novelty remains by definition unknown. The qualities that give rise to a dynamic attitude able to apprehend the future have nothing in common with a capacity for logical analysis; they require intuition and imagination, and even vision of the kind evinced by geniuses.

Major breakthroughs in any area invariably originate in a kind of inspiration that enables the discoverer to conceive of something beyond immediate appearances and familiar reality. A number of important inventions came about in this fashion, or as a result of dreams. The mathematician Henri Poincaré tells of how his important discoveries on

Fuchsian functions came to him "all by themselves," some during spells of insomnia, others as he was boarding a bus or strolling along a cliff's edge. He describes "those sudden flashes of inspiration, obvious signs of long prior unconscious labor; the role of this unconscious labor in mathematical invention seems incontestable to me."[1] Analysis and logical deduction come only afterwards, to verify and validate *a posteriori* a new idea.

The theory of catastrophe expounded by René Thom thus demonstrates that any system, once it has reached the end of its growth plan, sooner or later falls apart or is replaced by another – by something entirely different. In order to foretell this radically different future, we must make use of a capacity for imaginative, intuitive projection that takes us far from the beaten path. At the risk of seeming illogical or downright "zany" to those who confine themselves to extrapolating from current trends, we need more and more to cultivate abstraction in relation to immediate data in order to stimulate our capacity for creative anticipation, which is inherently "non-conformist" when it first comes to expression, but which is sometimes worth a Nobel prize.

Such an attitude presupposes that far from limiting ourselves to a single tool of analysis, we develop the art of modifying our view on a given issue by combining different approaches. We must not only make an assessment of the past, analyze the present situation, and estimate probable trends in the near future, as experts do, but also be able to imagine and undertake things that do not yet exist by turning our thoughts to more distant horizons.

A frame of mind concerned exclusively with managing current affairs is condemned to miss out on the major events of history. Who could have guessed at the turn of the century that the colossal power of the British empire would collapse, with America reaping the benefits? Who could have imagined in 1945 that Germany and Japan would turn into economic giants in just a few decades? None the less, harbingers of these developments did become detectable as the years went by. The only way to recognize them, and others in the future, is to pay careful attention to barely perceptible changes in direction that the cultural climate of the moment usually screens from our view, and to have a clear idea of desirable goals, even if for the time being they appear utopian.

FROM ANALYTICAL LOGIC TO SYSTEMIC THINKING

The belief that the world is composed of distinct, unrelated forces must be challenged. Submitting to the dictates of analytical logic leads to a specialization that fragments knowledge into separate fields. On the contrary, the future belongs to those who are able to shift from analysis to a synthetic vision, from conceptual reasoning to polysemous intelligence, and who master the skills of systemic thinking. Such a logic of the totality views all phenomena as the result of interacting networks of independent structures. It implies not only an interdisciplinary approach, but also a revolution in mental frameworks through which the individual begins to consider himself an integral part of a whole rather than an autonomous element.

In *The Fifth Discipline*, Peter Senge defines the concept of feedback as the ability of acts to reinforce each other or, conversely, to cancel each other out. This notion helps us to recognize the kinds of structures that indefinitely reproduce themselves. Senge concludes by saying, "In mastering systemic thinking, we give up the assumption that there must be an individual, or individual agent, responsible. The feedback perspective suggests that *everyone shares responsibility for problems generated by a system.*"[2]

The greater the complexity and the uncertainty in the environment's evolution, the more this comprehensive, long-term way of thinking proves to be relevant. It combines into an organic vision the multiple, often contradictory, torrents of information that pour down upon decision-makers, and thereby enables them to discover patterns, stumbling blocks, and the levers that can be used to remove them.

QUALITY OF VISION, A VISION OF QUALITY: THE JAPANESE LESSON

Exposure of the Western world to other cultures – through the mass media, travel, and international trade – has introduced us to previously unfamiliar galaxies of thought, particulary those of the East and the Far East. Now that Japan has imposed its presence as a world leader in matters of efficiency, yet without repudiating the basic elements of its ancient civilization, this is no longer the time for snickering, but rather for soul-searching – and for understanding.

A notion frequently referred to nowadays is that of "holistic vision," of systemic thinking and comprehensive perception, meaning a mode of thought that grasps all the organic interactions in a complex system instead of analyzing its various components sequentially. The Japanese are culturally more predisposed than

Westerners to thinking in holistic terms, to conceiving of phenomena in the context of integrated wholes.

Both cultures recognize the need for a deeply motivated vision to create the future, to give it serious thought. American management theoreticians distinguish between management, as it is taught in business schools, i.e. the art of running things properly, from "leadership," based on vision, which makes it possible to "do the right thing" rather than simply to "do things right."

In the field of economic planning procedures, we have seen first long-range planning methods, then participative management by objectives. The truth of the matter is that fads have come and gone in such rapid succession that very little is left in the end. The latest one seems to be anticipatory strategic vision.

The idea of creating enthusiasm by painting in glowing colors a major project able to draw on the energy of all amounts to using imagination so as to gain the broadest possible acceptance for a unifying belief in the company. The goal is no longer to take possession of employees' time and labor power, but to encourage them to commit themselves, body and soul, to the adventure the company holds out for them. This is admittedly an interesting way to instill team spirit and to stimulate initiative, but it remains inadequate.

The Japanese, in contrast, proceed quite differently and go much further. In a country lacking in natural resources, it was a matter of necessity in the postwar period to succeed in locally manufacturing products that were more profitable than those produced abroad so as to be able to export them in exchange for those products the country vitally needed. There was a collective sense of urgency in Japan about manufacturing quality products both for the home market and for export. In later years, however, the world economy began to suffer from excess production capacity in relation to demand, a situation of abundance that has profoundly redefined the issue. Thus, after giving top priority to a productivist logic based on necessity, the Japanese have come to reconsider the ultimate goal of business. In order to get their second economic wind, they know that they must be in a position to *justify* the race for production in such a way as to make people want to work and to stimulate competitive drive.

In the current Japanese outlook, a product is conceived of as a solution to the customer's problems, as a set of services that confer a positive image on the company and allow it to establish good relations with suppliers. Projecting a vision is a means for putting the company's efforts into perspective. The essential idea is that the company aims to serve the common good, first and foremost through the status it offers its employees, which fulfills the vital function of integrating them into society, then in relation to its customers, and lastly in the interests of the entire nation.

This comprehensive conception of business activity has resulted in mass production quality standards hitherto unparalleled in Western economies, where there exists traditionally a close correlation between quality and price. In contrast, the Japanese have succeeded in considerably lowering the cost of quality because they measure it both in general and precise ways. For example, they assess the effect that a decline in quality has on the entire industry chain (not only on the immediate buyer, but also on the distributor, the end user, after-sales servicing, maintenance and repairs after expiry of the guarantee, etc.). However marginal they may be, quality improvements are economically justified from this point of view, provided they are constant, lasting, and relatively inexpensive. They will thus be preferred to superficial changes in appearance or use of "noble" materials that, in light of their cost, would not sufficiently boost quality to be worth introducing.

Progress of this sort has been achieved because company members believe that by working hard, they contribute to general well-being, which stimulates and galvanizes them. The more clearly these goals of social harmony are defined and the more they are stressed, the easier it becomes to win the active support of everyone.

The difference between this system and the American approach is indeed striking. The "vision" that moves an American company goes no further than the promotion of its own products; in the last analysis, it remains limited to private, particular interests that in no way reflect an overall ideal of social well-being. This is a fundamentally individualistic outlook, whereas in the Far East (especially in Japan), an organic conception that takes the general interest into account guides company behavior.

At a time when developing a holistic point of view appears to offer the only means to apprehend the full range of interconnections that make up a complex system, it should be clear to us that the Japanese mentality opens the way to a much broader realm of awareness, and thus to a much greater strategic effectiveness.

LEARNING TO CHANGE MENTAL MODELS

Family upbringing and school education shape our image of the world and instill mental models that are difficult to modify in later life. In a rapidly changing world, where new discoveries are constantly challenging traditional assumptions, forms of education suited to the current situation are of vital importance.

Although quantum mechanics and holistic conceptions of the universe have indeed inspired many of the latest technological breakthroughs, these advanced scientific visions are still having a hard time penetrating our general way of thinking. It seems to be much more complicated to obtain the shift in outlook that they require than to conduct laboratory experiments. Old mental habits die hard, and people rarely give up age-old certainties without a fight. For even when the facts are plain to see, we still have to learn to recognize and to accept them, and above all to help the younger generation to become familiar with the key notions of tomorrow's world.

Just as technological tools, science, and social structures evolve, our view of the world must also be open to change and evolution. Nor is this merely a matter of increasing our ability to understand, since we must also be able to question the postulates implicit in our reasoning and behavior. At present, all kinds of techniques of mental dynamics are being developed to allow for ongoing, creative learning.

Our rationality is necessarily limited. The information we obtain remains incomplete and is never neutral, since it inevitably reflects the subjectivity of both the transmitter and the receiver. We can only examine a finite number of solutions; we are not in a position to choose the best possible one, but merely the most satisfying one, given the (limited) criteria that we have set for ourselves. The means condition the end and the available solutions shape our perception of problems, and thus also the way in which we deal with them. It is therefore essential to identify those features of the system that lead people to act in a particular fashion.

The ability to "shake off" acquired behavior patterns and to invent new, more appropriate ones constitutes a form of mental flexibility with which we are relatively unacquainted. In contrast, the frame of mind cultivated by Orientals in areas such as martial arts unceasingly focuses attention on the deficiencies and barriers in behavior that stem from the gap between reality and our perception of it.

In a context in which the essential resource is no longer short-term profitability, but human creativity, we should be giving absolute priority to an imaginative, sensitive form of intelligence as well as to the practical means for stimulating it. Only qualities such as imagination, creativity, and the ability to relate to others will enable modern society to adapt to change. From here on in, all efforts must be geared to developing comprehensive knowledge and to breaking down the barriers between skills and branches of learning so that people can practice the kinds of multidisciplinary approach that modern complexity demands.

Full encouragement should be given to group learning through dialogue, mutual emulation, and the strengthening of collective cohesion. In this way, new energy is constantly generated as traditional notions and dominant mental models are called into question. The goal is not simply to sharpen students' critical faculties and judgment regarding day-to-day choices, but to help them distance themselves with full lucidity from the more or less unconscious postulates that structure our thinking and reasoning processes, so that they can bring into focus the way in which thought functions under given circumstances.

NEW FORMS OF INTELLIGENCE

A number of contemporary authors advocate a diversification of the forms of intelligence. In his book *The Heart of Business*, Peter Koestenbaum lists eight different, yet complementary forms of intelligence that, in his opinion, we need to develop jointly if we are to achieve excellence in management.[3]

- logical intelligence
- somatic intelligence
- aesthetic intelligence
- transcendental intelligence
- marketing intelligence
- motivational intelligence
- the intelligence of wisdom
- team intelligence

Whatever we may think of this particular classification (several others might be imagined), the effort at reflection behind it is symptomatic of the need felt by numerous decision-makers and "front-line" people for widening their field of vision as much as possible.

In this regard, lateral thinking represents an intelligent tool (devised by Edward de Bono), the aim of which is to help people keep an all-too-present ego out of the way so that he or she can be freer to solve problems without being weighed down by thinking habits or personality traits. This does not mean neutralizing your feelings or personality, but merely bringing into bold relief the subterranean influence that they exert over thoughts you would like to consider objectively. The goal is to eliminate any emotional blocks that interfere with personal life or work.

Everyone sees a picture of reality that is distorted by the prism of upbringing, past experience, ideology, and personal prejudice. It ought to be possible, if not to take off these glasses, at least to relativize their importance by becoming aware of their existence. One possible method would involve systematically trying on other pairs of glasses in succession with a wide variety of colored lenses.[4]

- *White lenses*, which focus on pure facts and figures. The thinker attempts to be as impartial as a computer.
- *Red lenses*, which stimulate emotions and which give free rein to intuitions and hunches. The thinker has no need to justify herself.
- *Black lenses*, which foster systematic criticism. The thinker emphasizes everything that goes wrong.
- *Yellow lenses*, which encourage positive thinking and optimism. The thinker stakes everything on her wildest dreams.
- *Green lenses*, which reinforce originality. The thinker seeks all possible alternatives to the current situation or to obvious solutions.
- *Blue lenses*, which correspond to calmness and to rational control over thought. The thinker unifies her different previous visions, confident that she is holding the conductor's baton.

INCULCATING THE IMPORTANCE OF CREATIVITY

Greater flexibility, receptiveness, and broad-mindedness will undoubtedly prove to be the decisive leadership qualities of tomorrow. In Japan, for example, management training consists above all of teaching managers how to develop their potential, motivate their collaborators, foster creativity, and encourage innovation. This practical science clearly has no relation to the sterile cramming for exams or the obsessive pursuit of degrees typical of French education. In Germany, in-company apprenticeship programs are much more common than in France and produce far better results. Frenchman Daniel Goeudevert, former number two at Volkswagen, explained his rapid rise in German business by saying, "I built my career through successive apprenticeships, which would have been impossible in France, where once you have reached a certain level, the elite school mafia shuts everyone else out. In the French business world, looking for work with nothing but a measly degree in literature would have meant starting out with a serious handicap."[5]

In France, we dissipate energy and block upward mobility through a rigid, absurd screening system which functions in the opposite way to how it should. Instead of developing a wide variety of talent, it limits it; instead of accepting diverse modes of selection, it imposes a single pattern; instead of promoting a dynamic system of ongoing learning, it determines the entire career of people on the basis of their diplomas, although on-the-job experience and new skills acquired in practice are at least as important. In other words, the educational system does everything to discourage those human qualities that have primary importance in today's world, especially those required for ongoing training.

Henry Mintzberg has demonstrated how a procedural approach to management that is not centered on people "has managers walking on their heads." He says:

> Management has become a technical exercise based essentially on an analytical approach, whereas defining company strategy is above all a matter of synthesis. As for me, I believe first and foremost in the acquisition of knowledge and personal development; in the power of intuition; in an experimental, incremental approach similar to what you might encounter in learning; in listening to others with respect; in a word, I believe in being human.[6]

That we have created "human resource departments" does not stem merely from a desire to give a more catchy name to our classical personnel departments; it is also the sign that repetitive, routine tasks, whether in management or production, are steadily losing ground to innovative activities. The leading one is learning to optimize the creative potential of one's staff.

To do so, companies must take organizational steps so that their employees learn together in practice how to combine their skills and make full use of their capabilities. Sharing the assets that different disciplines offer in a dynamic of collective synergy is the best way to promote the growth of individuals, both in their careers and in the rest of their existence, and if need be, to help them change careers entirely. Integrated into the working day and vocational training programs, such ongoing, concrete, experimental, multidisciplinary group learning is now a necessity both for the modern economy and for the harmonious participation of individuals in society. Unfortunately, it stands diametrically opposed to the ossified, overly theoretical, individualistic, routine model that characterizes the vast machine designed to educate people – and to exclude people – to which French society so zealously clings.

In a rapidly evolving world, constantly updating knowledge is vital. This involves much more than providing occasional rehabilitation courses to employees; it is in fact a daily, unending requirement for the individual as well as for the company. In Japan, continuing education is an integral part of a person's career; it is considered an essential precondition for a person to be operational in an economy in which the primary raw material is information. In the United States, a good many companies have incorporated training programs into the working day. Not surprisingly, new graduates tend to be attracted to such companies. Training is also part of certain major corporations' information and internal communication policies (for example, Xerox trains 100,000 persons in three years). Some Japanese companies spend up to 8 percent of their total sales on training. For their overseas subsidiaries, this arrangement also offers a means to inculcate managers and other employees with the spirit and values of the parent company. When Nissan opened a subsidiary in the United States, its American training budget came to the equivalent of the subsidiary's entire payroll ($63 million).

All this underscores how important "intangible" investments are becoming. Things could hardly be otherwise in a world in which human beings and their creative capacities are the primary source of competitive advantage.

Notes

1 This quotation was taken from Arthur Koestler's seminal work on the conscious and unconscious processes at work in scientific discovery, creative

originality, and comic inspiration entitled *Le Cri d'Archimède* (Paris: Calmann-Lévy, 1965).

2 Peter Senge, *The Fifth Discipline* (New York: Doubleday-Currency, 1990), p. 78.

3 Peter Koestenbaum, *The Heart of the Business* (Dallas: Say Book Publishing Co., 1987).

4 This idea is derived from the hat example presented by Edward de Bono in his book *Thinking Hat* (Boston: Little Brown, 1986).

5 Quoted from an interview with *L'Expansion*, December 6–19, 1992.

6 Henry Mintzberg, "Pourquoi les managers marchent sur la tête," *La Tribune Desfossés*, June 9, 1993.

16

The Intangible as a Source of Meaning and Coherence

Men's hope is their reason for living and for dying.

André Malraux, *Les Conquérants*

Paying great attention to one's image, to communication, and responding to a need for meaning may not appear on a balance sheet, but they will determine tomorrow's results.

We must develop trust and human relations with as much care as they do in Asia.

Thought, desire, and action must be connected to each other.

Development of the company depends on the development of its natural, cultural, and human environment.

In a world of global interdependence, economic success is no longer merely a matter of accurate calculations and rigorous management. It also involves taking new parameters into account that are not directly quantifiable. The importance of non-material elements like training, service quality, or the ability to innovate have become fundamental. As part of a company's living capital, they should not be underestimated in any assessment of future performance potential.

QUANTITATIVE PERFORMANCE IS NO LONGER ENOUGH

To evaluate the strength of an economy or a company, it is no longer enough to enumerate the usual material and financial factors such as production capacity, market share, annual sales, or number of employees. In a world in which production techniques must constantly be adjusted to new conditions and everyone realizes how short-lived a technological lead can be, only qualitative criteria make a real difference. They are what enables a company to build up assets for the future and to respond better than others to the challenge of change. This challenge includes changing markets, which calls for adaptability, brand credibility, consumer trust, and efficient organization, both of the company and of its external networks. Yet it also involves changing values in society.

RESPONDING TO THE NEED FOR MEANING

The urban universe of industrial consumption has exuded a standardized way of life that deprives individuals of the ability to relate to their environment on a natural, daily basis. As information and trade become increasingly global in scope, everyone experiences growing uniformity and, as a consequence, a certain loss of meaning. Motivation declines, and people instinctively turn their backs on anything designed to have the same effect on a vast, "average" public.

In this changing situation, women play a decisive role. Representing 85 percent of all consumers, they have managed little by little to impose their way of consuming. They attempt to be sensible, and they often act upon feeling and devotion to their families. The rising influence of women has ushered in the "soft" era. We are currently moving toward a society that has reflex reactions of protection rather than conquest, one that tends to return to basics while rejecting whatever seems superfluous.

The fundamental contemporary desire is to choose one's existence, to control one's own life, and not, as in the past, to accumulate goods and to have unlimited access to services. People now want to establish a personal relationship with their surroundings and they unconsciously seek meaning in the daily use of objects. Product differentiation will depend in the future on whether or not the product can increase practical well-being, not on the quantity of services provided.

The intangible sometimes makes the difference, even to the extent of more than compensating for an initial quality handicap that an apparently low-technology product suffers. Thus, some laboratories have had unusual success in marketing relatively unsophisticated formulas, while focusing their advertising on attributes like the decision not to do animal testing, the use of natural ingredients, or recyclable packaging. Such products enjoy great popularity because they respond to the deep ethical expectations of a consumer convinced that by buying them, she is supporting a worthy goal and taking part in her own small way in a humanitarian, ecological movement.

Top-quality brands can participate in this phenomenon. Thus, Lancôme won new respect when it donated part of the proceeds from its luxury perfume sales to the legendary advocate of the poor and the homeless, the religious figure abbé Pierre, at Christmas time.

AUTHENTIC COMMUNICATION: IMPERATIVE NUMBER ONE

Nowadays, you have to "make things happen." Getting through to an audience (especially a TV audience) has become something of a fine art that requires making use of familiar images that represent reality. In the avalanche of audiovisual messages that pours down on a daily basis, the goal is to send out a signal that can retain not only the attention, but also the interest of those receiving it. Communication thus includes the influence exerted over people's minds in order to persuade them that the product being offered is up to date, important, and authentic.

Any collective organization, particularly a business, must devise a powerful, continuous, comprehensive, highly structured communication strategy: powerful because it must reach the entire potential market; continuous because the organization must constantly offer reminders of its presence and maintain a positive image in keeping with recent cultural trends; comprehensive because all aspects of a product (advertising, brand name, distribution, public relations, and even the "profile" of its creators) must be conceived of as messages; and highly structured because all possible means of communication must be considered (the press, audiovisual, posters, public performances, etc.) so that the organization can choose the right one at the right time.

In a sense, the reality and influence of any collective structure now depend on its media presence and its ability to put across a positive image, since our mass media society ultimately revolves around one big game of interacting scenarios. The spectator decides on what will happen next, whereas the actor must regularly change roles and costumes in order to stay in the limelight.

However, we have gone too far in the use of disguises, so much so that even children now know that you can't judge by appearances. It takes little time for myths to lose their power. Today's public expects "the real thing." Although communicators still retain the right to fabricate images, they must do so with a sense of humor, with meaning that reflects the true nature of the company, and with unambiguous authenticity.

STRESSING THE QUALITY OF HUMAN RELATIONS

Knowing how to listen to others, to make new proposals, and to communicate have become essential qualities. The first step is to perceive intelligently even the least conspicuous desires of customers. As André-Yves Portnoff puts it, "The modern service industry sees both the intelligence of the solutions offered and the intelligence of the customer's problems. The first challenge is thus understanding the customer, and even helping him formulate his wishes and his problems. Quality and psychological finesse in the communication between customer and supplier thus prove to be strategic components of business success."[1]

Certain aggressive sales techniques stand in the way of relations based on quality, respect, and understanding for the customer. By proceeding in such a fashion, salesmen often jeopardize future sales just for the sake of short-term success. For example, some suppliers manage to fob off vast quantities of goods on distributors, without taking into account the huge inventories that the latter are likely to be stuck with and that will convince them to stop dealing with the same suppliers. Furthermore, quality relations necessarily take time to establish. Constant changes in marketing teams lead to a weakening of collective memory and a certain ambiguity as to the part each participant should play. The same thing holds true with design staff, for example in advertising. A team's ability to take action, to learn together, and to go beyond previous achievements should be seen as one of those non-quantifiable assets that in the long run make all the difference.

THE COST OF TRUST

To Asians, a feeling for human relations is fundamental and "relationship capital" is the first thing to be cultivated. In the West, the cultural legacy of the notion of original sin leads us to consider man as basically evil, or at least untrustworthy. This explains why our legal systems contain abundant precautions, laid out in minute detail, for safeguarding our interests. We all contribute to creating a climate of mutual distrust.

In Asia, however, trust comes more spontaneously. In the philosophy of Mencius, a disciple of Confucius, the "fundamental goodness" of man has central status. Personal relations are valued, the underlying assumption being that they can only enhance business contacts and facilitate trade. This is the origin of a series of unwritten mutual obligations. The Japanese notion of *giri*, or "give and take," assures that people who know each other make commitments on their honor. To the extent that relations are based on trust and personal integrity, there is no need for contracts. When someone gives his word, others know that he means it. Everything rests on trust.

In Western culture, it ultimately matters little with whom you are dealing, since the legal framework has primary importance. Function is everything, and individuals are interchangeable. Thus, in the United States, it is by no means uncommon for a newly hired executive to settle into his office on his first morning and to begin putting on presentations in the afternoon. In Japan, a new manager is compelled to go through a long process of getting familiar with the context, penetrating concentric circles one by one; and once he has made himself known, he must at all costs avoid "rocking the boat," which would upset the delicate balance achieved and condemn him to start over from scratch.

All these intangible factors that we would do well to take seriously are generally hidden from view by the "Wall Street syndrome," i.e. mindless focus on quantitative parameters to the exclusion of all else. These intangibles that determine the quality of an organization include, among other things, the image of its president. Figures of the stature of Akio Morita or Lindsay Owen-Jones, who have solid media presence in their respective countries, give their companies a "profile" that raise their value. The same thing goes for networks of alliances that the company may build. When the Sisheido corporation signs a contract with a renowned university like Harvard for the funding of a number of research programs, the high-status students who benefit from this aid will clearly contribute to enhancing the company's public image. This is hardly a matter of facts and figures; it comes down to a "moral investment" that adds to the company's influence and prestige.

The point is not, however, to conceive the analysis of intangible assets as a replacement for traditional business analyses, but rather as an additional tool for investigating the positive forces of tomorrow.

THE VARIOUS GRIDS PROPOSED FOR MEASURING INTANGIBLE FACTORS

As we have seen, the era of undifferentiated mass consumption is over. The following points are what can still make a difference in this area.

1 The ability to provide varied, modular, personalized products for different life-styles.
2 The ability to monitor and to anticipate the evolution of customer tastes and needs.

3 The intrinsic quality of the product and the enjoyment that using it brings.
4 The quality and the breadth of the range of services provided in connection with the product.
5 The power of attraction of the product and the image of the company. Remember that it takes years or even decades to build a corporate image and to impose a product line (e.g. Chanel No. 5, Hermès, Mercedes); it takes much less time for them to lose their luster.
6 Communication that is both intelligent and suited to the target (using various advertising media and direct marketing).
7 Close collaboration with distributors as a means of obtaining immediate feedback on sales, and a climate of trust from end to end of the chain (i.e. right up to the consumer).

Regarding company organization, the key points are the following.

1 Consistency throughout the information system and all systems contributing to decision-making. The flow of information must be managed in strategic terms. This is not simply a computer problem (involving complete, accessible databases, etc.); the goal is to set up a form of organization that fosters optimal circulation of information throughout the company's value chain, including its distribution circuit and consumers.
2 A capacity for innovation, including research and development potential and the company's portfolio of patents pending.
3 First-rate technical know-how in production.
4 Superior management ability based on a system that organizes work through decentralization, autonomous units, and reducing bureaucracy.
5 Turning human resources to account by making full use of the specific skills of each employee and by instituting effective ongoing training programs.
6 An open, dynamic corporate culture involving both a clearly defined identity and a broad capacity for integrating people. A company's prestige and influence (which depend on subjective factors like the aura surrounding a name or the profile of its leaders) condition its ability to attract first-class talent.
7 A shared vision of goals. In the last analysis, the organization's quality and dynamism depend on its ability to get its members

to share both a clear vision of goals and the philosophy that is to guide future company development. A positive atmosphere at work, motivation, commitment, and enthusiasm cannot be obtained without an overall strategy that constantly fosters creative energy and team spirit.

The consulting firm M et A divides these different areas up into four basic categories: legal aspects (contracts, licences, patents, copyrights, confidentiality); image and communication (reputation, brand image, renown, customer loyalty, networks, databases); know-how embedded in the value chain (the know-how of employees, suppliers, and distributors, as well as the quality of design staff and management); and cultural factors (capacity for learning and changing, attachment to quality and customer service).

The relative weight of each intangible resource has been analyzed and the number of years required to replenish it has been evaluated.[2] It would seem that the most important ones are also those that it takes longest to reconstitute. Company reputation heads the list (more than 10 years), followed by brand image (6 years) and employee know-how (4.5 years). Cultural factors come in fourth place (2 years' replenishment time), ahead of networks (3.5 years) and equipment. Next come databases (2 years required to replace them), which in the past few years have taken on greater importance than supplier know-how, in spite of the 3 years needed to reconstitute it, and then distributor know-how (1.5 years).

In another study entitled "Identifying and analyzing intangible assets," Frank Petersens and Johan Bjurström have drawn up a chart representing the position of a company in light of its tangible and intangible assets (see figure 21.4 on p. 242).[3]

CONNECTING THOUGHT, DESIRE, AND ACTION

Productivity does not guarantee competitive strength; a company also needs quality and innovation (both in technical and marketing activities), qualities that depend above all on the behavior, spirit of initiative, and imagination of all its members, whatever their function. This leads us to the inescapable conclusion that the main component in excellence is the organizational and human factor. People are what can make a difference and achieve the combination of the three fundamental elements that constitute the famous Greek triangle.

- Logos: thought, reflection, anticipation of causes.
- Epithumia: desire in all its forms, mobilization, and appropriation.
- Erga: implementation, i.e. action and accomplishment.

PROSPECTIVE VISION GIVES CONTENT AND MEANING TO COLLECTIVE MOBILIZATION

According to Michel Godet, the three angles of the Greek triangle can be interpreted today, regarding business management, as prospective reflection, strategic will, and collective mobilization (figure 16.1).[4]

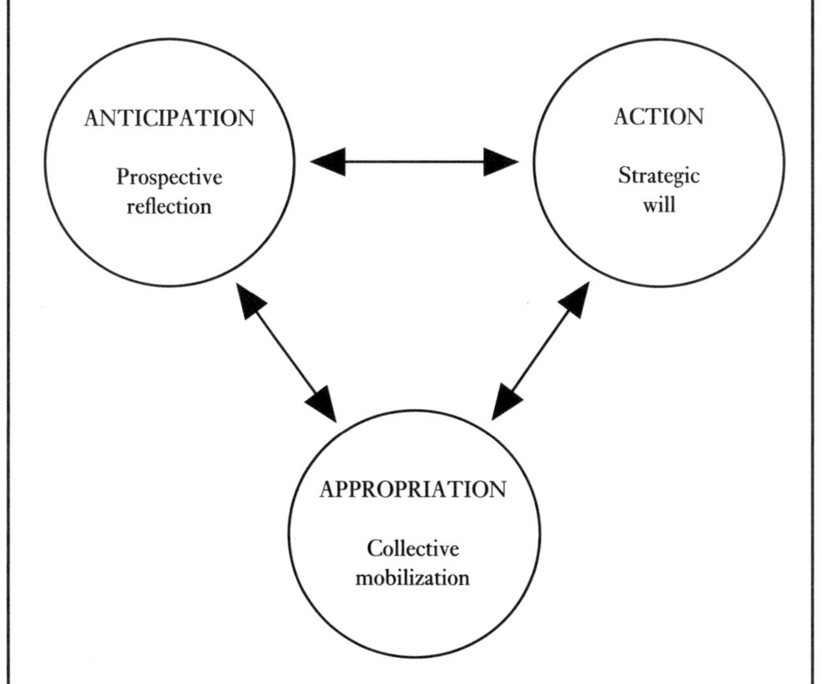

Figure 16.1 The Greek triangle (*Source*: Michel Godet, *From Anticipation to Action: A Handbook of Strategic Prospectives*, UNESCO, 1994)

OVERALL COHERENCE

Beyond the listing of intangible as well as tangible factors in success, we should constantly view the life of a company from the perspective of its relation to the environment in which it operates, whether the environment is human, cultural, or natural. What we are faced with is in fact a continuous series of interactions that only a systemic outlook can elucidate. Ultimately, what really matters is what people feel in a given situation. For example, a company quite clearly enhances its image by applying policies that show a concern for nature or by recycling the paper it uses. Although we now know that the plastic packaging industry contributes less to pollution than the paper industry does (witness the pollution of the Baltic Sea), we must none the less be aware of both objective factors and subjective conceptions (which are sometimes erroneous owing to the mental pollution that media hype sometimes produces). Thus, the company of tomorrow will have three "instrument panels": one for tangible assets, another for intangible assets, and yet another for its overall integration into its psychosocial environment.

Notes

1 André-Yves Portnoff, "La révolution de l'intelligence ou la libération du bon sens," working paper written for the review *Science et Technologie*, 1992.
2 See the tables presented by Richard Hall in his article, "The strategic analysis of intangible resources," *Strategic Management Journal*, 1992, vol. 13, pp. 135–44.
3 Frank Petersens and Johan Bjurström, "Identifying and analyzing intangible assets."
4 Michel Godet, in *Symposium de Prospective et Strategie*, Brazil, May 1989.

17

The New Hope Placed in Corporations

The corporation dominates society today the way the church dominated it in the past. This historical reality gives companies a major moral responsibility.

Peter Koestenbaum, *The Heart of Business*

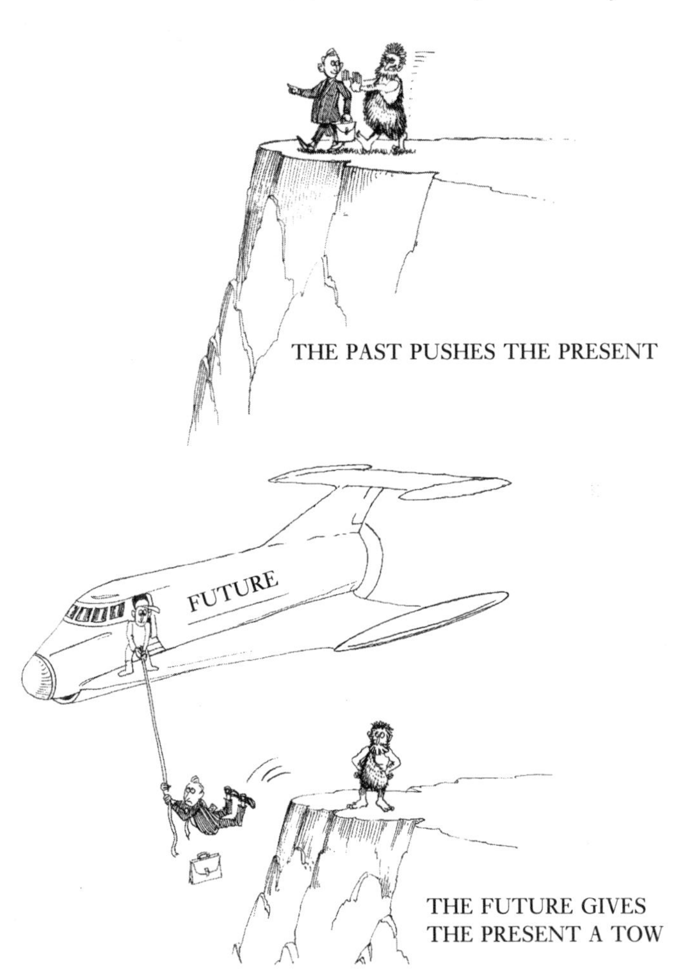

> *The corporation now has a broader mission to accomplish than before, since it is the institution that best represents the aspirations of people today. It connects them to society, embodies social consensus, and accepts change.*

> *The company of tomorrow will be a collective project worked out in common.*

The company of today looks increasingly like a surrogate for the family, the village, the government, and even the church. This is particularly true of large corporations, with their brand name, banner, and "company culture." Some of them end up assuming ethical or social missions that go well beyond mere business interests. Common in the United States and Japan, this phenomenon also manifests itself in Europe. For instance, the Swiss company Migros attempts to embody a moral rigor that reflects the need for standards and normative structures no longer provided by the present-day social context. Companies can develop a new, semi-religious fervor that draws its strength from the feeling of taking part in a vast international movement.

NEW PATTERNS OF DEVELOPMENT ARE EXPANDING THE CORPORATION'S MISSION

Far from being mere noble, disinterested gestures, such ethical concerns also affect a company's ability to motivate its personnel. A rapid survey of a number of "secondary problems" that have cropped up in addition to the usual goals of manufacturing, distribution, and sales should highlight for us the new obligations of today's businesses.

- A company can no longer remain indifferent to its influence on the environment and the localities in which its works are established. It will be held responsible for any pollution or disturbances to nature, the landscape, and residential areas.
- The company must take an interest in the means of transportation available to its employees and in their travel time to and from work, while arranging schedules that are well suited to working conditions. At a time when the majority of women have jobs, if the company fixes schedules with no regard for the family responsibilities (taking care of the children, picking them up from school, etc.) that its employees have to shoulder, it will be faced with rising lateness and absenteeism.

- In the present economic situation, the company has a crucial function to fulfill, that of creating jobs and furthering upward social mobility.
- In a society in which the school and university curricula of today often turn out to be obsolete tomorrow, the company can become the motor force behind ongoing education, providing training programs, refresher courses, and possibilities for retraining.
- Lastly, the company must develop cultural and leisure policies for its employees, perhaps even patronizing the arts or local sports teams.

Thus, in addition to the need for profits, companies must strive for new goals that in fact exist independently of each other. Business has a vital interest in clearly identifying them, for they all have economic implications.

A COMPANY WITHOUT IDEALS IS LIKE A SAILOR WITHOUT A MAP

At present, a company can no longer define its reason for being in mere economic and financial terms. It must also be able to formulate and put forward ideals that establish a clear-cut image for the company with a strong ethical flavor to it. One of the fundamental aspects of running a business involves making corporate ideals clear to all. The shift from *having* to *being* does not, of course, obviate the need for working every day and carrying out one's tasks. The point is to find a means to rally people and the appropriate way to convey this idea to all those concerned.

In this respect, companies that can give a clear, galvanizing answer to the question "Why work?" will acquire a substantial competitive advantage over those that can't, not only on the qualitative level, but also as regards quantitative business results. To be able to do so, they must come up with both the appropriate, sound formulations that are expected of them and creative measures that generate enjoyment, a new-found meaning in work, and that extra bit of "soul" without which no one has ever been able to move mountains.

A COMMUNITY IN SEARCH OF A SYSTEM OF ETHICS

Today, the quest for ethics is taking form and developing in the business world. Companies now represent the only collective cells left that can still capture people's imagination and tap their energy. This can be explained by their unquestionable organizing power and, by their flexibility, which enables them to move forward in step with technological and social change.

As Alvin Toffler has put it, "To begin with, any decent society must generate a feeling of community. Community offsets loneliness. It gives people a vitally necessary sense of belonging."[1] This need for belonging, satisfied in the past by family and village solidarity, is now focused on companies. Why? First of all because they represent the only organized collective entities that still seem to hold together, and, secondly, because the model they embody is located at the very point at which numerous present-day aspirations intersect.

The free-enterprise model is now accepted virtually throughout the world, both as a basic economic unit and as a means to organize social relations. For this reason, a company offers not only a local context (a job in a given environment) for integrating individuals into a community, but also an international framework, since the company is present everywhere and is connected to global technological, trade, and financial networks. Moreover, this dual identity (both local and global) reflects the values of today. It also embodies the ruling consensus in our society, which rests on three major points: utilitarian pragmatism, contractually based social relations, and the primacy of scientific knowledge and technical rationality.

In these areas, the business enterprise is the only institution that is constantly forced to accept and promote change in order to adapt, to foster creative dynamism, and to equip people to achieve it. Located at the point where the need for roots and the need for mobility and creative change meet, companies are the main force able to propose an orientation of our society.

THE DYNAMICS OF INTELLIGENT ORGANIZATIONS

In the new role distribution just mentioned, a company must obviously function above all as an organic whole with a community vocation and whose fundamental purpose is to help its members (as well as its machines and supply and distribution circuits) to keep pace with social, technical, and mental changes occurring. It thus has no other choice than to conceive of itself – and to operate – as a team of people learning together how to perfect themselves and to deal with the unending challenge of changing conditions. This is not only the business of researchers and decision-makers; the entire company must function in creative synergy.

A FEW VANGUARD ATTITUDES FOR DOING MORE THAN JUST SURVIVING

The average life expectancy of major corporations is 40 years (20–25 percent of them have been around since 1945, and 50 percent only since 1970). What might be called "vanguard" companies are those that are eager to learn more than merely how to manage previous achievements. In a continuous process of change and transformation, we have the choice between three possible attitudes.

- passive: we take change as it comes
- reactive: we wait before reacting
- prospective:
  pre-active: we prepare for anticipated change
  proactive: we act in order to hasten the change desired

Such constant leveraging of capacities for comprehension and innovation has various prerequisites.

1 You must grasp the nature of the forces of change at work so that you can survive in a chaotic period and stay on the right track.
2 Make the right moves for maintaining company prosperity, which will in turn contribute to overall development. To do so, you have to attract open-minded, creative individuals rather than conservatives.
3 You have to fulfill your responsibility for solidarity, which will also make it easier to get through this critical period.
4 People must be motivated by love, by the attention they receive, not by coercion and constraint. Sane companies attract sane individuals who design sane systems.
5 You should not hesitate to challenge the mental models that condition our perceptions by posing the right questions:
   What is our company's calling?
   What is its essence, its core, its *raison d'être?*
   What are its fundamental values?

What are its main assets and competencies?
What competitive advantage makes us different?
What steps should we be taking?

6 You have to build a shared prospective vision of the collective mission the company has fixed for itself in relation to its environment. In that way, everyone knows where they are going and can rally around a common project.

ASKING THE RIGHT QUESTIONS

By regularly conducting such analyses in a group context, in order to obtain broad support for the objectives defined, a company radically alters its collective frame of mind. Shared reflection on the long-term fate of the firm is both a continuous exercise in clear-thinking on whatever is not being done right, which has obvious benefits for those in charge, and a means to focus energy on specific, convergent goals.

The corporation of tomorrow will be a collective project worked out in common. In this new conception, which stresses the human side of economic performance and overall competitive drive, a company's success goes hand in hand with the development of the skills and the personal balance of its members. Why further the self-realization of employees? To quote Peter Senge, "People with high levels of personal mastery are more committed. They take more initiative. They have a broader and deeper sense of responsibility in their work. They learn faster. For all these reasons, a great many organizations espouse a commitment to fostering personal growth among their employees because they believe it will make the organization stronger."[2] Grasping the full implications of Edgar Morin's phrase, "The corporation produces the people who produce the corporation," companies concerned with staying in business must transform their organizational structures from instruments of control into tools that serve the individuals working for them.

Notes

1 Alvin Toffler, *The Third Wave* (New York: William Morrow and Company, 1980).
2 Peter Senge, *The Fifth Discipline* (New York: Doubleday-Currency, 1990), p. 143.

18

Organizations in the Service of People

Like jobs, people are becoming less interchangeable. Refusing to be considered as such, they have an acute awareness of their ethnic, religious, occupational, sexual, subcultural, and individual specificity.

Alvin Toffler, *The Third Wave*

The organization must grant everyone the freedom to get passionately involved with his or her work.

Stimulating creativity requires delegation, decentralization, and destruction of internal barriers.

A Japanese observer, Mr Matsushita, issued the following highly revealing judgment on the Western world. He predicted:

> We are going to win and the industrialized West is going to lose. There is nothing you can do about it, because you carry the seeds of your own defeat inside you. Your organizations are Tayloristic. You are convinced that you run your companies well by distinguishing between bosses on the one hand and underlings on the other hand, i.e. those who think and those who screw things in. To you, management is the art of transmitting the directors' ideas to the workers. To us, management is the art of mobilizing and bringing together the intelligence of all in the service of the company.

This outlook undoubtedly stems from an age-old culture which taught the Japanese that planting and harvesting rice takes the cooperation of everyone.

FROM MECHANICAL STRUCTURES TO ORGANIC STRUCTURES

In an economy increasingly centered on non-material functions and compelled to integrate complex ranges of data, the secret of managing such complexity lies entirely in the art and science of organization. The real problem is devising a way to weld into a dynamic whole all the circuits of information, creation, decision-making, and production. For this reason, it can be said that tomorrow's know-how will consist primarily in the organization of know-how.

Living systems, i.e. infinitely complex and precise organisms shaped by nature, provide unsurpassable models of a capacity for manifold reactions, for continual, spontaneous adjustments, and for inventive, sustained growth processes. They show us how to ensure the survival and unity of an organism faced with multiple demands and challenges.

When there is general agreement on goals, values, and playing rules, the mutual trust that thereby emerges serves to connect the different cells, just as occurs in living organisms. This cohesion, based on acknowledgment of the diversity of information and situations, is the ultimate goal toward which the economic cells of our time should be striving. To be sure, a comparison proves nothing in and of itself, and in any case, it would be impossible for us to imitate nature completely. Yet the fact remains that mechanistic logic, with its fractioning, repetition, and quantitative uniformity, is doomed by the prevailing conditions of our environment.

Complexity and constant change now make it imperative to develop a systemic perspective based on qualitative, organic logic. It should be added that such a perspective is the only one able to use mechanical processes as mere tools among others, an ability that mechanistic logic lacks.

In practice, this means that a company must be viewed as a living whole made up of interdependent, mutual relations, both internally and in its dealings with its environment. As far as organizational structure is concerned, rigid separation between functions must be replaced by a system that leverages all human potential existing in the company, the top priority in business today. In other words, the synergy between various objectives requires constant cooperation between people.

Up until now, companies were structured according to a mechanistic model; whatever desire they had to improve social, organizational, and environmental conditions was justified only by an "enlightened" concern for greater efficiency. Yet we now know that people are the main source of competitive advantage. It follows that their overall well-being – in private life as well as at work – contributes to the common good. Companies must thus foster the self-realization of its members without regard for immediate results, in the hope that people who feel fulfilled will subsequently have a positive influence on those around them.

ENCOURAGING EVERYONE TO APPROPRIATE THEIR OWN WORK

At present, an efficient system is one that allows everyone to contribute to the general interest by using the full range of his or her intelligence. This idea stands in stark opposition to a system based on resting on past accomplishments, passively following procedures, and strictly applying rules and directives. Paying attention to human factors and respecting individuals represent, in the last analysis, a potent force for management.

The need, for the individual, to invest his energy in the tasks he has to accomplish is a basic requirement in man's psychic make-up. The more we encourage this kind of appropriation, through which people feel responsible for what they do and go about it conscientiously (a conscientious attitude implies that the worker voluntarily, and thus freely, endorses the purpose of his work), the more we contribute to their mental and physical health as well as to their dynamism. Health should not be equated with the absence of illness; it should in fact be seen as the possiblity for a person to map out her own route, using all her faculties, in harmony with the community to which she belongs.

This opportunity for free, total involvement in one's work is the basis for true motivation; it is what leads employees to support the company's goals and to work creatively. Ideas, initiative, and creativity are forthcoming only from people who feel free, willing, and convinced that their jobs are worth doing.

WORK NEVER BOILS DOWN TO MERE EXECUTION

The Tayloristic way of thinking that still dominates the organization of work in the Western world turns out to be in direct contradiction to the idea of mobilizing employees' intelligence. Not only does it prohibit initiative and kill off creative resources; it also renders it impossible for a broad view of the whole and for team spirit to emerge from the multiple separate jobs on the organization chart – something that Cartesian brains love to refine endlessly.

Experience has more than demonstrated that defining job content as precisely as possible represents a rather futile exercise that fails to produce a single qualitative improvement.

To quote Dr P. Davezies:

> Whenever work is carried out, the worker executing it must deal with all the sources of variability that are not accounted for in his job description: variability regarding process, materials used, wear-and-tear of tools, changes in the material and human environment, and lastly the ups and downs in his own condition.
>
> Even if thinking on work has become ossified, practice never repeats itself exactly in the same way. Work thus never boils down to mere execution. It always entails a certain amount of interpretation, in the sense that directives must be interpreted, just as one would do in reading a musical score.[1]

Edgar Morin has pointed out in turn that in any structure, proper functioning presupposes "stubborn, underground resistance to the rules," since whenever workers launch a go-slow strike, i.e. obey the rules in literal fashion, operations soon grind to a halt. It should thus be recognized that employees never do exactly what is asked of them, and that a company's dynamic functioning depends precisely on this discrepancy.

FROM SUPERVISION TO TRUST

In one of the L'Oréal factories located in Orléans, we were able to verify how effective it can be to emphasize human potential. Previously, the employees did slipshod, careless work, generally seemed uncooperative, and absenteeism was rife. So we decided to introduce radically different methods of work. Each worker was given responsibility, small work groups were formed, production lines were rearranged in "U" patterns, and employees redesigned their own equipment.

All these reforms diminished the need for control and made possible a rise in efficiency we had never dreamt of. Two years after this reorganization, with no intervening change in personnel, the plant showed the highest productivity of any of the firm's factories. The lesson to be drawn is that by trusting front-line people and by guiding them toward assuming personal responsibility for their jobs, companies can achieve spectacular results.

The classic hierarchical model must be abandoned and replaced by one that allows everybody to take responsibility for himself and to play an active part in the development of the whole. A spirit of initiative, responsibility, and creative innovation can only take root when top management agrees to empower autonomous units.

STIMULATING THE ORGANIZATION'S CREATIVE POTENTIAL

Even though management and creation are contradictory terms (on the one hand, consensus, control, certainty, status quo; on the other hand, instinct, uncertainty, freedom, irreverence), it is still legitimate to speak of "managing" the creative phenomenon. What this means is inducing people to outdo themselves. Several general principles make it possible to stimulate the creative potential of the organization.

- Setting up a structure for fostering creative work (an artist must have the possibility to concentrate on his creative efforts instead of on managing his work).
- Fixing general directions rather than specific goals, while stressing that "the best way to anticipate the future is by inventing it."
- Encouraging thinking that goes against the current. Everyone should feel free to express their ideas without being penalized for them.

- Creating a favorable environment for differing aspirations and penchants (through office layout, the naming of specific rooms, etc.).
- Leaving room for emotion in the system.
- Encouraging staff members to assume responsibilities and to organize their own time. At IBM Germany, 450 managers work at home; at Apple, a number of designers only go to their offices once or twice a week.

To develop a team's creativity, a company should not underestimate the importance of making adequate time and equipment available. A group will accomplish a great deal if it is connected to the rest of the company, equipped with appropriate computer systems, and provided all its members can increase their knowledge. Results will be even more impressive if the team operates in a pleasant setting that fosters interaction and participation. It will be able to learn from its successes and failures as long as it can retain roughly the same personnel for at least three, four, or five years in a row. (All too many young people believe that if they don't get a promotion every 18 months, their honor is on the line.)

A BRIEF GUIDE TO INNOVATION

Innovation involves a wide variety of requirements, including the following.

- being in a constant state of alert
- being attentive to new ideas
- staying in tune with customers' wishes
- being at the junction of several technical areas
- facilitating the flow of information
- organizing symbiosis between research labs, universities, and business
- managing technological and marketing resources
- stimulating commitment throughout the company
- developing different forms of talent

People with diverse skills and character traits should be chosen for participation in innovative teams. For coming up with ideas, *lookouts* who pay constant attention to signals from their surroundings will help to enlarge a team's field of perception; *experts* will offer it their skills; and *inventors* will bring their creative ability to bear. For formulating and spreading ideas, *speakers* are essential. Lastly, for putting ideas into practice, *project coordinators* will be selected on the basis of their ability for commitment. Aimed primarily at stimulating and coordinating initiatives, their efforts will require unfailing support from a group of *achievers* who have no qualms about creative destruction and transgressing norms.

BREAKING DOWN BARRIERS TO PAVE THE WAY FOR INNOVATION

The dynamics of creativity are at the heart of today's competitive challenges. For this reason, organizational configuration and management choices must reflect them.

To simplify things, we might say that in times past, companies were structured around three main functions: a production function (factories, products), a sales function (customers), and an administrative, financial function (administration and accounting). Then, to adjust to heightened competition and the emergence of global markets, they became more sophisticated, adding three new functions to the initial organization: research and development, upstream from production; marketing, upstream from sales; and human resources.

It should be admitted that in order to achieve satisfactory performance levels in the first three functions, companies have above all to gain total control over the regular, repetitive, routine aspect of work. Conversely, the essential tasks assigned to R&D, human resource departments, and marketing include the ability to anticipate and take hold of emerging trends, make technological breakthroughs, establish beachheads in new markets, and take human factors into account.

This explains why such departments attempt to get the most out of the creative potential of their members. The tendency has clearly been to separate these different functions along the lines of the scientific management of labor devised by Taylor and to organize them much in the same way that production is organized, aiming at total quality, zero faults, etc., and hiring engineers expressly trained for particular specialties.

In the meantime, however, we have entered into the world of the intangible, in which "everything is related to everything," one where the key notions have become cohabitation inside the company and coordination of different teams. Each of the various jobs and functions in the firm calls for its own forms of behavior and psychology which must now adjust to each other instead of being in perpetual conflict.

This is why it is vital for the more routine functions in production or administration (even if such concepts are currently evolving under the influence of modern information processing) to find a *modus vivendi* with those functions that demand creativity above all, and that thus imply constantly new, unique situations.

The only way to reduce conflicts is to help everyone to understand and to assimilate the requirements and specifics of the area in which they work. For this reason, companies have the obligation to break down barriers between functions and to conceive of the organization as an integrated whole; otherwise, they will continue to waste resources and energy.

DELEGATING ROUTINES IN ORDER TO MAKE THEM MORE CREATIVE

A starry-eyed, eccentric inventor would probably exert a disruptive influence if he were to work on the assembly line, whereas his behavior would meet with greater acceptance in a design department. The point is that there are different mindsets that should be fostered according to the nature of the job to be performed; no value judgment is implied. Just as human beings have both an *animus* (masculine) and an *anima* (feminine), there are creative aspects to ordinary production work and routine aspects to research.

According to the findings of an American study on time devoted to routine and creative tasks in companies, American managers split their time about equally between the two kinds of work in 1980 (with creative work slightly in the lead at 52 percent), whereas eight years later, things had gotten seriously out of balance. They were now spending a mere 37 percent of their time on creative work; routine functions had climbed to 63 percent of their time.[2]

This study reveals that managers in fact spend a considerable amount of time carrying out routine tasks. These tasks may involve dispatching and handling written materials, in which case the ratio of routine to creativity is about average (65 as opposed to 35 percent), getting access to information (70 as opposed to 30 percent), or, worst of all, problem solving (74 as opposed to 26 percent).

The way in which we judge performances strongly affects the areas on which people concentrate. Unfortunately, as a result of the "Wall Street syndrome," which leads some executives to focus their attention on short-term financial results, most employees concern themselves almost exclusively with routine, reactive work. They have the distinct impression that they will be judged primarily for their short-term contribution to sales and profit margins, in other words, to quantitative growth, even if that compels them to neglect long-range goals, to forget about updating their knowledge, and to dismiss "intangible" forms of evaluation. To put it bluntly, they follow the line of least resistance, since it is obviously easier to do familiar things over and over again than to learn something new. Managers are also afraid to delegate too much responsibility to their staff by training them. They don't seem to realize that delegation is an outstanding way of galvanizing energy, since it brings deep emotional satisfaction to those empowered.

A large proportion of these routine tasks, which seem so reassuring because they can be tangibly measured, could be left to subordinates, thereby freeing up executives' time for more creative work. It has been estimated that managers could delegate 70 percent of their routine work (for example, 70 percent of the 63 percent figure mentioned above) and that, in the United States, this failure to delegate occasioned an aggregate loss of $315 billion in 1988.

In many cases, we tend to give priority to urgent work, rather than to truly important work, i.e. delegatable rather than creative tasks. What is urgent yet relatively unimportant should, however, be delegated, and the same holds true for what is important but not urgent. Only tasks that are both urgent and important deserve a manager's immediate attention.

Managing the future means achieving a better balance between creative and routine work. The organization chart of some bold American companies already includes positions for a creative development director and a routine operations director. The existence of these two positions – with equal status in the company hierarchy – indicates to what extent creativity and day-to-day operations take on the same importance in the minds of contemporary American managers.

DECENTRALIZING AS A WAY TO ENCOURAGE CREATIVITY AT ALL LEVELS

Decisions must be made faster and faster, and increasingly in collaboration with front-line operations. They thus depend on a circuit of autonomous, yet interrelated agents. In reality, effective decision-making requires that the decision-maker be relieved of a number of other functions.

The by now famous principle of subsidiarity, a concept invented by the Catholic Church and subsequently adopted by the European Community, involves delegating responsibility to the lowest possible level at which it can be assumed. In such a system, every participant is recognized as an essential part of the whole. When applied to the individuals who work in a company, this principle helps them to achieve a sense of fulfillment, because it attests to the trust placed in them and to the attention and respect they enjoy.

Delegation and decentralization offer a response both to the desire of individuals for autonomy and to the challenges of complexity. In the long run, specialization and centralization lead down a bureaucratic dead-end. As Michel Crozier put it, only man has the flexibility required for dealing with and reducing complexity.

In the age of computers, decentralized organization has become a necessity. Distributed computing is pointless unless the power to use one's own intelligence is also properly distributed. Today's communication technologies imply decentralized, network organizations and freedom of expression, without which they are simply useless. Computer-programmed machines lend themselves to production in small units, small batches, and small companies; they signal the demise of mass production, gigantic factories, and monotonous drudgery. The time is now ripe for customized products, and thus for the service industry.

Decentralization implies clear definitions of everyone's role on the basis of his or her particular skills. It also encourages personal responsibility and motivation. The definition of goals and of the means made available to each employee requires constant exchanges of information and consultation, with the ability to listen and to engage in dialogue taking on as much importance as the aptitude for team learning. Everyone has part of the solution, but only the group as a whole can organize and exploit the creative resources of its members in the pursuit of shared objectives.

Such a process inevitably meets with resistance. We have all been trained for segmented tasks, and working on a project that makes simultaneous use of all the available human qualities runs counter to that education, however much everyone acknowledges in theory the need for such reform.

In order to win support for company goals, managers must also become versed in the art of communicating and spreading information as widely as possible. The days in which information retention offered the illusion of power are over; at present, it is hardly conceivable to give orders without indicating the how and the why of what is being requested. This approach is the only one that enables every collaborator to understand the role he plays in the company and to sense the utility of his work. In other words, meaning enhances efficiency. This also underscores the need for breaking down barriers between functions. The greater the communication flow, the less each department or sub-unit will be tempted to consider itself the hub of company activity, and the more "cross-pollination" will occur between the job experience of different people.

Creating this kind of coherence between particular activities through a system of clear information and freely accepted involvement of all is only possible to the extent that everyone finds reasons for living and deep fulfillment in his work situation. The aim of any company should be to put into practice an ethical vision regarding the personal development of each and every one of its members. Such an undertaking is the precondition for individual creativity and the overall well-being of the company.

Notes

1 Dr P. Davezies, "De l'épreuve à l'expérience du travail," in a Symposium on Labor Medicine at the Hôpitaux de Lyon in 1991.
2 Richard W. Larson and David J. Zimmey, *White Collar Shuffle: Who Does What in Today's Work Place* (New York: Amacom, 1990).

19

The Art of Leadership: Involving Everyone in Creative Work

Managers fight fires. In contrast, leaders light fires.

Perry Pascarella and Mark A. Frohman,
The Purpose-driven Organization[1]

A leader is no longer the captain of the ship, but its architect.

The solitary hero is an outdated myth; what is required today are team leaders who know how to rally everyone around a powerful vision.

A great leader can be recognized by his ability to criticize his own behavior.

In those euphoric years of quantitative growth and market conquest, the dominant image of what constituted a company director was the semi-autocratic boss whose power derived from superior skill, which he had acquired at a precise point in time, and whose value could be measured by the annual increase in sales. His methodical, rigorous way of running the company was based on clear planning of quantitative objectives and an organization chart that spelled out a strict division of labor. Authoritarian, austere, and rigid inside the company, Machiavellian in dealing with the outside world, the director's management style was based on power relations as well as on his urge to assert unquestionable supremacy.

THE CHANGING NATURE OF MANAGEMENT

This portrait is rather outdated, even if it remains partially accurate to this day. Obviously, getting tangible results and knowing how to win out in a world of power relations continue to be fundamental capabilities for any company president. Yet in the 1990s, competitive edge no longer depends solely on such forms of "excellence." The model of the effective manager is changing.

Although management still is the art of running a business with competence, authority, shrewdness, and efficiency, these qualities no longer guarantee success in and of themselves. In an unstable, perpetually shifting period, a leader must also be a kind of prophet who dares take more risks than in the past.

We can no longer reason as though personal and technical skills can be acquired once and for all. In a world that is changing faster and faster, such skills depend on an ability to digest an unending flow of information and to become familiar with new developments. Market intelligence and the ability to evince the required qualities call for constant updating of strategies. Whereas tried-and-tested marketing formulas used to suffice, flexibility, inventiveness, and a feeling for human relations are now required.

Lastly, to the extent that running a business depends above all on innovation and contact with customers, establishing close relations with trading partners, sub-contractors, and customers themselves is of the utmost importance, as is smooth coordination with all activities situated upstream from production. The goal is thus to be able to weld into a single movement the entire chain of contributors, which can only be accomplished by involving all of them in the dynamics of participation, i.e. by decentralizing responsibility. Flying alone is sheer suicide.

A NEW IMAGE FOR THE DECISION-MAKER

Both economic and sociological evolution have generated new authority models. Just as the extension of education and the increase in individual autonomy have whittled down traditional attachment to and respect for major public institutions, they have weakened dominant business structures.

In and of itself, the *de jure* or *de facto* power of a company president no longer gives him the effective authority he needs in order to "mobilize his troops." To do so, he must first "win his stripes" by gaining the confidence and support of his personnel. If he fails in this endeavor, he will obtain little more than passive obedience on the part of the majority, or the devotion of sycophants acting out of ambition or fear of losing their jobs. Thus, functional power, however essential it may be, must be reinforced by a personal form of authority that subordinates perceive as a source of inspiration and an impetus to collective action. The task facing a top manager consists not only in running things properly, but also in creating positive feeling in his immediate environment.

The great men of yesteryear, those solitary heroes always ready to go it alone, are a dying species. Today's leaders are those able to build and to maintain strong relations of mutual trust at all levels of the company. They generate practical solidarity in the service of common goals and weld their organization into a sort of organic whole. Given the current business context and the dominant values today, credibility and effective action are the qualities that count the most; technical competence has become secondary.

FROM CAPTAIN TO ARCHITECT

In these troubled times, a popular ideal is the one embodied by the former Purchasing Director at General Motors who moved on to Volkswagen, Mr Lopez de Arriortua. He conveys the image of the tough manager who never lets anyone push him around. This man, who succeeded in getting all his collaborators to wear their watches on their right wrists so that they could be reminded at every instant just how much the world has changed, symbolizes the efficiency of short-term solutions and high-powered management style.

Today's corporate leaders would do better, however, to take their inspiration from impresarios, whose function requires skillfully managing the creative efforts of individuals.[2] At times, they play the part of coaches, since creativity is not a management process, but a learning process. At other times, they have to raise their voices, because creativity demands iron discipline from everyone involved. In any case, the behavior of impresarios shows that a "boss" must alternate between an admiring and a demanding attitude. His contribution is to bring about the convergence of promising ideas and activities.

In Western society, leaders are heroes that enjoy the confidence of a group of people who have much less confidence in their colleagues and themselves. They are supposed to make all key decisions and galvanize their troops.

This is a simplistic conception, however, for a leader's task is both more subtle and more important than this. He or she is not the ship's captain, nor its navigator, helmsman, nor even its first mate. He or she is the draftsman who draws up the ship's blueprints, ultimately a much more vital contribution. A wise decision to tack will have little positive effect if the ship's design makes it unmaneuverable.

Corporate leaders are now in charge of building organizations in which all members can continue to extend their ability to grasp complexity, clarify their thinking, and expand their mental models.

FOLLOWING THE MUSIC OR DIRECTING IT? LESSONS FROM THE CONDUCTOR OF AN ORCHESTRA

Peter Drucker has compared the contemporary corporation to a baseball team (each player concerns himself with his own performance, without paying attention to what the others are doing), to a football team (where the goal is both to react flexibly to the opposing team's movements and to position yourself according to who has the ball, the latter being, however, the only one who touches it, while the other players wait their turn), to a string quartet (whose perfect ensemble playing takes years of practice together), or to a symphony orchestra, in which Drucker sees a model for the organization of the future. "Several dozen, even several hundred highly qualified people play together," he explains. "And yet there is only one boss, the conductor, without any intermediate management level between him and his musicians. The accent or predominant role is given to some member or other of the team based on circumstances, the tasks to be accomplished, or the specialty of each player, not on the basis of his rank on team."[3] And although there exists a "first violinist," his job is not to command the second.

The value of these observations is not limited to the aptness of the metaphor employed, for conductors have a great deal to teach us. Benjamin Zander, conductor at the Boston Philharmonic, likes to tell the story of the recording of a symphony in four movements under the direction of one of his colleagues. Three movements could be recorded in a single day, but since it was by this time 7 p.m., it was decided to postpone recording of the last movement until a later date. Unfortunately, the conductor was to die in the intervening period. So impressive was his interpretation of the first three movements that the members of the orchestra were sufficiently moved to decide to record the last one without a conductor as a final homage to him. The listener, however, cannot fail to notice just how much the fourth movement is lacking in the lyricism that can be so clearly heard in the preceding movements. Suddenly, the music, now no longer conducted, but merely followed, somehow sounds lifeless. What is missing is the stimulation, the vision, that only a conductor can bring.

Thus, the conductor – the only participant who produces no sound – is none the less the one who determines the outcome and the success of the whole. Depending on the tempos he indicates, he achieves widely differing interpretations that affect the listener's mood in as many different ways.

Benjamin Zander also tells how he stimulated the playing of one of his pupils, a Taiwanese instrumentalist who was ranked 68th out of 70, who felt like an anonymous stranger in the midst of a symphony orchestra. Zander took this pupil aside to inform him, despite his protests, that he had to get A grades from then on. Stimulated by this challenge, the pupil began quite suddenly to play much better than before.

A TRUE LEADER IS CONCERNED FIRST AND FOREMOST WITH INSPIRING CREATIVITY

Like the conductor of an orchestra, a company director must channel group energy, while drawing out the creativity of all team members. Creativity is not something that can be decreed; it can only be released. It depends on the intensity of the personal commitment and interest felt by participants. As is well known, a slight touch of passion can produce genius. If this flame is not kindled in the hearts and minds of individuals, they are unlikely to give more of themselves than is usual. Creation can thus be traced back to a deep-going motivation that derives from belief in the object of one's efforts. Developing such profound support for the goals of a company is no minor art.

Usually, corporate leaders attempt to motivate their personnel by means of impassioned speeches, bonus or profit-sharing schemes, or seminars during which top management's plans are explained to lower-level managers. This approach, however, only serves to impose from the top down a set of goals that are supposed to inspire those who will have to achieve them. Such leaders also seem to be unaware that the primary source of motivation comes from within each participant.

A GALVANIZING VISION REQUIRES THE INVOLVEMENT OF EVERYONE

There is nothing clumsier and more ineffectual than imposing a "prefabricated" vision. If, however, you involve as many people as possible in working one out, they will consider it their own project and the expression of their own values. In addition, by making use of the specific skills of everyone in collectively defining group objectives, you reinforce the self-confidence of participants and increase the energy that they will invest in the project.

The most urgent task for a company leader is thus to instill a clear view of the company's goals and values into its members and to be able to transform it into a truly shared vision. As Peter Senge points out,

> A vision is truly shared when you and I have a similar picture and are committed to one another having it, not just each of us, individually, having it. When people truly share a vision they are connected, bound together by a common aspiration. Personal visions derive their power from an individual's deep caring for the vision. Shared visions derive their power from a common caring. In fact, we have come to believe that one of the reasons people seek to build shared visions is their desire to be connected in an important undertaking.[4]

This common compelling vision is the basis for a consensus on the answers to be given to six essential questions.

1 What is the company's "calling," i.e. its specific identity and its position in the economic and social environment, as indicated in particular by its own history and culture?
2 What are the implications of this calling and what is the central project, i.e. the overall objective that emerges from it and that the company plans to reach in the coming five or 10 years?
3 What are the core values that the company will have to defend and embody in this connection, and what corporate image does this convey to the general public?
4 What strategy should be implemented in order to fulfill these requirements, i.e. what intermediate objectives are to be achieved and what is the value chain to be set up?
5 What are the rules of internal organization that this strategy implies (procedures, organization of work, information and training circuits, etc.)?
6 What is the mission (or mission contract) established for every participant, every independent team, or every department in the company and the degree of initiative and creativity expected of the different elements in the value chain?

The role of a corporate club in this effort is first and foremost to put forward a general framework, an overall aim to be pursued. It is up to the club to work out the ship's blueprints and to chart the sailing course, i.e. to select the core ideas, values, and strategic thrust that are to serve as an inspiration to the work of the entire organization. In a sense, the corporate club could be said to vouch for the creative tension that must be maintained between the conditions of daily reality and the distant horizon to be reached. Its task is thus central to stimulating the whole group's dynamics and carrying out the adjustments required by circumstances.

A shared vision is not an immutable "treasure-hunting map." It must constantly be modified to reflect changes that occur on the economic, social, political, and cultural fronts. As Bent Namias wrote, "Far from being a definitive conclusion, vision is an element in a continual process that involves orienting the organization according to realities that emerge from the surrounding world. This can best be accomplished in the framework of systematic organization of knowledge acquisition."[5]

THE SMART COMPANY: AN ORGANIZATION BASED ON SHARED LEARNING

Working out a compelling, shared vision implies that all those concerned should feel that they are involved in the information flow that underlies the vision and allows for ongoing adjustments in it. The whole company should be conceived of as a "comprehensive brain" selecting and assimilating data necessary for the organism to function properly.

The world is far too complex to be apprehended by one or two individuals. A corporation cannot be reduced to a handful of thinkers on the one hand and a mass of order-takers on the other. It must achieve constant synergy of skills and viewpoints. Fueling creative collective energy means regularly reaping the benefits of the potential for intelligence that every collaborator possesses and that can express itself when certain tasks are assigned to him or her. This also implies that everyone should have the organization's shared vision clearly in mind and feel responsible for its overall attainment, not merely for carrying out his or her own limited tasks. A worker is more likely to put his heart into his work if those who give him a stone to cut tell him that he is participating in the construction of a cathedral rather than saying that the general aim is to build a wall, or merely to cut a stone. In such a case, he goes from drudgery to artistry in full awareness of his role and capabilities.

By placing its trust in its members and bringing them together on the basis of clear playing rules, the community can tap the resources of all and make use of their imagination and intelligence in pursuit of results that are far greater than those that each individual could achieve alone.

The isolated individual acts in keeping with the conception he has of his situation, a conception reflecting ideas and habits that he can hardly shake off. He has a hard time accepting alternative points of view or of imagining two rival working hypotheses. In contrast, a collective structure becomes a genuine "thinking machine" when it accepts a multitude of viewpoints and encourages expression of and comparison between differing conceptions of a given reality.

Yet in order to bring about this alchemy of intelligence based on a collective effort at reflection, a company must develop the art of dialogue. According to David Bohm, dialogue implies "the free flow of meaning," in which, contrary to what obtains in discussion, no one attempts to win. And everyone comes out ahead.

Once this conception of the smart organization has been accepted and applied, the company no longer functions as an aggregate of more or less coordinated individual jobs, but as a network of constant interconnections. It is this network structure that enables the group's internal energy to circulate freely and to enrich everyone's work in an interactive fashion. Tearing down barriers based on narrowly defined functions and competition between individuals is a way to allow everyone to benefit from what the overall group has to offer – and to obtain greater motivation as a result. When the general meaning underlying individual contributions receives adequate emphasis and appears clearly to everyone, the members of a company feel linked to one another in a common undertaking.

FROM MERE ENROLLMENT TO ACTIVE CO-RESPONSIBILITY

Enrollment is a matter of freely choosing to support a vision, whereas the word commitment "describes a state of being not only enrolled but feeling full responsible for making the vision happen."[6]

In their paper, "Developing citizenship for active organization," presented at the Ecology and Work Conference in Pittsburg on June 6, 1991, William Pasmore, Gary Frank, and Bob Rehm put forward a diagram showing a progression by stages, running from the conventional system of control exercised over the employee to the commitment of the volunteer, the conformity of the disciple, and finally the co-creation of the citizen.

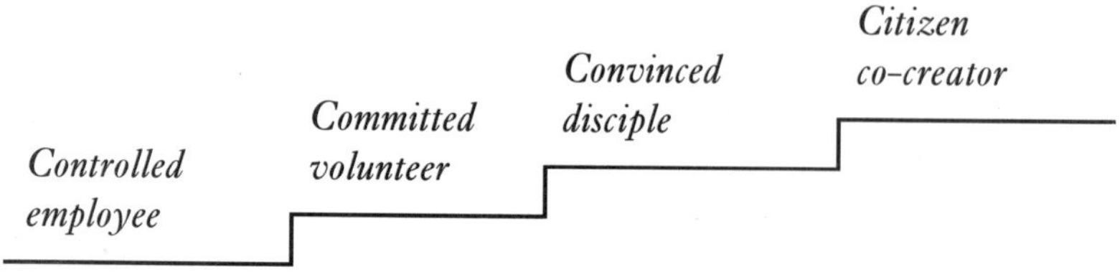

Controlled employee	*Committed volunteer*	*Convinced disciple*	*Citizen co-creator*
Employee	Member	Partner	Co-owner
Contractual	Volunteer	Disciple	Citizen
Need for security	Social needs	Personal esteem	Self-realization
Passive	Involved	Cooperative	Collaborative
My job	Team	Unit	Organization

Uniform	Receive information	Share information	Create information
Low value	Acceptance of values	Values in harmony	Value-oriented
No power	Little power	Empowerment	Full authority
Opinions not taken into account	Opinions not highly regarded	Opinions listened to	Opinions preponderant
A single skill	Multiple skills	Multiple functions	Overall skill
Days	Months	Years	Decades
Working hours	Based on skills	Salaried employee	Involved

REAL LEADERSHIP IS THE ABILITY TO QUESTION ONE'S OWN BEHAVIOR

Whereas in the bureaucratic model, everything rests on the infallibility of the leader "who sees all and knows all," and who is the only one able to make proper decisions, in the model based on synergy, consensus, and networking, the leader must at all costs avoid shutting him or herself up in an ivory tower. By opening his or her mind to the broadest possible horizons, he or she can sense at every moment what adjustments are required for dealing with a changing reality. Such an approach presupposes both humility and a pragmatic, constructive attitude that remains wary of *a priori* judgments.

FAREWELL TO PAST SUCCESS

Freedom of thought, the freedom to march to the beat of a different drum, is the basis for creative activity. A system that values only success, while discouraging any risk-taking, encourages people to follow in the footsteps of respected elders, to copy outmoded success stories instead of inventing those of tomorrow. The problem, however, is that trying to repeat the accomplishments of the past is a sure-fire way to fail and to condemn a company to stagnation.

In such a value system, it will not even do any good to try to change the people involved, since the constraints of the system are still there in force, reproducing the same paralyzing effect.

A solution currently in vogue is to call in consultants – specialists unacquainted with the way the company's frame of reference operates and thus in a better position to discover its flaws. Yet this new trend also reflects the relative inability of companies to train their managers to question their own behavior.

Peter Drucker pointed out in this connection that "if you occupy a position for over ten years, you start defending your own past and run the risk of doing damage." He then went on to say that France's "debacle" in World War II could be explained in part by the notable age difference between the French and German officer casts.[7]

Indeed, the majority of France's generals in 1940, being mentally prepared to win World War I all over again, did offer a clear, if pitiful, confirmation of this observation. Yet prior examples in military history reveal a much wiser attitude. In the army of the former Austro-Hungarian empire, a special decoration was awarded to those officers who achieved victory by disobeying the orders of the high command. And going even further back, as far as the Mongol invasions, the great conqueror Genghis Khan guarded against the harmful influence of entrenched habits of success in an even more expeditious manner. If one of his generals won two brilliant victories in a row, he was removed from his position for the next battle!

MANAGEMENT IN THE SERVICE OF PEOPLE

Thus, the logic of new forms of value – quality, intelligence, creativity – lead to an entirely different conception of a company director's role, which now primarily involves coordinating a team's efforts. This is why a leader must give top priority to integrating individuals and in general to human concerns.

It is for him to embody the collective vision, to affirm the identity of the company and the ethical values it conveys both to its members and to public opinion. The leader must also ensure that real synergy takes place inside the company, considering it the only means to optimize the skills of all collaborators and rally them around a long-term shared project. Lastly, he has to maintain the coherence of communication between the various partners and give a powerful impulse to group learning, which is so vital in the present period of technological upheaval.

Needless to say, all of this presupposes a personal "profile" defined essentially by a broad humanistic background, a multidisciplinary outlook, and a willingness to listen to others, to grant them time, and to share decision-making responsibility with them in a desire to maintain internal cohesion.

Seen in this light, the art of management is to avoid getting caught up in the day-to-day running of the company, which should be delegated as much as it can be, so as to be able to focus entirely on major objectives and on keeping things on the right track. To remain alert in this way to means and ends, a corporate leader must rigorously organize his or her time, which will enable him or her to concentrate on essentials, to be on the lookout for innovation, to do regular prospecting on changing market conditions, to pass on vital information, and to keep his or her troops constantly mobilized.

These goals can only be reached if we realize that people are the primary source of competitive advantage. In the future, companies will above all have to solve the problem of making people as "comfortable" as possible. Up until now, energy was channeled into meeting the requirements of the organization. Tomorrow, it will be necessary to foster human fulfillment if companies are to have a strong creative impact.

Notes

1 San Francisco: Jossey-Bass, 1989.
2 See John Sculley with John A. Byrne, *Odyssey: from Pepsi to Apple* (New York: Harper and Row, 1987).
3 Interview in *L'Expansion*, June 1993.
4 Peter Senge, *The Fifth Discipline* (New York: Doubleday-Currency, 1990), p. 206.
5 Bent Namias, "Visionary leadership – how to re-vision the future," *The Futurist*, September–October 1992.
6 Senge, *The Fifth Discipline*, p. 218.
7 In an interview with *L'Expansion*, June 1993.

20

Waking the Sleeping Giant

The world is a sea whose shore is our heart.

Chinese proverb

With its greater focus, the East will continually astound us once it starts moving.

Let's get our focus back! Wisdom and action are not mutually exclusive; they reinforce each other.

The human brain is a giant that is not exploited to full capacity.

We need to take a longer view of things, instead of being obsessed with apparent emergencies.

Every leader is a role model.

We must move from work as constraint to profession as fulfillment.

Man is the ultimate solution and justification.

When China awakens, prophesied Alain Peyrefitte, the world will shake. That day has come. Isolation behind the Great Wall is a thing of the past. The recent opening of China has forcibly thrust it into the modern world, where it has no intention of playing second fiddle.

WESTERN EXPANSION, EASTERN CONCENTRATION

The Chinese have not substantially changed over the past 3,000 years. They invented schooling, gun powder, and the compass, inventions which others (mere barbarians, to boot!) then made use of to invade China.

If China is called the Empire of the Middle, there is good reason for it: the country is organized in centripetal fashion. Chinese houses are inwardly focused. In the middle, there is the ancestors' temple. Needless to say, China is the center of the world, and Peking the center of China. Between the four temples of Heaven, Earth, the Sun and the Moon, we find Tienanmen Square, in the center of which is located the tribune from which the master of the Empire of the Middle expresses himself.

The emperor is thus the only one allowed to occupy the center and to set this gigantic nation in motion, to the outermost bounds of the Empire. When the aged Deng Xiao-ping decided to break the country out of the straightjacket that half a century of Maoism had imposed on it, the entire overseas Chinese community mobilized to place its financial power in the service of the country's economic reconstruction. They were manifestly unperturbed by the regime's continued insistence on appending the word "socialist" to the market economy it was actively developing.

In contrast, the West is characterized primarily by centrifugal forces, which explains why it must constantly negotiate agreements like the GATT or the ALENA in order to consolidate its unstable cohesion. Historically, what occurred is that the West set out to conquer virgin lands, sending its missionaries everywhere possible, only after a long winter in the arts and sciences. In essence, it constructed its form of modernity in flagrant contradiction to its own cultural foundations. Western society achieved levels of pragmatism and efficiency that made it the envy of Asia (since strength and power naturally command respect). Only later did the Asians realize that at our "vital center," there was nothing.

The Chinese were subjected to Western "gunboat diplomacy," an experience that was to traumatize them for a long time. They realized that in order to safeguard their independence, they had to borrow arms from the West, without, however, letting themselves be subjugated in the process.[1] Thus, when the Chinese apply and improve upon formulas developed abroad, they treat them as an additional floor to their cultural edifice that does not change its basic structure.[2]

WHEN THE SON OF HEAVEN FAILS TO REFORM THE EARTH

It was during the reign of Ts'ai-Tien (who lived from 1871 to 1908) that China failed its attempted modernization and experienced the humiliation of foreign occupation. Having ascended the throne at the age of four, he vainly considered himself the emperor of the "Great Renewal" and had to accept, against his wishes, the name of Kuang Hsü, or "Glorious Succession." Victor Segalen, who presented the emperor in his book *Le Fils du Ciel*, has his character express in poetic terms the centripetal problematic: "It is time to get out of Us, and Us out of the Palace. Are we our slave forever? And see. And discover!"[3]

Segalen's emperor tries to follow the suggestions of his adviser K'ang Yu-wei, who adroitly justifies the reforms he is proposing in the following terms: "it was subsequently necessary to get back from other peoples what they had stolen from us . . . In doing so, he observed that the most beautiful speeches expressed in new phrases what we already knew; that they had promulgated nothing that our authors had not previously written; and that taking occasional inspiration from their sayings was a sure way of going back to the ancestors and prolonging the immutable series."

Kuang-Hsü ultimately failed in this endeavor as a result of the hostility of the mandarins and his aunt, the Empress Dowager Tseu-Hi. His adviser was decapitated, and he himself was shut up in the Palace of the South Island, which no bridge connected to the mainland. Thus cut off from the world, the deposed monarch was even stripped of any responsibility over his own daily existence. A double was brought in, blamed for everything, and beaten in his stead.

The emperor, whom tradition concealed from the sight of his subjects since time immemorial because of his function, that of reflecting celestial harmony on Earth, thus found himself doubly isolated. He was gnawed by philosophical questions that have a strangely contemporary ring to them: "Who will answer for the emptiness of my self? Who will clad me in a solid coat of armor? Who will teach me who I am?"

REUNIFYING WISDOM AND ACTION

It may just be possible to explain the enormous difference between the Oriental frame of mind and ours by positing that the two cultures do not rely on the same cerebral hemisphere. Asians may make greater use of the right hemisphere, the seat of imagination, emotion, dreams, colors, while Westerners tend to specialize in the left hemisphere, which makes possible logic, language, numbers, analysis, and order. As a result, Westerners can be thought to have trouble grasping the deeper meaning of existence; in fact, they are just as unconcerned with this problem as the Chinese, dominated by the right hemisphere, were with conquering the world.

To excel in the present-day sphere of physical matter and production, Asians have no other choice than to stimulate the long-dormant left part of their cerebral functions. Thus awakens the sleeping giant, which turns out to be no other than the reunified brain.

Profoundly shaped by the legacy of Ancient Greece, our civilization contrasts the deep thinking of the wise man who withdraws from the world with the vanity of the man of action, who is compelled to draw his sword and cut the Gordian knot. In the West, the individual is not even asked "How?" or "Why?" Confucianism, however, believes, as Bob Aubrey points out, that wisdom and action reinforce each other and enrich each other. The Master thus taught the following: "Only when one knows where one stands can one be calm. Only when one is calm can one achieve tranquility. Only after achieving tranquility can one have a peaceful rest. Only after achieving peaceful rest can one deliberate. Only when one can deliberate can one reach one's goals."[4]

The essential difference between the two cultures can be seen in their relationship to time. In the Far East, although time may vanish, the future will always be mastered in the long run. Only independent views of contingencies and momentary circumstances are capable of rallying people. The ultimately rather superficial introduction of Marxist ideology in China did not alter the basic nature of the Chinese soul. The Communists achieved victory above all because they raised high the banner of national resistance to the Japanese invasion. Confucianism survived the Cultural Revolution (which was unleashed by the "emperor" himself and never really threatened Chinese unity). The reason is that it is not so much a religion as a social morality and a humanistic philosophy, even a philosophy of education that stresses harmony between individual acts and the general good.

KICKING THE URGENCY HABIT

For an Eastern mind schooled in the values of duration, our focus on the short term is indeed surprising. "One of the ironies of management in the West is that the higher up a manager is located in the company hierarchy, the more concerned he is with short-term results," notes Masaaki Imai.[5] And it seems clear that our horizon has been getting even closer in range since history started accelerating a few years ago. Whether we blame the mass media, over-abundant information, the melting away of ideologies, or the tyranny of three-year payback, the fact remains that we are all now living in a climate of emergency and short-term goals. The problem is compounded by the end of the Communist regimes, which has taken us out of "a threatening world that was none the less essentially free of real risk, and thrust us into a world devoid of any major threats, but fraught with risk," as Alain Minc has pointed out.[6] We have the impression that we must respond immediately to these new risks under the pressure of events, a pressure that leaves us no time to step back and examine the problems in depth. No one puts forward utopias today. There are too many gaps to be closed.

The irony of our epoch is that actual threats do exist, perhaps more than ever before – but they can only be apprehended in a long-term perspective. I am referring to pollution, the hole in the ozone layer, the international drug trade, the decline of education, increasing debasement of products, and fanatical cost-cutting. No emergency measure will ever be able to combat them. No national government will either.

Rapid social and economic transformations in our immediate environment have generated turbulence and risk situations that call for quick strategic decisions. In this respect, "what is disturbing in this turbulence," states Peter Drucker, "is not so much the turbulence itself as the fact that we react with the logic of yesterday." As long as we hear the alarm signals only faintly and the mental models to which we remain unconsciously attached prevent us from discerning the real causes of the impasses we have reached, we will be incapable of making strategic choices.

Michel Joras has rightly pointed out that "we have moved from a fixed society in which thought (philosophy, religion, culture) and production (mechanical, organized, modeled, repetitive) were experienced as separate areas to a shifting, uncertain society. In such a society, business and political leaders must give up the idea of managing order on the basis of models and adopt management controlled by chance."[7]

Decision-makers have a frantic pace of life that is hardly conducive to serious thinking on essentials, on long-range perspectives. They thus tend to forget that at their level of power, there are no real emergencies, just people in a hurry, and that in today's world, there is no stress, just stress-producing thought.

A LEADER IS ABOVE ALL A ROLE MODEL

Anyone who is a prisoner of constant emergency as well as of habits and social obligations rarely finds the time to reflect on the meaning of his or her life. If such a person has business leadership functions, however, he or she must raise this kind of question in relation to the meaning, the mission, and the philosophy of the company he or she is in charge of. The first step is to build a personal vision and an ethical code that guides his or her own life, then to call upon his or her colleagues to do the same thing inside the company.

Leaders should be role models, and their private life should offer a positive example of balance. Yet what do today's leaders generally follow more closely: the ups and downs in their bank account or the direction in which their relationship to their children is heading? And are all those leaders who so readily introduce sweeping transformations in their companies also prepared to change themselves? There is clearly nothing more important, when the goal is to encourage others to question their own behavior, than to go about this task yourself honestly and diligently. The quality of management cannot be separated from the quality of the manager, which ultimately boils down to the quality of his or her life.

Returning to the most ancient Indian traditions (after all, there exists a "yoga of disinterested action"), Dr Jagdish Parikh has demonstrated that for a manager, mastery, located "between involvement and detachment," is fueled by his personal development, and that in reaching the highest step, that of spiritual development, he discovers inner joy as well.[8]

It often takes a heart attack, a child with a drug problem, or deep grief in the family for the essential questions to come to the surface. Thus, Vice-President Al Gore became committed to ecology and was prompted to write a book following a tragic car accident of which his son was a victim. The same kind of experience often turns out to have played an important part in the rougher life of many artists. Bruised by existence, they experience an unusually high number of flashes from their right brain hemispheres that open the way to a different state of consciousness.

Be that as it may, we all have two eyes that give us stereoscopic vision, two ears for hearing acutely, and two hands for transforming matter. To understand the world around us, we also have minds and hearts, reason and intuition; everyone is gifted with a brain divided into left and right hemispheres. If the right one fails to develop, how will we ever be able to see things in perspective?

Whenever dramatic life events force our hearts to open up, our consciousness receives unsuspected new riches, and we realize that, previously, we were in turn like sleeping giants.

There is a Chinese ideogram signifying both heart and mind. Western dualism would be quite incapable simply of grasping this concept. This strikingly shows how difficult it is for our civilization to conceive of a harmonious world.

WORK IS NOT OFTEN ENOUGH A FULFILLING EXPERIENCE

If today's leaders, who are subjected to mounting stress and who are painfully aware of just how many problems elude their control, can't find true happiness in spite of the undeniable satisfaction they derive from their positions, life can only be even bleaker for their subordinates.

Most people don't work for the right reasons. What impels them to get up every morning and set out for work, where they usually go to great pains, is simply the idea that they are lucky to have a job. Their horizons and creative potential are correspondingly limited. They learned long ago how little impact they have on the way the business, political, or even trade union world develops. Getting them to realize that they have the means to play a creative role in their own existence is thus no easy task, and in any case, a self-development program cannot be imposed from above.

Nevertheless, the most fundamental challenge now facing managers is providing their employees with all the conditions they need to achieve autonomy in their daily lives, to develop their sensitivity and spirituality. This implies building organizations in which people feel free to work out visions in cooperation with each other, in which questioning and a commitment to truth are the rule, and in which people know that they are expected to question the *status quo* every day, not out of a desire for systematic opposition, but out of a concern for constant improvement.

On the basis of personal ethics and self-mastery, we can develop a shared corporate vision. Otherwise, in the absence of mental models that can both unite people and provide meaning, employees who experience work as constraint and drudgery rather than as calling and fulfillment will derive no real benefit from the new powers they have been granted. In such a case, all the attempts at empowerment in the world will merely increase both the level of stress in the organization and the need for additional management efforts to maintain the cohesion of the system.

If there is a clearly recognizable ethical philosophy underlying it, a shared vision becomes something much more concrete than an idea. It becomes a force in people's hearts. It provides both the goal and the energy for reaching it. Throughout my career, I have often observed how right Willis Harman was when he said, "Sane people work in sane companies and create sane products."

Everything depends on people. For too long, we believed, or wanted to believe, that other parameters might have greater importance. We had high hopes indeed for machines, technology, and information processing. Yet the fact remains that all roads lead us constantly back to man. The ultimate solution lies with people and only people, just as the seeds of our own destruction do.

In so far as the function of artists is to warn us, in symbolic and prophetic fashion, against the fate that awaits us, we would do well to recall the powerful images that film-maker Federico Fellini bequeathed to us in his last films. In *Prova d'orchestra*, symphony musicians argue away in the orchestra pit while the very walls of the opera house are cracking. In *E la nave va*, the members of high society who have embarked on a cruise to cast the ashes of a renowned woman singer into the sea are suddenly confronted, on their luxury ocean liner, with an influx of poor, yet joyful Serbian refugees who upset their microcosm as the first canon shots of World War I can be heard. Bearing these images in mind, let's take a fresh look at Europe, with its fragility and its pride in its past accomplishments. As Machiavelli warned, "It is impossible to convince a man who succeeds by applying his own methods that he could do better by changing. It is in this way that the fate of a man changes: because the world changes, but not he."

The value of a system can be measured by the happiness it brings to those who construct it. That the free-enterprise system is being questioned today – at a time in which it is the only candidate still running – has less to do with any passing, cyclical slump that it periodically suffers between two booms than with its apparent failure to make people happy.

Homo economicus possesses a large head, a big belly, and a wilted soul. The reason is that since the start of the industrial revolution, our leaders have given priority to the company's body (its results) at the expense of its soul, meaning the values that sustain it. Malraux wrote that "the twenty-first century will be religious or it will be nothing." This message can be translated for the benefit of our corporate directors into a similar warning that may serve as a conclusion to the present work: in the third millennium, the free-enterprise system will be visionary or it will be nothing.

Notes

1 This concern for independence, which continued for a long time in the guise of Maoist "self-reliance," today takes the form of a distrustful attitude toward foreign capital. As for the dazzling success of the Asian "tigers," it stems fundamentally from national policies that encourage individual savings, offer government assistance and protection to domestic companies, and purposely maintain the national currency at a low level in order to stimulate exports.
2 The profound upheaval in contemporary Chinese mentality is due infinitely less to exposure to Western values than to the shock wave that has battered the traditional Chinese family structure since the rise of the single-child family.
3 Victor Segalen, *Le Fils du Ciel* (Paris: Flammarion, 1985).
4 For this quotation from Confucius, see Bob Aubrey and Bruno Tilliette, *Savoir faire savoir* (Paris: InterEditons, 1990).
5 Masaaki Imai, *Kaizen, Les Clés de la compétitivité japonaise* (Paris: Eyrolles, 1989).
6 In an interview on radio RTL, November 20, 1993.
7 "Pour une nouvelle approche du processus du management de l'entreprise agressée" and "Le concept d'information prospective," *Annales des mines*, April 1990.
8 Jagdish Parikh, *Managing your Self* (Cambridge, Mass.: Blackwell, 1994).

PART IV

Lasting Prosperity

21

Seven Keys to Lasting Prosperity

Let us endeavor to get the future to pull the present, rather than hoping to use the past to push it.

Philippe de Woot, Strategy Professor at the University of Louvain,
Afplane Conference, 1992

THE TRICKY ART OF MANAGEMENT

- *First key*: constant promotion of *innovation*
- *Second key*: evaluating performance potential in terms of *tangible factors*
- *Third key*: evaluating the potential of *intangible factors*

- *Fourth key*: elaborating a strategic *vision*
- *Fifth key*: giving the *individual* an essential function in the system
- *Sixth key*: integrating individual fulfillment as a means of increasing the company's *creative influence*
- *Seventh key*: balancing "*doing*" and "*being*," efficiency and ultimate purpose

It should be said, now that we have reached the end of this book, that most companies and corporate leaders do show a rather strong awareness of some points on the above list, which will be enlarged upon in the coming pages. The problem, however, is that the new complexity that characterizes our postmodern society can only be mastered if we simultaneously use all the levers we have at our disposal. Only by simultaneously incorporating all the above points in a synthetic corporate vision can a company ensure its survival in a balanced fashion.

Short-term pressure, the temptation to pull off some short-lived feat, the frenzy of achieving performances that are evaluated in the wrong way may prompt many executives to write off several of our seven keys as secondary, or even pointless preoccupations. A phrase of Molière's should serve here as a final warning: "We are responsible for what we do, but also for what we do not do."

Today's consumers want communication, and thus transparency, at all levels. This explains why the behavior patterns of the postwar boom decades now tend to be inverted in the way indicated by the following diagram.

THE INVERSION OF VALUES: FROM CONSUMER SOCIETY TO COMMUNICATION SOCIETY

Values of the consumer society		*Values of the communication society*
Technical performance	→	Practical utility
Fashion, novelty,	→	Service quality and product
showiness	→	intelligence
Bulk purchases	→	Selectiveness, fixing of priorities
Loosening of constraints	→	Concern for coherence

Autonomy	→	Human contact, conviviality
Quantitative power	→	Cohesion and security
Segmentation	→	Comprehensiveness
Consumer-spectator	→	Interactive partner
Every man for himself	→	Ecological, humanitarian solidarity

DYNAMIC INTEGRATION OF FACTORS OF CHANGE

Integrating change in a dynamic way means using information on foreseeable developments to update company operations and organization constantly. This can also be seen as an ongoing capacity to record and assimilate new data, and, of course, a willingness to carry out immediately the technical and structural changes that they imply.

According to Arie de Geus, "your ability to learn faster than your competitors might well be the only competitive advantage you can bank on." This advantage is closely correlated with the ability to define new priorities and an aptitude for collective learning that should be instilled in the entire organization. In business, "hell is what is seen too late" (Whitebread). Like uncertainty and complexity, sharp breaks make existing pressures increasingly random, and thus particularly dangerous. At a time when most of our management tools and criteria for judging performance essentially involve forecasting, we have to accept a change in logic and the need for establishing the broadest possible networks. In this way, we have a chance of immediately exploiting the opportunities that arise and thereby of winning.

In this context, the new role of leaders consists first and foremost in conducting long-term thinking, in developing a compelling vision that includes the most ambitious scenarios, and in building the present in accordance with the future. It is always preferable to get it partly right through approximation rather than to get it all wrong with rigorous planning. In any case, with the new "management of the unpredictable," we can learn to discover the right road, the most promising projects, and to eliminate those dubious ideas that create the illusion of being good. Applying the guidelines laid out in this book should facilitate such an undertaking.

To summarize these new guidelines for managerial practice, I encourage the reader to make use of seven evaluation keys that I consider essential.

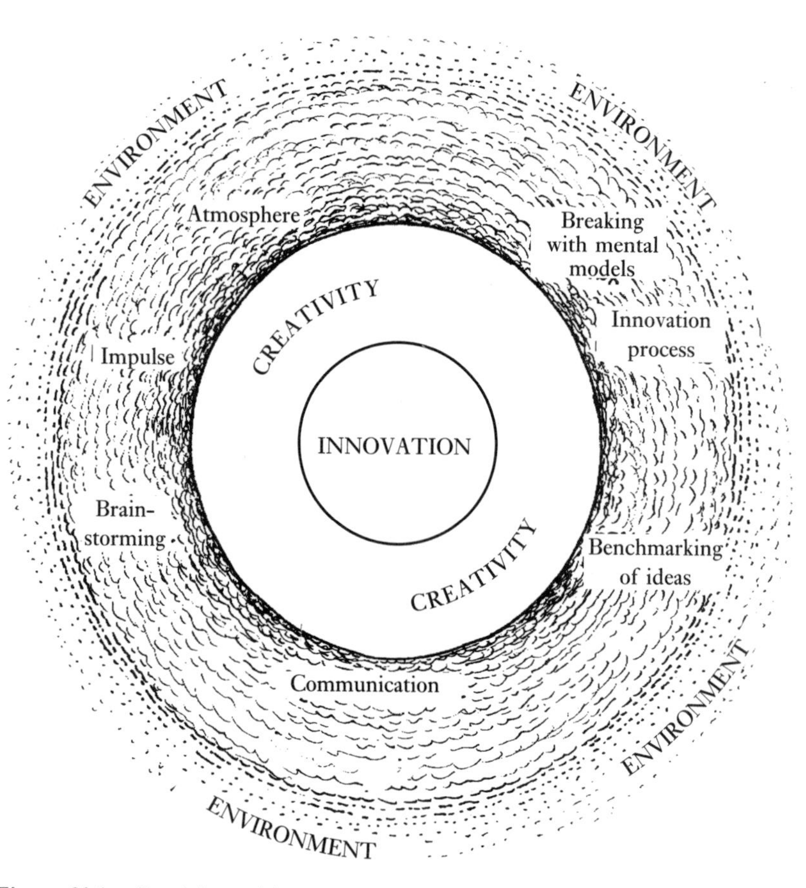

Figure 21.1 Creativity and innovation

FIRST KEY: CONSTANT PROMOTION OF INNOVATION

Figure 21.1 illustrates the necessary connection between creativity and innovation. The only way to achieve ongoing innovation is by developing a corporate culture that tirelessly encourages creativity. Fostering creativity and thereby innovation has become a major challenge for companies today.

We should recall that creativity is a thought process that generates ideas, while innovation results from the application of these ideas. However, only a small number of ideas actually lead to innovation. It might take 60 ideas before a true innovation emerges. This is because there is no need to prove the utility of an idea, whereas an innovation must produce concrete results, i.e. continual improvements in the company, its products, and its services. For this reason, the ideas generated by the creative process must be evaluated, with the ultimate criterion obviously being customer satisfaction.

There are several prerequisites to managing the innovation process in a structured, consistent fashion.

- *The climate.* The goal is to foster a working atmosphere inside the company in which creativity can thrive.
- *The process of creative planning.* Innovation must come from top management, whose task it is to develop a compelling vision and to plan the future direction of the company.
- *Tearing down barriers.* In a large number of companies, too many barriers, the chief one being a ubiquitous bureaucracy, keep ideas from circulating. Senior management should therefore audit information circuits, zero in on obstacles to creativity, and do its utmost to eliminate them.
- *Stimulating idea sources.* Ideas can be found either inside the company, particularly when appropriate structures have been set up, or outside the company (customers, consultants, competitors, etc.). To take possession of them, the company should proceed in a systematic fashion, conducting regular research on innovation going on elsewhere.
- *Innovation stimuli.* Recognizing and showing appreciation of the ideas of all collaborators is an excellent way to encourage creativity, without necessarily resorting to financial incentives or other material benefits.
- *Communication procedures.* Every member of the company is a potential source of ideas or is in possession of useful information derived from observing the external environment. Everyone should therefore know to whom and in what way they can transmit their ideas, and everyone should be encouraged to do so. Communication procedures have no existence in and of themselves. This is particularly true in multinationals, which have the opportunity to obtain "cross-fertilization" of ideas from widely different environments and cultures.
- *Idea evaluation procedures.* Once a company has organized in such a way as to collect and generate ideas, it must be able to sift and assess them quickly. The inability to give concrete, systematic expression

to ideas and the decline in motivation that results from it constitute a major hindrance to the development of creativity.

- *Innovation management.* Proper management of innovative ideas demands a capacity for assessing the degree of innovation attained during a given period. Such a system should allow the company to learn from its recent failures and successes. Furthermore, the best way to stimulate creativity is to show that ideas are actually put into practice.

SECOND KEY: EVALUATING PERFORMANCE POTENTIAL IN TERMS OF TANGIBLE FACTORS

Companies are currently judged above all according to quantitative measures such as balance sheet, financial performance, operating account, price/earnings ratio, real estate assets, plant and equipment. What we have here is the famous Wall Street syndrome. Under pressure from the financial community, this view of performance has deeply affected management options. The problem has been compounded by the increasing mobility – and precariousness – of company presidents, which leads them to sacrifice the long term and to focus on short-term gains, which often bring substantial benefits.

It should be emphasized, however, that all companies have a certain potential for excellence and innovation that cannot be reduced to quantitative criteria like the ones just mentioned. The propensity to innovate, the importance attributed to research and development and to marketing are all tangible elements that strongly condition a company's future dynamism. In order to conserve and develop this potential, the company must assess and rigorously analyze all tangible factors that, if properly used, would enable it to make constant progress (cf. figure 21.2).

Thus, a company should monitor the following factors on an ongoing basis, if need be by setting up specific units for studying them: internal rivalry in its industry or industry segment; potential inputs; the role of government authorities or pressure groups; and alternative products. It should also carry on regular dialogue with buyers and suppliers so as to achieve a community of interest, or even a genuine alliance that could contribute to shared prosperity (as in the Japanese example).

The company must be fully cognizant of the strategic limits to its sphere of activity and attempt to analyze as accurately as possible its own current or potential capacities as well as those of its competitors.

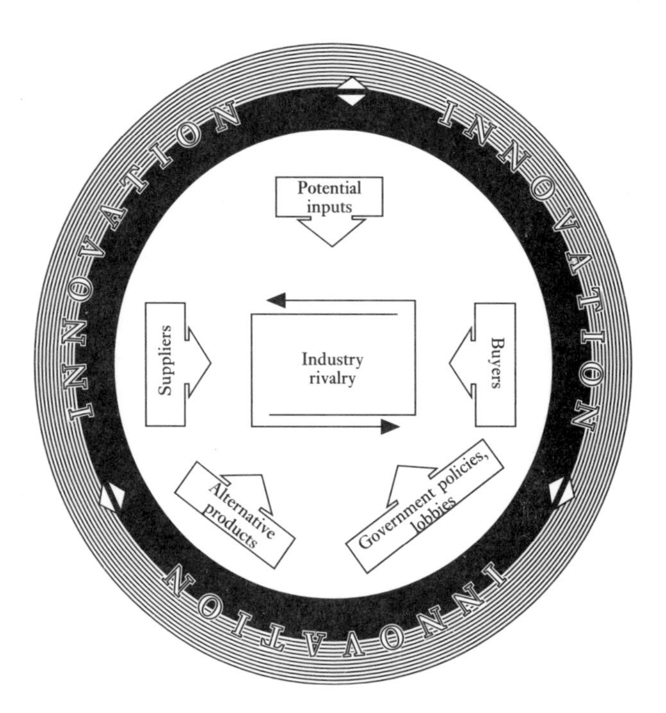

Figure 21.2 Improving tangible aspects in order to maintain competitive advantage (*Source*: based on Michael Porter, *The Competitive Advantage of Nations*, New York: Free Press, 1990)

Industry rivalry
How intense is competitive rivalry?
Price wars
Distribution of growth among different industries
Concentration of competitors
Product standardization
Competitors' strategies
What are the major changes?

Potential inputs
What are the potential inputs in the industry?
How might the industry react to them?
Entry barriers/entry costs
Ability to retain customers

Buyers
How much bargaining power do customers possess?
Customer sensitivity to price
Concentration of distributors
Upstream integration of customers
Changes in criteria for buying

Alternative products
What alternative products are there?
How likely are they to reach the market?
What risks would their emergence entail?
How capable is the industry of adjusting to new techniques?

Suppliers
How much bargaining power do suppliers possess?
Concentration of suppliers
Downstream integration of suppliers

The technique that I advocate for conducting such an evaluation is benchmarking, i.e. the art of using the best available practices as a basis for comparison (cf. figure 21.3). For those companies that have the courage to try it, this method can provide a revolutionary tool. The goal is to define a number of parameters that make it possible to draw up a chart of the company's strengths and weaknesses as well as to identify the main players in the industry under study. The next step is to single out the best one of all, to study its performances, and thus to determine in what areas the company is most in need of upgrading.

The main points to be considered in such an assessment appear to be products and services offered, technological level, downstream integration, distribution channels, distributors, customers, service applications, and global reach.

THIRD KEY: EVALUATING THE POTENTIAL OF INTANGIBLE FACTORS

All too often, the evaluation of a company depends on purely quantitative criteria. Yet in a world in which production methods must constantly be updated, in which competition is increasingly fierce because of the short-lived nature of technological gaps, these criteria prove to be inadequate. Intangible assets are now what distinguishes a company and ensures its survival.

The company's reputation, its role, its image, its name, its culture, the creativity of its teams, its skills and competencies, its management ability, its capacity for anticipation and questioning, the loyalty of its customers, its networks: these are its intangible assets. They may at times be difficult to evaluate, but they none the less determine the company's inherent value – and its future.

As figure 21.4 shows, the current situation of companies A and B by no means prefigures how they will fare in the future, which depends essentially on their respective intangible assets.

In light of today's changes and upheavals, of the rising complexity that companies must deal with, and of the problem of managing the unforeseeable, companies need to set up genuine "observatories" of the future (see figure 21.5). The goal is to monitor change in three broad areas: technology, markets, and society. Each of these research units should be able to feed information to management, and thus to help improve the quality of operations and decision-making.

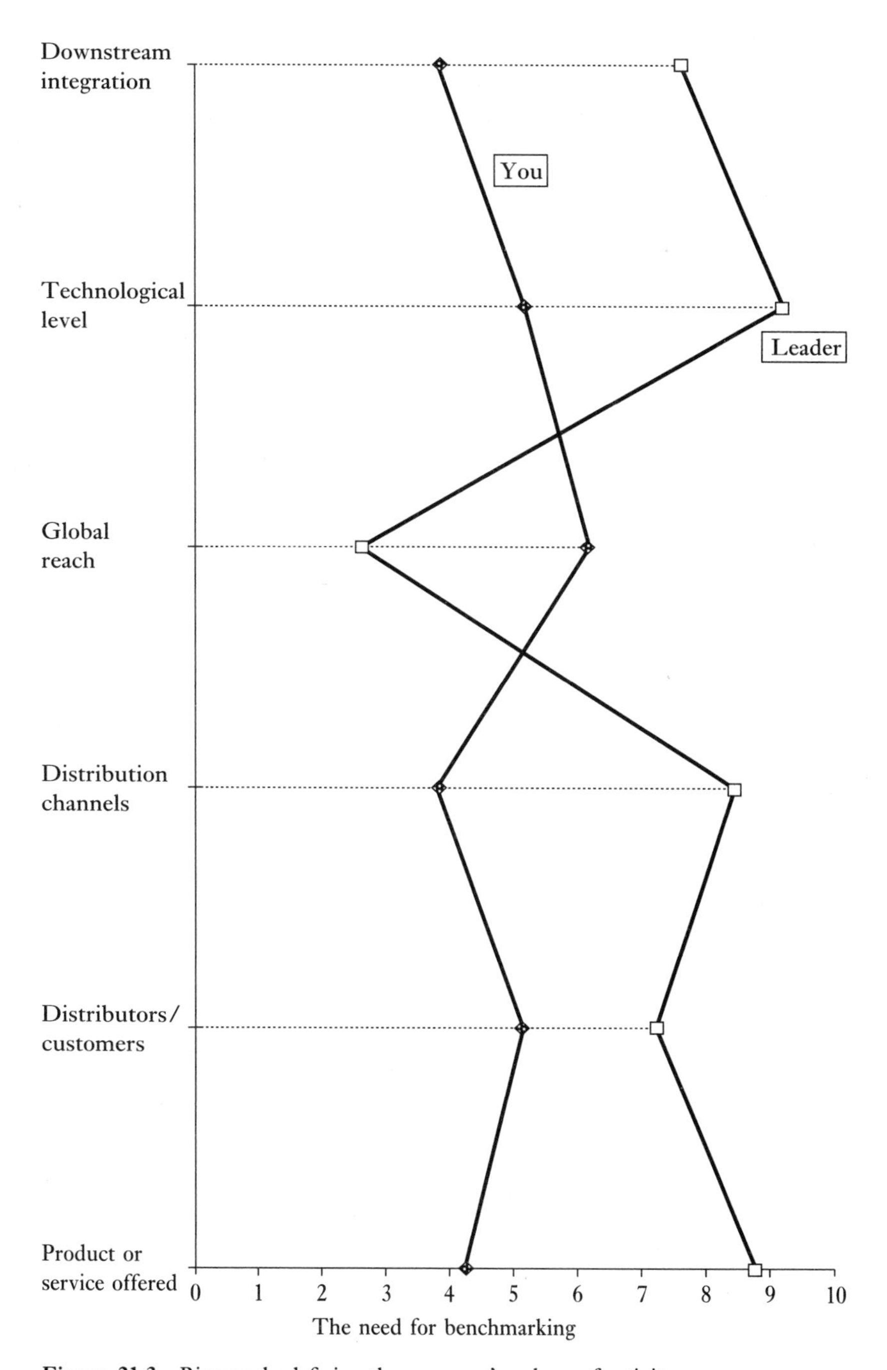

Figure 21.3 Rigorously defining the company's sphere of activity

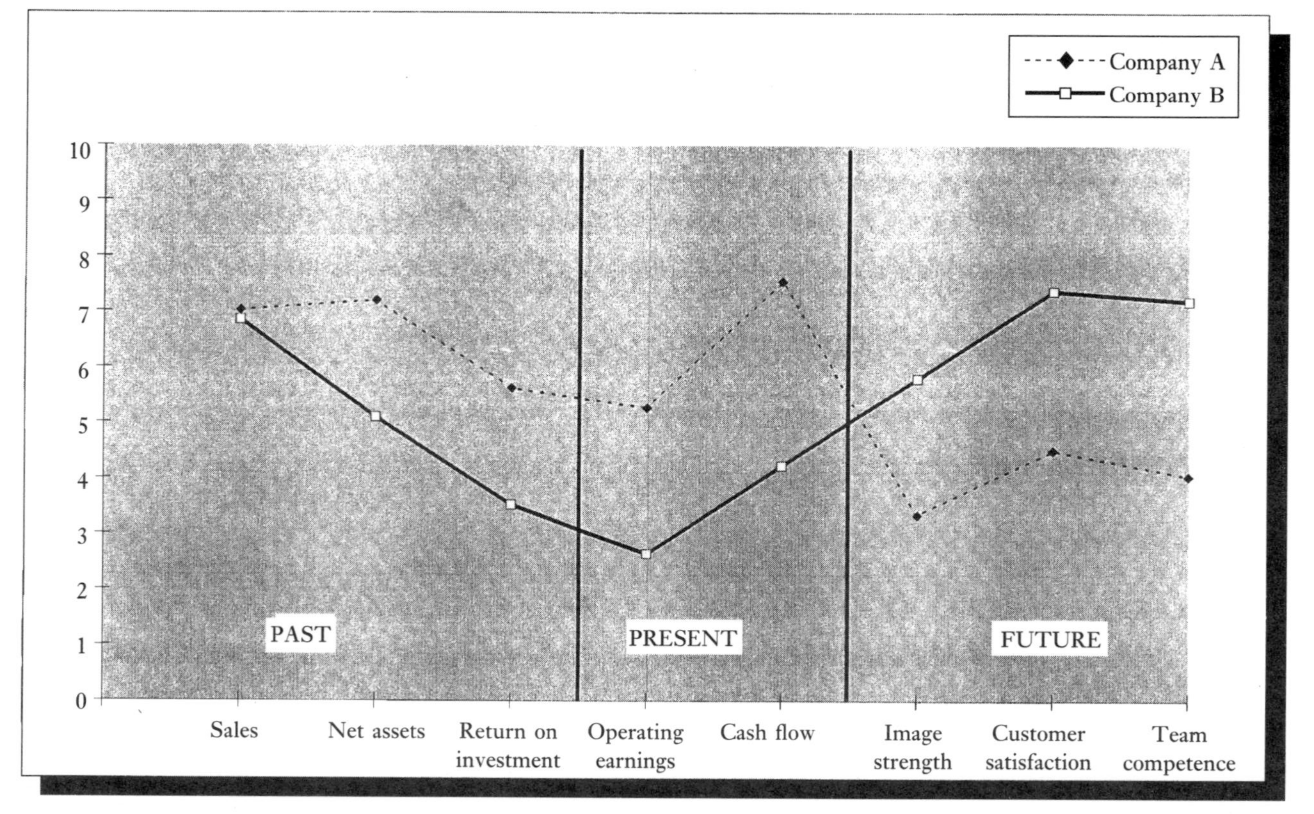

Figure 21.4 Taking intangible assets seriously (*Source*: Frank Petersens and Johan Bjurström, "Identifying and analyzing intangible assets")

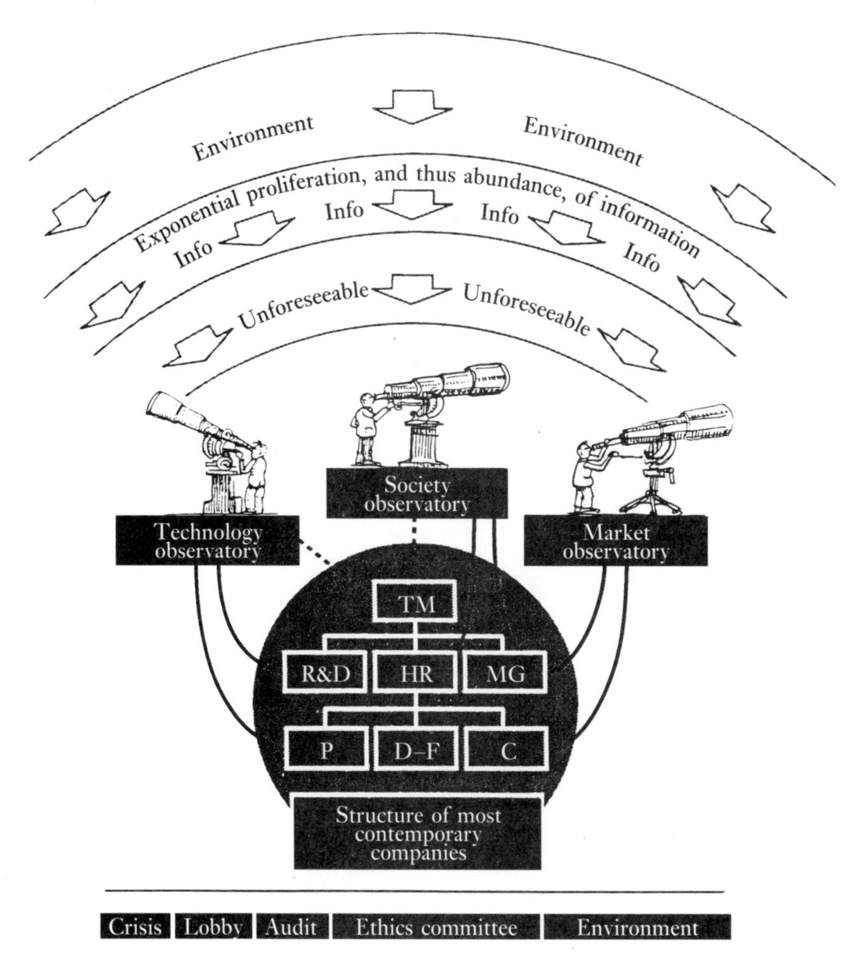

Figure 21.5 Controlling and organizing company information through "observatories" of the future

FOURTH KEY: ELABORATING A STRATEGIC VISION

We know the past. We must analyze it, and we often do a decent job of it. This is the province of decision specialists and problem-solvers. As regards the near future, we can certainly make an effort at anticipating it in linear fashion. But what about what happens ten years from now? Since we can hardly hope to foretell the future without being wide of the mark, the obvious solution is to invent it. Only those companies that think seriously today about where they want to be in 20 years have any chance of making the right decisions.

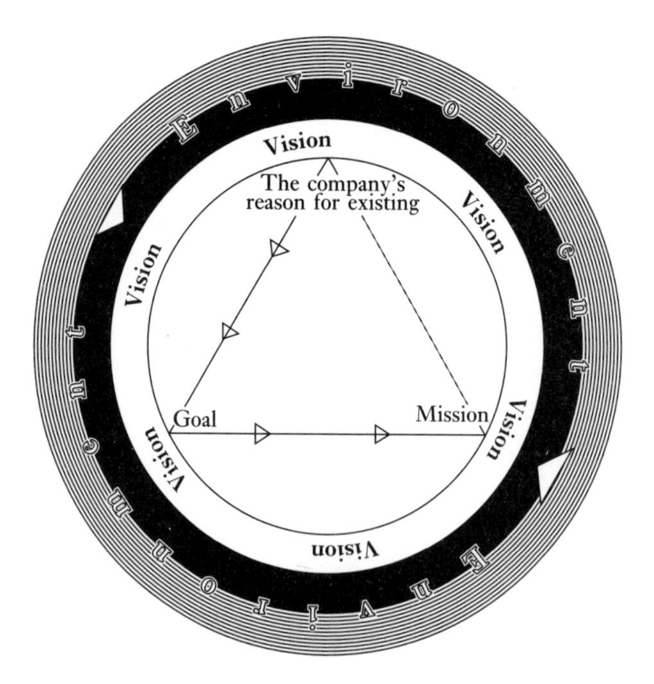

Figure 21.6 The need for vision

If the intention is to construct the present on the basis of the future, then we absolutely have to project a vision – the clearest one possible – of what such a future will be made of. A corporate vision sets a goal shared by all company members. It spells out the company's reason for being, for it defines its direction, its objectives, and its mission, while giving due weight to its core values (see figure 21.6). Although such a vision takes the environment and human factors into account, it must not be influenced by the ups and downs of the moment.

FIFTH KEY: GIVING THE INDIVIDUAL AN ESSENTIAL FUNCTION IN THE SYSTEM

In a society in which techniques and innovations become rapidly obsolete, the primary source of competitive advantage is people. Yet in so far as companies show concern for the human factor, it is usually from the standpoint of improving the organization's functioning. In such a view, the individual is the central element in a closed system that defines the organization's rules, stipulates job descriptions, dictates social relations, and places the individual in a given workplace.

The fact remains, however, that people are increasingly alive to their environment, both inside and outside the company. They are looking to find a meaning to their lives that might also enable them better to understand the world. To respond to these legitimate aspirations, companies cannot limit their goals to achieving maximum efficiency. They must also develop a genuine view of their future able to galvanize their members and to guarantee their self-realization.

To accomplish this in a world in constant flux, companies must deal with internal constraints by making use of external elements, identified by their various research units ("observatories").

Individual behavior should be considered the decisive factor in a process of change. In other words, significant change in an organization is only possible to the extent that the members of the organization adjust their behavior and maintain it in this modified state over a long period. The key to successful change thus lies in figuring out how to motivate people, although it should be recalled that traditional systems of evaluation heavily condition their attitudes, for individuals adapt themselves to the work structure or framework in which they happen to be and to the various signals it sends out to them. The work structure affects three areas in particular:

- expected performance
- expected results
- expected recognition (valence)

This framework can be broken down into four dimensions: technology, social factors, organizational factors, and physical setting. Figure 21.7 presents this idea in graphic form. The company's vision, goal, and mission are the factors that foster and maintain the coherence of these four dimensions. Likewise, the individual is the interface between the organization's dimensions and the results it produces. Therefore, the behavior of individuals in an organization should be adjusted only after the specifics of these four interrelated dimensions have been, for they shape considerably what people do at work and the consistency of the signals they receive.

Given how complex the functioning of an organization can be, it is no easy task to locate its breaking points and balance points. Although we vitally need to identify the roots of the problem, the complexity of the situation allows us to perceive only the tip of the iceberg, and any dysfunctions we may observe result from a set of problems rather than from an isolated point.

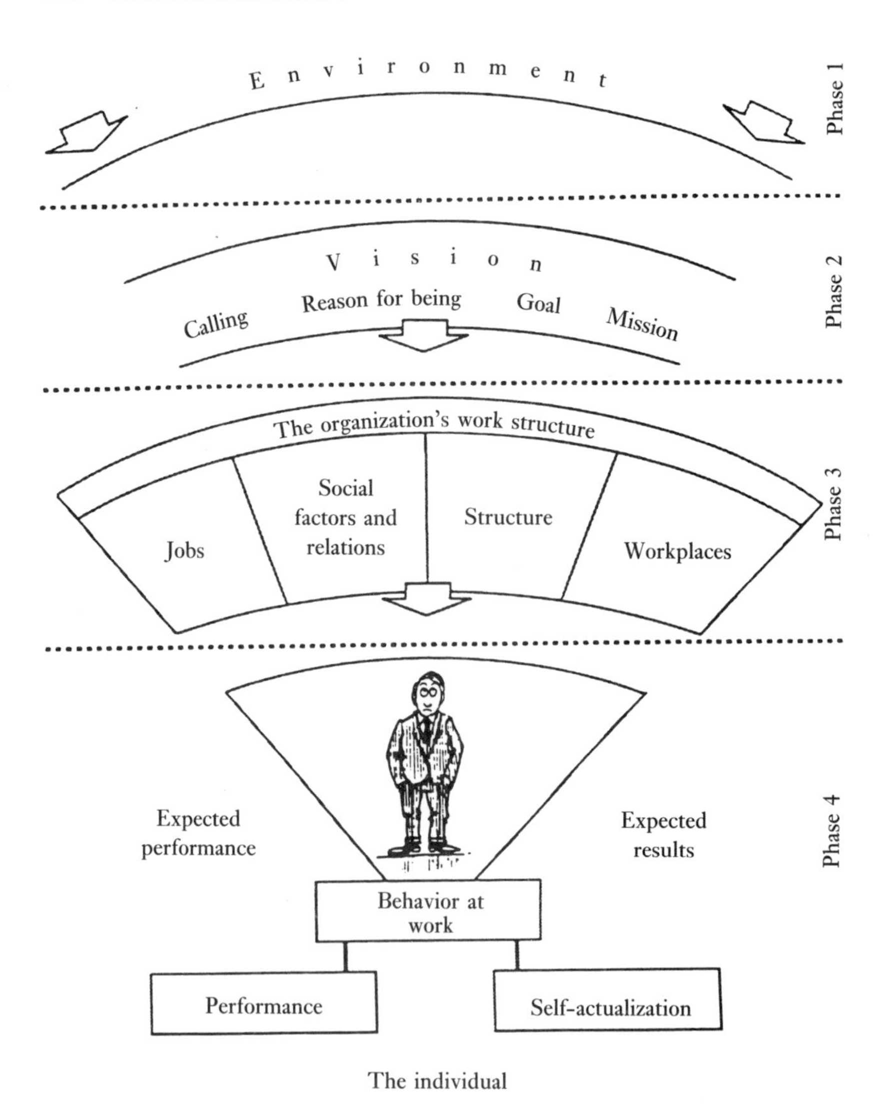

Figure 21.7 The individual: the heart of the company (*Source*: adapted from Jerry Porras, *Stream Analysis*, p. 72)

SIXTH KEY: INTEGRATING INDIVIDUAL FULFILLMENT AS A MEANS OF INCREASING THE COMPANY'S CREATIVE INFLUENCE

A company can survive only by achieving satisfactory performance. Today, however, the human factor is the primary source of performance.

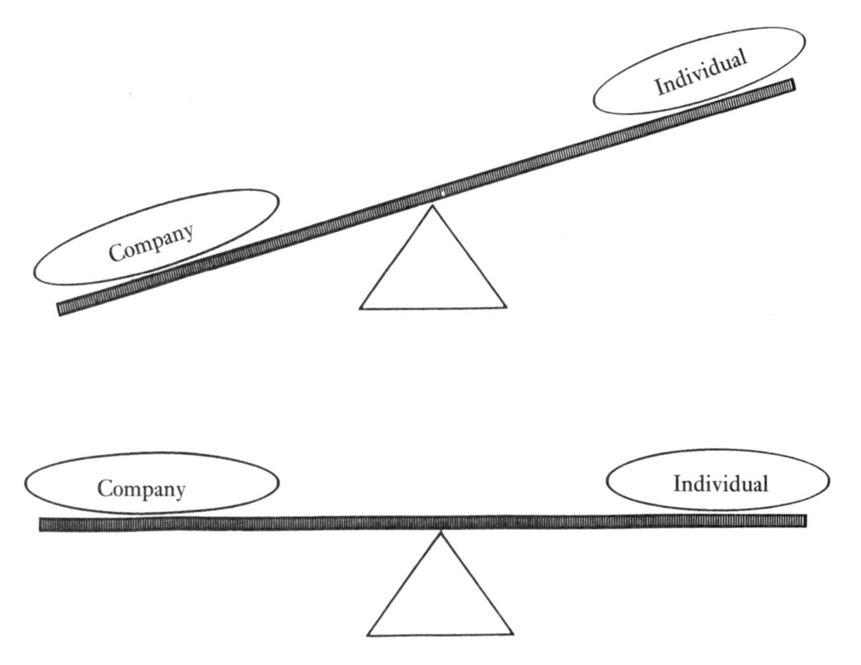

Figure 21.8 Balance between the company's need for efficiency and the aspirations of the individual

Fostering individual fulfillment and a climate of creativity have become a vital necessity for companies.

In the past several years, we have seen management models come and go that only consider people in terms of their contribution to the organization. Yet this is no longer enough. The task at hand today is to achieve balance between the company's need for efficiency and the aspirations of the individual, as illustrated in figure 21.8. Such a meeting between individual projects and the company project offers the best possible guarantee of creativity, and thus company success.

SEVENTH KEY: BALANCING "DOING" AND "BEING," EFFICIENCY AND ULTIMATE PURPOSE

Focusing only on efficiency to the exclusion of the organization's ultimate purpose may mean jeopardizing the future of the company by imprisoning it in a short-term oriented form of management. The real

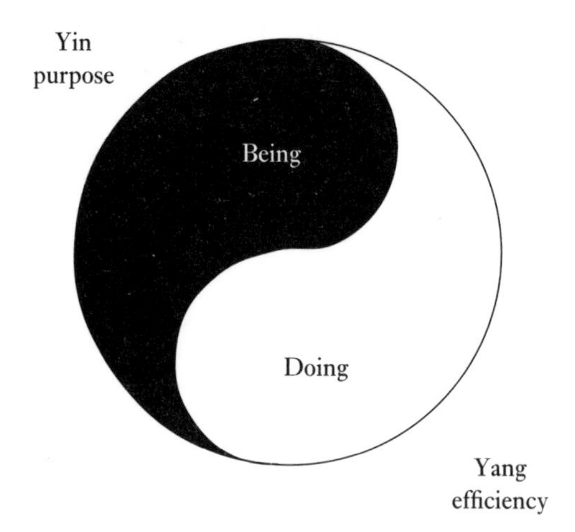

Figure 21.9 The Yin and the Yang (an idea suggested by the seminar held by the Management Centre Europe in Brussels, October 1, 1992, particularly by Richard Tanner Pascale, Tony Buzan, and Vanda North)

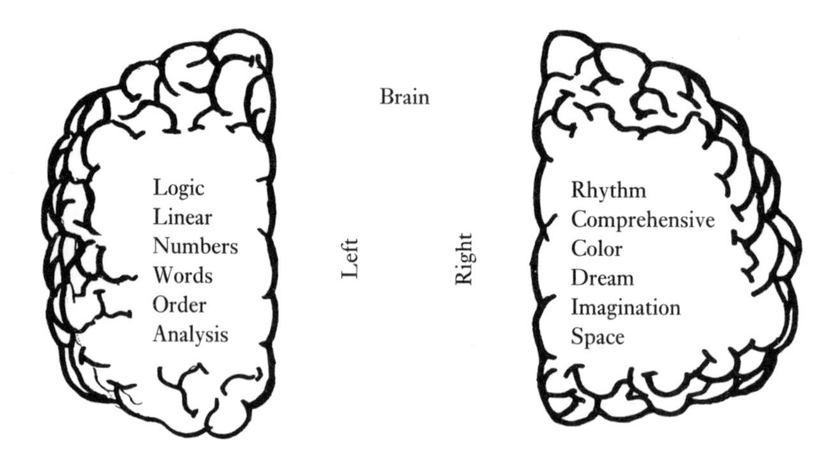

Figure 21.10 Dominant traits in the two cerebral hemispheres (an idea suggested by the seminar held by the Management Centre Europe in Brussels, October 1, 1992, particularly by Richard Tanner Pascale, Tony Buzan, and Vanda North)

goal, however, is to achieve balance between doing and being, or rather "being better" (see figure 21.9).

It would seem that we use a mere 5 percent, or even 1 percent, of our brain capacity. Thus, from a pure efficiency standpoint, it can be said that we use only the left hemisphere of the brain, i.e. its logical, analytical region (see figure 21.10). The risk is a dangerous atrophy of the immense creative potential offered by the right hemisphere, the seat of imagination, dreams, and intuition.

Achieving creative harmony means developing our intellectual capabilities in their entirety.

Appendix

REPETITIVE AND NON-ROUTINE FUNCTIONS: A DELICATE BALANCE

Predominantly repetitive, routine functions	*Predominantly creative, non-routine functions*
Nature of work	
Action	Reflection
Defined steps	Undefined steps
Sequential steps	Non-sequential steps
Repetitive tasks	Non-repetitive tasks
One right way	Several right ways
Product-oriented	Idea-oriented
Process of simple transformation	Multiple transformations
Predictions possible	Predictions difficult
Clear, shared goals	Multiple, competing goals
Readily available information	Hard-to-find information
Nature of success	
High output	Efficiency
Technical perfection	Human perfection
Measurable productivity	Non-measurable productivity
Physical technology	Knowledge technology
Standardized information	Non-standardized information
Limited specialization	Extreme specialization
Reproductive	Oriented toward profit realization

Nature of decision-making	
Fully operational specifications	Only partially operational specifications
Rules of application	Inhibitive rules
Logical decisions	Intuitive decisions
Experience useful	Experience inadequate
Decisions imposed by the hierarchy	Decisions based on consensus
Authority based on position	Authority based on competence
Nature of the context	
Short-term horizon (short cycles)	Long-term horizon (long cycles)
Stable environment	Unstable environment
Results defined in advance	Results defined along the way
Drops in performance	
Repetitive	Unique
Obvious	Hidden

In this list,[1] I have attempted to highlight the main differences between repetitive, routine functions, i.e. rational ones, and those that have an irrational character (creativity). The problem is that the former are situated downstream from the latter. Adjustment is not easy, for in one case, work is based on certainty, and in the other case, on uncertainty; the tangible as opposed to the intangible.

Thus, in the field of research, there is always a lag between the emergence of an idea and its appearance on the market. Conversely, in production, the watchword is to "get it done right now." Projects must have official approval, choices must be made, and questions must be settled once and for all. A research worker always wants to perfect his or her formula. Yet it is essential to stop the process sooner or later so that people located all along the value chain can do their jobs and deadlines can be met.

In a similar way, marketing departments often have to present new projects to production management, which must be able at a certain point to choose one of them, even if new ideas are still coming in. Clarity and precision are needed, and decisions must not meet with eternal questioning.

Let's now compare two truly creative functions: R&D and marketing. Getting them in phase with each other is more difficult than it might seem. Furthermore, when you look at them closely, you realize that they don't function in the same way and that one projects a particular image on the other. Once again, there is a need for breaking with certain mental models.

COMPARING R&D AND MARKETING

	R&D	*Marketing*
Work environment		
Structure	Necessary vagueness Established tradition Stable, specialized positions	Well defined *Ad hoc* tradition Rotation of individuals
Methods	Scientific, non-codified	Creative, codified
Databases	Systematic and objective	Unmethodical, largely subjective
Work and time pressure	Essentially internal How long will it take?	Essentially external How long have we been given?
Job criteria		
Hypotheses	Random New ideas What can we improve?	More reliable Great ideas How can we frame them?
Main criteria	Pursuit of quality	Quantitive results
Staff quality		
Training	Broad scientific	General, with a particular specialization
Experience	Broad, deep	Disparate

Notes

1 See William Pasmore and Kathleen Gurley, "Enhancing R&D across functional areas," in R. Kilmann and I. Kilmann (eds), *Making Organizations More Competitive* (San Francisco: Jossey-Bass, 1991), p. 371.
2 "This is not dreaming up a frame, but framing a dream," Robert A. Burgelman and Leonard R. Sayles, *Inside Corporate Innovation: Strategy, Structure, and Managerial Skills* (New York: Free Press, 1986), p. 66.